PRINCIPLES OF TECHNICAL MANAGEMENT

WILLIAM A. COHEN

Principles of Technical Management

a division of American Management Associations

Library of Congress Cataloging in Publication Data

Cohen, William A   1937–
    Principles of technical management.

    Includes index.
    1. Engineering—Management.   I. Title.
TA190.C64   620'.0068   79-54829
ISBN 0-8144-5580-8

FIRST PRINTING

PREFACE

Technical management probably began in prehistoric times. A talented Neanderthal spear-sharpener discovered that in addition to his technical achievements, he could manage others of his tribe to accomplish superior spear sharpening and was subsequently assigned these duties full time. He discovered that certain management skills helped considerably in getting the tribe's spears sharpened efficiently. A knock on the side of the head proved necessary for one of his technical people, while an approving grunt served to keep another on the right track.

Many factors that had little to do with the technical aspects of sharpening a spear boosted the quality and quantity of his output. He discovered that output was highest when the spear-sharpening group did its work together at certain hours, rather than when every sharpener worked on his own. He discovered that quality was maintained and output actually increased when periodic breaks in the work were scheduled. He learned how to recognize good potential spear-sharpeners by the size of their hands. This kept him from wasting valuable training time on Neanderthals who could never quite acquire the skill to do a good job. He learned that tribal members were much more eager to volunteer for spear-sharpening duties if spear-sharpeners were given larger portions of meat at mealtime. He learned that planning ahead was far better than trying to get control of the work after it had already started. In short, he learned how to manage spear-sharpening for maximum effect with maximum efficiency.

Spear-sharpening may not be considered much of an impressive technical process today. But the importance of management in accomplishing any technical task requiring more than one person is obvious. Without technical management, man could not build aircraft, produce in quantity, develop computers, or go to the moon.

Further, the importance of technical management can only increase since the technological base itself is growing rapidly. A great explosion of technology has occurred since World War II, with the simultaneous sprouting of many billion-dollar industries such as computers, electronics, plastics, television, space, and energy. As technical goals have been achieved, expectations of further technical progress have risen. For example, the American moon landing resulted in expectations for additional national goals in space, including trips to Mars and Venus, a space shuttle, and a space station. For these reasons, there is a growing demand for good technical managers.

Meanwhile, the technical sophistication of what is being done makes the manager's role more difficult. For example, it wasn't too long ago that an engineer or scientist could be knowledgeable about all the technical aspects of what might be considered his job. Thus, when he became a manager, he could easily adhere to the old maxim: "Don't ask your people to do anything you can't do yourself." It is rarely possible to follow this rule today. Most technical managers find that there are many things individuals reporting to them can do that they are not even remotely qualified to do. This phenomenon, with its implied problems, is confirmed by Peter Drucker in *Management: Tasks, Practices, Responsibilities.* * Drucker describes the growth of the knowledge worker and the knowledge organization as requiring the restructuring of not only jobs but the organization's design.

Despite the importance and complexities of technical management, it has not always been given sufficient attention as a field of study. Experts in management have not delved into this area as thoroughly as they have other areas, such as general management or marketing management. Technical managers, for their part, have been reluctant to apply general management principles to a technical discipline. Many regard management as a social science—not necessarily precise, not necessarily qualifiable, and grossly inexact when compared with mathematics, physics, or any field of engineering. Technical professionals who are involved in creative research may regard the notion of technical management as nonsense, feeling that events will just happen and cannot be controlled or managed. Most technical professionals who have become expert managers have not encouraged the acquisition of managerial knowledge by others. Indeed, managers of technical organizations, unlike most other classes of professionals, generally consider their technical reputations to be more important than their reputations as technical managers. In this unwelcome environment, it is not surprising that few managerial theorists have rushed to accept the challenge.

As a result of this situation, many, perhaps most, engineers and scientists promoted into positions of technical management responsibility find themselves unprepared for the tasks now demanded of them. Years of training and education are required before the technical profes-

* Harper & Row: New York, 1974.

sional is permitted to practice in his or her field. Yet this same professional may be thrust into management without a single day of orientation, education, or training for the new responsibilities.

Some believe in the philosophy of sink or swim: new technical managers either succeed or they do not. But in most other fields, the concept that "leaders are made, not born" prevails. For example, the military profession, which sometimes has a crucial need for instant managers in battle, scorns the sink-or-swim concept. Potential as well as present managers are taught management principles.

Others believe that only through experience can technical managers be developed, that there is something inherently wrong with studying or reading about management. Of course experience is essential, and one can learn much from it. But many managers don't remain long enough as technical managers to acquire the experience. If they do not perform well immediately, their management responsibilities are taken from them and they are returned to the straight technical work from whence they came. Even those managers who survive the learning-through-experience process may never achieve their full potential because of their lack of education about management. Meanwhile, the company, the manager's organization, and the manager himself suffer. It has been said that experience may be the best teacher, but the tuition is very high. Perhaps nowhere is such a price paid as in technical management.

Obviously, then, it would be foolish for a newly promoted technical manager, or an aspiring technical manager, to sit back and expect to acquire knowledge through osmosis. But what options exist for aggressively pursuing knowledge in this field? The technical manager can seek management education through a college or university, either through an "executive program" or, more formally, through an M.B.A. For many, this is an excellent solution. But a major drawback is that the program will rarely be oriented toward technical management. Therefore, to a great extent, technical management students will have to use their own judgment in applying general management concepts to their functional specialties. Further, because the thrust has not been toward technical management, students may spend an excessive period of time distilling what they need to know from the sum total of instruction presented.

Another option is to attend short courses or seminars conducted by such organizations as the American Management Associations. Since these courses are oriented toward specific functional areas and tasks, they are successful in providing solutions for the specific problems with which the managers they instruct are faced. The current AMA catalog, for example, describes 23 different courses under the general heading of technical management. The problem here is that it would be physically impossible for a manager to attend all the courses, and it is difficult to predict which courses will be most valuable in a given year.

This book was written to fill the gap between these two options: the nontechnical, conceptual learning provided by the academic world, and the more specific, but necessarily narrower in scope, instruction provided by short courses designed for operating managers. While management concepts are noted in passing, the focus is on application. The purpose is to show how these concepts can be applied to solve the technical management problems with which you are confronted and to provide you with the knowledge you need in order for you to make successful decisions.

The book, however, cannot make your decisions for you. Every circumstance, opportunity, organization, and problem is different. There are a thousand and one variables, and no one can assess the situation as clearly as the technical manager on the firing line. The book will simply help you to think through the problem more clearly and to enable you to arrive at an optimal course of action.

I think that after reading this book you will agree that the potential for improving your department or unit is considerable, even if you are already moderately successful. Why is this? At least part of the answer is that many questions that can and will make a difference have never even been asked. For example, have you ever asked yourself such basic questions as: What are the objectives of your organization? Is your organization structured to accomplish these objectives, or are you really set up to accomplish something entirely different? How do you measure how well your organization is accomplishing its objectives? Other questions you should ask may or may not have a quantifiable answer. Examples of these might be: How do you compute the productivity of your professionals? How do you determine efficiency? What is a professional worth? Organizational improvement may be possible because the measurements you are using are wrong, because you aren't using a measurement you could be, or because the answer itself is irrelevant.

This is an aspect of the book above and beyond simple managerial problem-solving—the realization that there is more to management than fire-fighting, that without solving a single additional problem, you can enhance the effectiveness and efficiency of your organization by an integrative analysis of what you are doing and how you are doing it.

William A. Cohen

CONTENTS

PRINCIPLES OF TECHNICAL MANAGEMENT

CHAPTER 1

The Scope, Responsibilities, and Functions of Technical Management

You can't execute your responsibilities as a technical manager effectively or efficiently until you have determined the potentials and the limits of the technical work of your organization. Why is this? Unless you know the scope of the work you are supposed to be doing, you do not know if you are doing the work you should be and in the manner you should be doing it. You only have a limited amount of resources. If you are expending them outside the scope of your work, you are not operating efficiently, and you risk being ineffective as well.

Let me give you a specific example of what I am talking about. A design department of a large aerospace company spent about 20 percent of its resources doing what amounted to applied research. It wasn't that the applied research work was unnecessary, but a special department already existed to do precisely that work. This was a misallocation of funds, because the work could have been done better and more cheaply by the department that was set up to do it. In addition, this would have freed additional people in the design department for design work. The manager of the design department was eventually replaced, and his replacement analyzed the scope of the department's activities. The result was that this department was able to operate on a lower budget and yet produce more and better design work, focusing on the work that it could do best.

To define the scope of your organization's activities, you should ask yourself: "What are the responsibilities of the organization I am managing? What is it we are supposed to be doing for the company?" Or, if the organization you are managing is a company: "What is it my company is supposed to be providing? Why do we exist?"

Several years ago, a West Coast manufacturer of diving equipment decided to enter the toy industry with a miniature version of one of its diving masks mounted on a toy diver that could be made to submerge. The toy industry was booming; an overcapacity existed in the company; the machinery (though not the tooling) was available to make the toy; and as a small bonus, it was felt that the toy would help to promote the company's other products. This toy venture ended in failure primarily because the product was outside the scope of the company's reason for existence. The toy was not normal to the company's product line, the toy market was a totally unknown entity, methods of distribution were unfamiliar, and even efficient manufacturing methods for toys were not the same as those required for the manufacture of diving equipment.

THE IMPORTANCE OF SCOPE FOR TECHNICAL MANAGERS

An awareness of scope is important at every level of management. If you head a reliability department, your people should stick to reliability. If your engineers are doing design work or sales work—no matter how well they are performing—they are working outside the scope of what your technical area should probably be.

Some technical managers encounter a serious pitfall regarding scope. They have defined the scope of their organization's activities, yet they depart from their own guidelines because:

> The organization that is supposed to do the work won't do it, won't do it fast enough, or won't do it very effectively.
>
> or
>
> A particular scientist or engineer prefers to do work that is outside the scope of the organization's activities.

Consider the first point. Emergencies will sometimes arise that will necessitate your organization's doing work outside its normal scope. But if emergency becomes habit, you have a problem—and it won't be solved by your organization's doing work that should really be done by someone else. Say the responsible organization won't do the work, or won't do it quickly or effectively enough, and you have gotten nowhere by talking with the manager of the responsible organization. It is your duty to take the problem up through your chain of command, because:

1. If you're having problems with this organization, other organizations in the company are probably having problems with it as well. If every organization in the company adopts the solution of working outside its scope of activities, the cure is probably worse than the disease.
2. It is usually more efficient for you to spend time fighting to get the responsible organization to do its job than to gear up for this special task within your organization and do the work yourself every time the task arises.
3. The responsible organization is staffed for this job; you probably are not.
4. You are taking your people away from what should be the main effort of your organization.

There is one exception to the rule of not doing someone else's work. This is when the overall manager of the subsidiary organization and the head of the organization in question also know what is taking place. This exception will be covered in Chapter 2. But the general rule stands—don't do someone else's work.

Now consider the second reason for violating scope. Why shouldn't you allow an engineer or scientist to do something outside the scope of your organization's activities so long as it is on the person's own time? First, it probably won't be on the person's own time for long if you allow him or her to use company equipment, facilities, or resources. Second, if an organization exists to do the job, your engineer may be interfering with that organization's operations. Third, and most important, you are detracting from what must be your main effort—those required activities that are demanded of your organization by the company or by an outside "customer" that you serve.

I once knew a president of a small engineering company in the electronics industry. He violated this concept repeatedly. Reliability engineers worked on R&D. R&D people spent their time on product development. Salespeople struggled with organizational problems. Even the president recognized that this was a tremendous waste of resources, and it caused some real organizational problems as his people stumbled over one another and essential work went undone. I asked him once why he permitted this situation to go on. His answer astounded me. It was his policy, I was told, not to discourage any of his people who had ideas that might benefit the company.

Such a goal might have been accomplished without going to such extremes. A suggested idea could be turned over to the appropriate group for evaluation. Or, if the individual was qualified and willing and the idea had merit, he or she could be transferred to an appropriate organization on a temporary or permanent basis to work on the idea.

Permitting work outside the scope of your organization's technical activities, no matter how skilled the individual may be at this work, means that some work within your organization is not being accomplished. It means possible duplication of the work by some other department. And it means a dilution of effort outside of your required activities.

Keeping the activities of your technical organization within the proper scope will:

- o Result in efficient allocation of resources, since your organization will do what you staffed it to do and what it does best.
- o Help ensure that your people's efforts are directed toward the achievement of established objectives.
- o Assist in maintaining morale, since rewards can be clearly tied to an individual's performance within the agreed-upon scope.
- o Save the company's resources by avoiding possible duplication of effort.

THE RESPONSIBILITIES AND FUNCTIONS OF THE TECHNICAL ORGANIZATION

In the age of technology, few technical tasks are unimportant. Accordingly, when a technical organization fails to execute properly its responsibilities and functions, the consequences are usually quite severe.

For example, the Ultra-Strength Company was founded on the development of a new process, yet it almost collapsed after initial success as a result of failure to execute that very task properly. Ultra-Strength was founded by two young engineers whom we'll call Joe Smith and George Hamel. Smith and Hamel had previously been with a large company, a division of which was engaged in producing various types of nonmetallic armor for the U.S. Army. Working on their own, they had developed an idea for producing ceramic armor at a much lower cost than their competitors. Failing to sell their idea to their management, Smith and Hamel quit to form Ultra-Strength. The success of Ultra-Strength was immediate, and within three years they were making a good profit and had captured 30 percent of the U.S. market. Ultra-Strength's success was due to development of the proprietary low-cost process for producing the ceramic armor. The period of growth—extending into three years after the company's founding—had been devoted mainly to marketing activities. Also, the process had been further refined to improve the quality without raising cost.

At this point, Smith and Hamel decided to do three things to promote the expansion of their company: capture a greater percentage of the U.S. market, get into the foreign market for armor materials, and introduce a new armor product. Six months after Ultra-Strength initiated this strategy, another company introduced a new ceramic armor material that was significantly more effective than the old one. The manufacturing process Smith and Hamel had developed could not be applied directly to the new material. Usage of the old material declined as the U.S. market dried up with the end of the war in Southeast Asia. Within two years, Ultra-Strength was in trouble, and it was saved from bankruptcy only by acquisition by a larger competitor.

Was this only bad luck? Ultra-Strength's function, on which its success was founded, had been the development of a better way to make an existing product. It was not that its product was better, only that it was cheaper. Nor did Ultra-Strength possess unique marketing know-how, nor a much improved armor product. New, improved products are inevitable. In fact, the introduction of this new material was no secret; it was expected and was known even to Smith and Hamel. Had Ultra-Strength concentrated its efforts on developing an improved method of processing the new material before it was introduced, as it did with the earlier material, it could probably have repeated its earlier success and improved its marketing position.

Ultra-Strength did not err by exceeding the scope of its work. Clearly the strategy decided on to promote expansion was within the scope of Ultra-Strength's business. Ultra-Strength's problem was that it did not understand its function in the scheme of things; that is, the primary reason for its existence and its success.

The Ultra-Strength lesson is that every technical manager must fully understand the responsibilities and functions of the organization. A technical organization is responsible for one or more of five basic functions:

1. To provide technical, scientific, or engineering consultation or service to other organizations in the company, or to an external customer.
2. To develop new products, processes, or materials that will be better or cheaper than the current product, process, or material used.

3. To improve current products, processes, or materials so that they will be better or cheaper than what is currently used.
4. To conduct research.
5. To manufacture something.

In addition, a technical organization may be responsible for developing and maintaining a reputation for superior technical performance.

THE IMPORTANCE OF AVOIDING COMPANY SUBOPTIMIZATION

The execution of the technical organization's responsibilities and functions cannot be separated from overall company goals. Accordingly, you as a technical manager must ensure that your organization performs its responsibilities in a way that supports the company's objectives, even though this may require that your organization carry out its tasks less than optimally. Optimization of the performance of your organization may sometimes constitute suboptimization so far as the broader interests of the company are concerned. Suboptimization of your organization's performance may be justified if it supports the optimization of higher company goals.

How might this work in practice? Assume that you are manager of research and development, and that a project is organized external to your organization. You are asked to let three of your key people be transferred to the new project on a permanent basis. To do so will downgrade your ongoing R&D effort. Do you agree to the transfer or not?

At your level of management, you are not in a position to evaluate the tradeoffs between the potential gain to the company by successful and timely completion of the project and the potential loss to the company by decline in the ongoing R&D effort. You must not arbitrarily seek to optimize the performance of your own organization, by insisting on retaining the three individuals, while disregarding the goals of the company. This might suboptimize the performance of the company as a whole. Instead, you should make the effect of the transfer of personnel on your current R&D work known to the individual who is in a better position to evaluate and who is responsible for making this decision. Whatever that person decides, you must discharge the responsibilities of your organization within the limitations placed by your company's operations and goals.

In larger companies this is true at every level of organization. The unit manager must consider the section goals as being of greater importance, the section manager must bow to the department's goals, the department to the subdivision's, the subdivision to the division's, and the division to the company's.

CLARIFYING THE RESPONSIBILITIES, FUNCTIONS, AND OBJECTIVES OF A NEW JOB

Any technical manager faces considerable risk in assuming a new position in that he may not understand what it is he is supposed to do or what it is he is responsible for. This may be due to erroneous assumptions about what the boss wants or about what the job consists of, or a tendency to continue to perform the functions of a previous job while neglecting the required functions of the new job.

To minimize this potential danger, you as a technical manager with new responsibilities and functions should take the following four actions.

1. Discuss the new responsibilities, functions, and objectives with your boss.
2. Think through the responsibilities, functions, and objectives on your own.
3. Review the responsibilities, functions, and objectives with your boss and document them.
4. Periodically review the responsibilities, functions, and objectives on your own and with your boss.

Discuss the New Responsibilities, Functions, and Objectives with Your Boss

Before accepting any new responsibilities you should make every effort to understand exactly how your boss defines these responsibilities and how he or she feels about them. The mere fact of your being made a project engineer does not define your responsibilities. The term project engineer means different things to different people. Even if you are the former deputy replacing the old project engineer, the boss may have made this change partially to alter the former responsibilities and functions of the job. Therefore, the first step is always to talk to the boss and find out what he or she wants. Don't assume anything. In this meeting or series of meetings, also find out what the organization's objectives will be, how much authority you're going to have, and what other conditions exist that may not be readily apparent. Try to find out everything that could affect your functions or responsibilities. Don't depend on memory; take notes. Tell the boss you'd like to think through what has been discussed and would like to schedule an additional meeting after you've had time to review all the facts.

Think Through the Responsibilities, Functions, and Objectives on Your Own

Go over your notes after your initial meeting and think things through. Check the following:

o Do you have sufficient authority and resources to accomplish the objectives that you are going to be responsible for? If not, what additional authority or resources do you need?
o Are you being asked to accept responsibility for actions that can best be handled by some other organization or manager? In other words, is your organization the most appropriate one to perform the functions and be responsible for attainment of the objectives outlined?
o Are there things you should be responsible for that you are not? Make a note to discuss these further.
o Are there undefined or hazy areas in functions, objectives, responsibilities, or any other aspect of the work? Note these down for future discussion.

Think all these issues through carefully. Where additional information is needed that can only come from your boss, write down the questions that you plan to ask at your meeting. Consider each possible answer he or she may give to your questions, and apply the known facts to make a list of recommendations wherever possible.

Review the Responsibilities, Functions, and Objectives with Your Boss and Document Them '

When you have completed this self-review process, you are ready for your next meeting with your boss. The purpose of this meeting is to finalize your responsibilities, functions, objectives, and other aspects of your new work prior to accepting responsibility for it. You have thought the problem through and are ready to make specific recommendations, depending on additional information from your boss in all areas.

Most of your recommendations will probably be accepted. Some will not, because of information you did not have that your boss will give you. A few may be rejected with little explanation. Be alert for these—there may be things your boss cannot or prefers not to tell you. Once you are certain that your boss understands your recommendations and your reasons for them, you should not press the issue after a decision is made.

You should again take notes, and your meeting should end with a list of responsibilities and other aspects of work that you both understand and agree to. It is usually advantageous to get these agreed-upon points in writing. But for various reasons, this is not always possible. Depending on your particular situation, you might ask your boss if he or she would object to your sending a memorandum to confirm these points so that you will both have it to refer to in the future. You would then send him or her a memorandum containing a list that begins something like this: "This memorandum confirms responsibilities and other aspects of my new work that we agreed to at our recent meeting."

You can best judge whether proposing such a memorandum to your boss is appropriate or not. Another technique is to write the memorandum to the file, with a copy to your boss.

Periodically Review the Responsibilities. Functions, and Objectives on Your Own and with Your Boss

Nothing remains static. Also, a "first cut" assessment of the new work, no matter how thorough, is never perfect. Therefore, make plans with your boss to formally review the responsibilities and functions of the new job again after one month, three months, and six months. Ask yourself the same questions and make new recommendations regarding the important aspects of the work.

As you follow these steps in assuming the responsibilities for new work, you will find that both you and your boss have a much clearer idea of what functions, responsibilities, and objectives go along with your particular technical management assignment.

YOUR BASIC RESPONSIBILITIES AS A TECHNICAL MANAGER

As a technical manager you have responsibilities in many different areas, depending on the job, the company, and other factors. But there are three responsibilities that you will always have regardless of your situation. These are to company goals, to your subordinates, and to yourself.

Responsibility to Company Goals

Responsibility to company goals must come first because you, your subordinates, and your organization are all dependent on company survival and performance. This does not mean that to uphold company principles you must be ready to do battle in a physical sense, or that you are required to lie, cheat, compromise your ethical standards, or sacrifice your family life for the sake of the company. What it does mean is that on your list of work or career priorities, company goals come first—before your personal ambitions, before the vacation schedule of your subordinates, before pay raises, before friendships, and before either your own desires or the desires of your subordinates. And, as noted earlier, you should not strive to optimize the performance of your own organization when this may result in suboptimization of company performance.

Managers who do not place their responsibility to company goals first are not being true to the obligations for which they are being paid. Failure to meet this responsibility can cause a critical failure in the company and hence hurt all members of the company, including the technical managers themselves.

Responsibility to Your Subordinates

Once you have faithfully executed your responsibilities to company goals, responsibilities to your subordinates come next. Without question, responsibilities to your subordinates come before responsibilities to yourself. If you are unwilling to place the welfare and problems of your subordinates above your own welfare and problems, you should seek employment as something other than as a technical manager, for this order of priority is inherent in the position. Without your technical subordinates you have no reason for existence, no job to perform, nothing to manage. Your subordinates' function is to perform the technical work. Yours is to manage the performance of that work. Therefore, your subordinates' welfare and problems constitute the core of your managerial function. Your subordinates will expect you to execute that function, including looking out for and defending their interests. If you do not do this you will not be able to function in your full capacity as a leader or manager.

A manager who places his own interests above the interests of his or her subordinates cannot expect those subordinates to place company interests above their own. The technical area being covered by these subordinates will suffer, company performance will suffer, and technical employees will eventually feel the effects of this decline. As a technical manager, you must keep in mind that it is primarily the performance of your organization—and not your individual performance as an engineer or scientist—that is important.

Responsibility to Yourself

This managerial responsibility may be of lower priority, but it is an essential one. If you do not fulfill your responsibilities to yourself or to your family, you will soon have personal problems and difficulties that will detract from the time and effort you must give to managing your organization. If you refuse to look out for your own interests within the company, you might not be in a position to help attain your company's goals or to take care of the interests and welfare of your subordinates in the future.

Along these lines, consider Mickey B.'s story. Mickey was an aeronautical engineer working for a large aerospace company. A combination of World War II expansion and Mickey's considerable talent as a leader thrust him into an engineering management position relatively early in his career. Mickey was good at the job. He pursued the company's goals relentlessly, working late hours every night. He consistently defended the interests of his subordinates, and with his help, many were promoted into responsible positions in the company. At the war's end, Mickey was one of the few young engineers retained as a manager, and his company continued to use him in what had become his speciality, reciprocating engines. Mickey maintained the pace, working long hours at his job. He was looked up to by his people and respected by everyone.

As jets began to replace reciprocating engines, Mickey was one of the first to be given the opportunity to attend a six-month course that would prepare him to lead an engineering group working with the new engine. But Mickey turned this down, pleading his current workload. Within a year, he was asked to go again, but again Mickey indicated that for the company's sake, he could not. Twice more he was encouraged to attend a qualification course for jet engines, but he always refused. Finally, he was called in by the head of his division. His accomplishments and value to the company were extolled. He was shown plans for expansion into jets and a record of the decline in the older reciprocating engines. Mickey nodded in agreement. He explained to the division head just how much he wanted to go to the jet engine course, but still could not because of his current responsibilities. He did, however, agree to attend the course at the first opportunity.

In 1968, Mickey left the reciprocating engine group he had headed for more than twenty years. It was the last such group in his company. Today, people whom Mickey trained in the early days occupy senior managerial posts in the company. Mickey is still respected by everyone, but although he was always an outstanding line manager, he has held one pedestrian staff job after another for the last ten years. Mickey never found time to attend that course, and thus never became qualified to head up a group working with what became the company's main product line. This same lack of qualification has limited the contributions he has made in the staff positions he has held. Mickey fulfilled all his responsibilities as a manager faithfully—that is, all but one. He failed to fulfill his responsibility to himself.

A manager who totally neglects legitimate responsibilities to himself will invariably cause his company to suffer over the long run, since he will not reach his full potential and will not make the contributions to the company's operations that he might have made. The code of managerial responsibility is a tough one to live by, since it must be balanced against other responsibilities. But if you are to lead a technical organization, it is the only philosophy that will ensure your ultimate effectiveness as a manager.

Balancing the Three Responsibilities

If you do not put your company's (or your organization's) goals first, you endanger your operations and will ultimately be unsuccessful as a manger. If you don't put your responsibilities to your subordinates above yourself, you will not succeed as a manager. If you do not take the necessary time to fulfill your responsibilities to yourself, you will not succeed as a manager either. For success, all three responsibilities must be fulfilled.

These principles are interrelated and have to do with the issue of company suboptimization discussed earlier. Think back to that R&D department which stands to lose several key personnel. The company's goals come first, but then come the goals of your own organization. What if you were asked for your opinion about whether one of your key individuals should be promoted into a job that is nonessential now but that in the long run is an essential stepping-stone to greater things? In arriving at a recommendation, you must think of company and organizational goals, the goals of the individual, and your own personal goals.

Many of the decisions you make as a technical manager will have to do with personnel, and they are seldom simple. In the example above, the priority of responsibilities can be used as a guide. But each situation is different, and only you can weigh the different factors and reach a decision.

But your problems are not over even when the decision is made. What if it is decided that for the higher good of the company, the key individual cannot be promoted into the stepping-stone job? Do you tell the person that he was even considered for the promotion? If the key individual knows he was considered for promotion and you have decided not to promote him because he is key to your operation, you'd better be able to give him a good estimate as to when and under what circumstances you are going to allow him to be promoted.

Consider another example. An opportunity comes to send only one individual from your organization to a course on some aspect of your operations. Do you send anyone at all? Do you send a manager, or do you send an engineer? Do you send yourself? Here again is an important people decision that is more complex than it might first appear. Sending anyone but yourself could, depending on the type of course, generate hard feelings. It might give the appearance of favoritism, or it might suggest that you feel the individual lacks training or knowledge in that area. If you send yourself, you might create the impression that you are going to take advantage of all such opportunities. Your reaction to the course will influence people's view of it too. Unless you return and announce that the course was worthless, the mere fact of your attendance will add to its attractiveness for people in your organization.

Any time you make a people decision you should consider your priority of responsibilities: company or unit goals, your people, and yourself. Once you get in the habit of basing your decisions on these criteria, you will find that the people in your organization will recognize it, respect you for it, and in many cases emulate your behavior. Can you imagine the difference between an organization where members place themselves last and the objectives of the organization first, and an organization where members do the opposite of this?

CHAPTER 2

Organizing for
Efficiency and Effectiveness

Efficiency and effectiveness are the keys to good management. To be effective means that you accomplish your initial objectives. The efficiency component measures how well you do this—how quickly and cost-effectively you achieve your goals, and how well you use the resources that are available to you. Efficiency and effectiveness go hand in hand to help determine your organization's contribution to the company's performance, as well as your personal performance as a technical manager.

The structure of your organization is the starting point for achieving efficiency and effectiveness. One may debate the issue of whether organization, personnel, or some other factor is most crucial to the achievement of efficiency and effectiveness, but a few minutes of reflection will demonstrate that regardless of *relative* importance, the structure of an organization is an essential building block. For example, the same United States whose government was unworkable under the Articles of Confederation became effective, and even reasonably efficient, under the different organizational structure defined by the Constitution.

Government projects being worked on by the engineering department of a prominent government contractor were plagued by slippages and overruns. In desperation, the company reorganized along product rather than functional lines. The slippages and overruns stopped.

A major foreign aerospace company was developing its first home-designed aircraft as a project within its engineering division. The project slipped months, and then years. The vice president of engineering was fired. Finally, the project was reorganized around a systems program office reporting to top management. The program was brought under control and became a technical as well as a financial success.

While organizational structure wasn't the only reason for the turnarounds in these examples, we can see that if we want to promote organizational efficiency and effectiveness, we must start with an appropriate organizational structure.

THE IMPORTANCE OF DEFINING OBJECTIVES

The first step in designing an organizational structure for efficiency and effectiveness is to establish or confirm your organization's basic objectives. This may appear obvious, or trivial, but it definitely is not. It is amazing how many companies and technical groups have been founded and structured with no consideration at all for what they are supposed to accomplish. Structuring your organization without establishing, confirming, or reconfirming its basic objectives goes beyond "putting the cart before the horse." It's more analogous to shooting an arrow before you know what your target is, or starting an important journey without having decided on a destination. You must precisely define the main objectives of your organization before you can do anything further about structuring it in a sensible way.

The method of defining your organization's objectives is not complex. It is similar to defining the responsibilities, functions, and objectives of a new job as shown in Chapter 1 and consists of only two actions: talking with people and thinking.

You should talk with people even if you believe your organization's main objectives are a "given" from your boss. Even your boss may not understand the whole problem, and what you think your boss means may not be the same as what he or she actually means. Also, managers of other organizations in your company that will affect or be affected by your organization may contribute facts of which neither you nor your boss are aware. Finally, you may gain insights from your own subordinates regarding your organization's objectives.

After gathering all the information you can, your second task is to analyze the facts and opinions you have obtained and decide which are likely to be valid and which are not. Think the problem through until you can recommend to your boss what your objectives should be and why. This should be done whether your organization is new or old and established.

Ron Z. was a newly hired vice president of research and development in a medium-size, high-technology company doing business primarily with the federal government. Ron's boss, the president, said:

"As I see it, your main goal is to develop certain types of products that the company can market in the near term—the next three to five years."

The vice president of finance, in a conversation with Ron, congratulated him on his appointment and said:

"As I see it, your main goal is to get us on track with these government-funded programs. We're overrunning and losing a lot of money on all of them."

During a meeting Ron had with the vice president of one of the operating divisions, this vice president commented:

"As I see it, your main goal is long-range research—developing the products that will be the company's bread and butter five to ten years from now. My own engineers handle the near-term stuff."

And in a meeting Ron had with one of his engineers about current allocation of time, he heard:

"Most of our time is spent performing various engineering services for the product divisions."

Ron's thinking through of the problem led him to confirm to the president that the basic objectives of his organization should be new product development for the near term through company-funded and government-funded programs. All such programs were transferred to Ron's organization, and engineering services were performed by the operating division engineers. This early definition of organizational objectives was the basic direction taken by the research and development division for the next five years. It led to a 1,100 percent growth in research and development sales within three years and the acquisition of new business that had the potential for quadrupling the company's then-current production sales.

Different organizations will have different main objectives. Your objective could be to develop proprietary products, to engage in scientific research, or to acquire government contracts. Or your goal might be related to technical support, quality assurance, reliability, or engineering sales. Whatever your objective or objectives, they should be clearly expressed, written down, and agreed upon by you and your boss.

BREAKING YOUR MAIN OBJECTIVE DOWN INTO TASKS
AND SUBTASKS

Once your main objective or objectives have been established, you can begin to think about how you are going to accomplish them. A single major objective may be of such magnitude that it is difficult, if not impossible, to accomplish. But a major objective is made up of subcomponents, and each of these tasks is smaller, less overwhelming, and easier to accomplish than the overriding objective.

For example, consider Ron's objective of near-term new product development. He might choose to break this objective into tasks involving identification of potential new product candidates, screening, selection of products for development, development plans, and the actual execution of the new product development. Each task is then further broken down into subtasks. For example, the development task might be made up of research, design, mock-up fabrication, building of a prototype, limited test, limited production, and operational test.

Having accomplished a breakdown by task, Ron has a much better understanding about the kind of organizational structure he will need. He will have forced himself to think through such questions as: Will his organization do its own marketing of its R&D services to the government, or will a company marketing department do this, or will these responsibilities be shared? At what point will testing be finished and will the operating division become involved in producing and marketing the product? How much flexibility and how much stability will Ron's organization need? Will the organization be primarily a research organization, a systems development organization, or a sales organization? How much interface will be required with other company organizations?

Answering these questions once, however, is not enough. The technical manager may need to rethink the organization's objectives, tasks, and subtasks from time to time.

The Importance of Continued Mission Review

No environment in which any organization functions is static. As time goes on, the work of an organization will change to be compatible with its environment and the situations it faces. These changes may or may not necessitate a full restructuring. Peter Drucker has observed that reorganization is major surgery. Like major surgery, it should not be undertaken without good reason. However, changes in the environment, the marketplace, or the product may necessitate anything from minor organizational tune-up to a major reorganization.

Therefore, an appraisal of the organization's main objectives, as well as the tasks and subtasks needed to accomplish them, must be under constant review by the organization's manager. Only in this way can he or she maintain an understanding of the tasks and current objectives of the organization. Such an understanding is essential not only if the organization is to be structured to perform most efficiently and effectively but even if it is going to survive.

Should a Charter Be Drawn Up?

A written charter formally establishes an organization and outlines its objectives, the scope of its work, its authority, and its responsibilities. It serves as a framework for good working relationships.

Once you have agreed with your boss on what your organization's goals will be and completed the definition of tasks, a written charter cleared by your boss can greatly assist you in your job by:

- Providing clear documented guidance for your people on where the organization is going.
- Alerting other organizations in the company as to your responsibilities and authority.
- Ensuring that both you and your boss understand what it is you will be doing.
- Providing guidance on ways of resolving conflicts (over roles, responsibilities, etc.) between your organization and other organizations.

The best time to get a charter is when an organization is just being established or when you are just taking over as the organization's manager. However, it is almost always possible to obtain a charter if you can present valid reasons as to why you need one.

Usually it is to your advantage for your organization to have a written charter. However, there are situations in which is is better not to have one. For example, your boss may be intentionally allowing your organization to encroach on the work responsibilities of other, collateral organizations. Under these circumstances it is unwise to make your encroachment conspicuous. Or perhaps you are one of many similar technical subunits that report to a larger technical organization which already has a charter. Under these circumstances, your responsibilities, authority, and scope of work may be so obvious as to make development of a charter unnecessary. Finally, the nature and scope of your group's work may be such—or may be changing so frequently—that a charter would have to be written in too general a fashion. In this case it would be little more than decoration and would provide no advantage to your operation. It might even provide disadvantages.

Consider whether it is to your advantage to have a written charter, and if it is, ask for one.

THE CONCEPT OF THE TRADITIONAL ORGANIZATION

Traditional organization theory introduces the concepts of line and staff, an understanding of which is essential to structuring any organization. Line personnel are the people who take actions and make decisions that are related directly to the objectives of the organization. Line personnel form a "chain of command" in which decisions and orders are passed down from the top of an organization to succeeding lower levels to the very bottom working level. Responsibilities and authority are typically very explicit and clear-cut. There is no doubt about who reports to whom or about what authority and responsibility managers at each level have.

Staff personnel provide advice, assistance, and recommendations to line personnel. Staff is not in the chain of command. According to traditional organization theory, anyone who is not line is staff.

A good example of traditional organization is the military. Figure 1 shows the organization of a typical infantry battalion. Note the lines of authority and the pyramided structure reaching its pinnacle with the battalion commander. Also note the staff at every level of the organization down to platoon level.

Many companies and technical organizations are organized along traditional lines. Figure 2 shows an engineering division. Note the similarities to the organization of the infantry battalion.

According to traditional organization theory, there are two kinds of staff: personal and specialized.

Personal Staff

Personal staff members are individuals who are assigned to a particular manager and have no specific duties or responsibilities except those assigned by their boss. Personal assistants, for example, have no official authority except that which derives from the authority of their man-

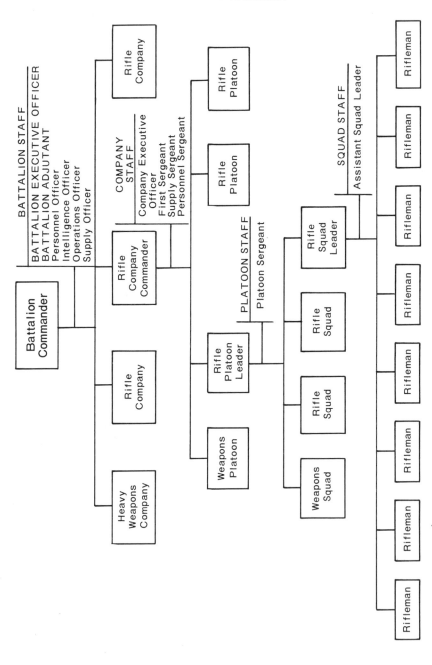

FIGURE 1. Typical infantry battalion organization.

FIGURE 2. An engineering division.

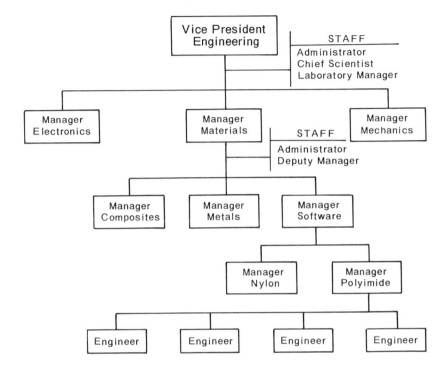

agers. A secretary would be personal staff. So would an "assistant-to" at any level. Neither office has any authority on its own. However, if a manager instructs a secretary or an assistant-to to arrange a meeting of all senior subordinate managers, within the limits of that assignment the secretary or assistant-to has authority to do the job.

Specialized Staff

Specialized staff members differ from personal staff members in that they perform necessary functions that require special skills, training, education, or experience. Moreover, they may have authority over their own specialty areas as a result of their background. Yet, the functions are not directly related to the organization's business. In the military, specialized functions are performed by the surgeon general, judge advocate general, chaplain, and so on. In industry, the functions might be finance, personnel, law, contracts, or even research and development.

A specialized staff can continuously develop and execute plans and projects pertaining to its specialized function, while at the same time freeing line managers to concentrate on day-to-day operations and to make use of the data developed by the staff when appropriate. A specialized staff can also advise the line managers in the organization on a continuing basis. Thus a personnel manager may work across the board to advise line managers of government hiring requirements or current competitive compensation within the industry. Finally, members of the specialized staff may be assigned by line managers to perform certain work pertaining to their specialities. For example, a research and development department might be directed to explore the technical risk in developing a new product.

Traditional organization theory has been altered slightly in recent times in consideration of the fact that certain of the specialized staff may be "staff" to the larger organization but "line" in accomplishment of their own function. The head of research and development, for example, may function as staff in advising the manager (the president) of a manufacturing company. However, within his own R&D organization, he may manage considerable resources in people, capital, and facilities and head his own chain of command in order to perform the R&D function of developing new products. Therefore, the R&D manager of a company may at once be operating as a line manager and as a staff adviser.

THE PRINCIPLES OF TRADITIONAL ORGANIZATION THEORY

Certain principles of traditional organization theory have evolved and are considered basic to achieving a successful organization. These principles include:

1. Responsibility should be given only with a commensurate amount of authority.

2. Each position should report to only one other position, so that every individual has only one boss.

3. Clear lines of authority and responsibility should be established from the top to the bottom of an organization.

4. A limited number of individuals should report to any one manager, defined by the number the manager can control effectively and usually thought to be nine or less. This is known as the "span of control."

5. The design of the job should determine the selection of personnel rather than the personnel determining the design of the job.

6. Responsibility or authority for carrying out a task should not be divided among different managers.

7. A superior who delegates authority for accomplishing a task to a subordinate is still accountable for the task's being performed properly.

The traditional theory of organization has served reasonably well as a model for structuring and operating an organization successfully. However, in recent times behavioral scientists have entered the picture and criticized traditional theory. The theme of their criticisms is not that a traditionally structured organization won't work, but that a group of human beings can be organized to work better.

The basic criticisms of the behavioral scientists are:

○ The principles of traditional organization theory make demands on individuals that are at odds with their psychological needs. For example, the narrow specialization of tasks inherent in a traditional organization may be incongruent with an individual's desire for variety.

○ The principles of traditional organization theory are derived from an incorrect basic assumption: the idea that people dislike work and responsibility and therefore must be closely supervised if they are to perform organizational tasks properly. In fact, many people do seek responsibility and do enjoy work. Therefore, principles based on a theory to the contrary cannot take advantage of the maximum potential for work inherent in every individual.

○ A traditional organization provides for no communications between the manager and his organization as a whole, only between the manager and his immediate subordinates. Therefore, information going down from the top, or coming up from the bottom, is by necessity filtered. It may not represent a true picture of what the communicator actually desires to communicate. Defenders of traditional organization might refer to mass meetings of an organization's personnel, during which the manager could distribute down-going information without a filter, or the fact that a subordinate manager could bring the communicator with him to a meeting with a superior manager to ensure the accuracy of up-going communication. The first point might be refuted by pointing out that a mass meeting is not usually the day-to-day method of communication and if it were always used, would interfere with the chain of command. There are also some problems with the idea of a subordinate manager bringing a communicator to a meeting with a superior manager. Further, the decision to include the communicator is really up to the subordinate manager and is not inherently provided for by the organizational structure. The bottom line is that the traditional organization may lead people in the middle to distort information or to keep it to themselves.

  ○ Traditional organization theory does not integrate many dimensions of managerial and employee behavior. For example, leadership and motivation are treated as separate entities in a traditional organization—tools that must be understood and manipulated to improve the working of the organization. They are not part of the organizational structure itself.

  ○ Traditional organization theory assumes that human beings always act rationally. Therefore, it follows that management should be concerned primarily with formal and official actions that will make things come out right. In this view, one issues a directive, it proceeds down through the chain of command, and it is followed. But in real life we know that individuals do not always act in a rational manner. The directive put in at one end of the system does not always result in the exact desired action coming out the other end. Varying alliances and informal organizations grow within a formal organization and must be dealt with in some way. Managers may be wasting their time if they keep trying to achieve the impossible: make their people fit into the "rational" world as they see it.

  ○ Many people question the assumption that human beings prefer the security of clearly defined paths as against freedom to determine their own approach. This certainly isn't true for all of the people all of the time. Many individuals flourish in a less structured atmosphere.

  ○ Traditional theory makes a questionable assumption about authority—that its source is always at the top, and levels below the top can obtain it only as it is delegated downward. Even this reasonable-sounding assumption has been found to be untrue at times. Some types of authority exist by virtue of a person's expertise, or even his or her personality. Such an individual may be in any organization and at any level. In 1938 Chester Barnard wrote a book called *The Functions of the Executive.** No armchair theorist, Barnard had been president of the New Jersey Bell Telephone Company. He advanced a number of arguments that questioned traditional organization theory. One point he made was that the issue of whether an order has authority depends not necessarily on who gives the order but on whether it is accepted by those who receive it. Later research proved this observation accurate.

    In summary, whether one agrees or disagrees with the behavioral scientists, it is true that some assumptions made by traditional manage-

*Cambridge, Mass.: Harvard University Press, 1968.

ment theorists have been either proved wrong or proved right only some of the time.

NONTRADITIONAL SOLUTIONS TO THE ORGANIZATIONAL PROBLEM

The nontraditional human relations theory of organization places less emphasis on the strict, traditional pyramided structure of division of responsibility and authority in which each person is responsible to only one boss. Instead, the emphasis is on group interaction, in which all individuals are in constant contact through membership in different groups within the organization. Advocates of the human relations approach favor:

An emphasis on teamwork and development of voluntary cooperation.

Voluntary self-reliance and responsibility.

Enrichment or enlargement of jobs rather than narrow specialization.

Accountability to peers rather than superiors.

Enlargement of the span of control to encourage delegation.

An emphasis on group rather than individual decision-making.

Use of informal norms rather than total reliance on rules and regulations.

No doubt many of these solutions sound like prescriptions for organizational disaster. In practice, many of these unorthodox ideas have worked, and still are working, reasonably well. As an example, consider the task solution.

The Task Solution

Perhaps the first deviation from traditional organization theory was the task organization, an organization coming into existence for only a temporary time period to accomplish a certain well-defined task. Again we might look to the military for examples. In the military, task forces and detached commands for accomplishing specific missions or objectives may have predated the inception of traditional organization. The Doolittle Raiders group for the bombing mission against Japan during the early months of World War II was a task organization. It ceased to exist after the completion of its mission. For that matter, the Japanese forces that carried out the raid on Pearl Harbor were also a task organization.

In industry, we have had milder forms of task organization for some time. For example, there have been various types of committees set up to do various things over varying periods of time. The task organization enables management to draw individuals from the entire parent organization. Because the members of a task organization may come from different levels of the parent organization, information can be disseminated at several levels simultaneously. Because the organization is temporary, unneeded resources can be redirected as soon as they become superfluous to the solution of the problem. Also, task organizations enable a greater number of individuals to gain higher-level managerial experience sooner than they can in the more fixed, permanent traditional organizations. Perhaps the most sophisticated form of task organization is the matrix organization. This will be discussed later.

Criticisms of the Human Relations Theory

Despite some outstanding successes, many managers and modern organization theorists regard at least some of the human relation theories as incorrect, if not downright stupid. They argue that:

- These theories assume that all problems can be reduced to the human level and ignore the restraints imposed by technology, job design, the market, the formal (as opposed to informal) power structure, and other factors that can have a significant effect on how an organization operates.
- The informal structures advocated sometimes result in greater psychological conflict and role ambiguities than are present in a traditional organization.
- The theories erroneously assume that resources are always available on an unlimited basis to do what is required.

TRADITIONAL ORGANIZATION OR A HUMAN RELATIONS ORGANIZATION?

The two approaches to organization are usually not compatible, and yet both claim universality. Since research has netted support for both approaches as being best, the observant student of organization has been left in a bit of a quandary. This dichotomy with its attendant conflicting claims gave rise to yet a third theory of organization, known as contingency theory. The thrust of contingency theory is that there is no best approach for all organizations and that the theory chosen should depend on various situational factors, including the environment the manager is in and the circumstances he or she is facing.

Contingency theory tells us to use our heads. What is totally correct for a manufacturing company staffed largely by nondegreed employees may be totally wrong for a research firm made up mainly of Ph.D.'s.

THE RISKS OF SWITCHING THEORIES MIDSTREAM

Contingency theory raises an important question. If the traditional organization theory and the human relations theory can apply to different firms at different times, should not one or the other be used—on a continuously changing basis—as environmental and situational factors facing the firm change?

It is true that new conditions may make the organizational structure in use seem nonoptimal, at least from a theoretical point of view. And, as will be shown later, there is good reason to associate alternate theories of organization with a firm's stages of growth. However, another factor must be taken into consideration: the effect of change itself on the organization's efficiency and effectiveness. Change is intervention, and intervention even with good intent can lead to negative results in both the short and long run. For example, a change in structure in going from application of one theory to another might cause the unwanted resignation of a key executive, or the loss of an important customer.

This factor, the factor of change, acts as an overriding check against continual organizational alterations. It means that regardless of how well meant a change is, or how much logic dictates this change, its possible negative effects must be carefully weighed against the hoped-for benefits.

DESIGNING A SUCCESSFUL ORGANIZATION: THE IMPORTANCE OF OBJECTIVES

To recapitulate the points we have covered so far, step 1 in designing any organization is to determine the organization's main objectives and work to be done. Step 2 is to choose an appropriate theory of organization. We can design a traditional organizational structure with clear lines of authority and responsibility, or a human relations structure that may cut across organizational lines, employ a span of control of indeterminate number, and be built around nonspecialized divisions of labor.

To a given operating manager, it makes little difference whether a theory has universal applicability or does not. What is important is its applicability to the manager's organization. And the only criterion for this applicability is success in attaining the established objectives. The type of organizational structure selected must be that which offers the greatest probability of success.

For example, if you head up a project organization, your primary requirement for success is to complete the project successfully—to get the job done. Effectiveness is more important than efficiency. It is no use doing the job economically if you either do not finish it or find that when you finish the result doesn't work as it should. On the other hand, if you are an engineering testing organization, competing with other firms offering a similar service, the primary requirement for success may well be efficiency—an emphasis on economic operation.

Therefore, in thinking through what kind of structure you want, the basic objective of your organization must still be foremost in your mind. The different types of organizational structures described below will all work well in suitable situations and circumstances. Which ones will be appropriate for you will depend on your main objectives and on the work done by your organization.

CENTRALIZATION VERSUS DECENTRALIZATION

The issue of centralization versus decentralization must be resolved regardless of whether the traditional approach or human relations approach is used as the theoretical underpinning for your organizational design. Centralized decision-making means making decisions at the highest level possible within the company. An example might be a firm with many plants in which all basic decisions and policies are made at headquarters. There are certain advantages of centralization. Important decisions are generally made by those people in the organization who are most qualified to make them. (This assumes, of course, that the more competent and experienced people in the organization are located at the top.) Usually the decision-makers in a centralized organization will be located where they are readily accessible to one another. This makes coordination easier and increases the likelihood that a decision will support overall company interests rather than the interests of any one group or division of the company. Centralized organizations require less total staff, since general staff support can come from headquarters rather than each suborganization being allocated its own. Other forms of duplicated effort can also be eliminated, as many functions can be performed at the control location.

Finally, centralization permits various types of standardization that are frequently advantageous. For example, if a company has standardized operating procedures throughout the organization, managers can be transferred from one division to another more easily because less time will be needed for familiarization with new procedures. Frequently, materials or equipment can be purchased more cheaply for all of the divisions of the organization simultaneously if the material or equipment is standardized.

In a decentralized organization, responsibility is delegated as far down the organization as possible. One of the primary advantages of decentralization is that the individuals who are most directly concerned with the work to be accomplished can make the decisions related to it. Decisions may be made by people who have greater knowledge of specific conditions and problems. This is the reason multinational corporations are usually decentralized. Local conditions vary so much that centralization of compensation, buying, or even a single overall corporate policy may not be possible.

In addition, under decentralization there is a much more rapid response to changing situations. In a centralized organization, it takes time to collect the information required for a decision and send it to higher headquarters; for headquarters to request additional information; for this information to be collected and sent back; for higher headquarters to make the decision and send it back down to the subordinate unit; and for the subordinate unit to implement the decision. If the situation changes much during this process, several reiterations of the process may be necessary—or the decision may have disastrous consequences because it is based on obsolete information and is no longer appropriate to the changed situation. With a decentralized structure, decisions can be made and implemented more rapidly.

Another advantage is that decentralization promotes management development. More managers are needed in a decentralized organization than in a centralized one, so there are many good learning opportunities for individuals who are candidates for higher-level management later in their careers. Finally, decentralization may provide greater job satisfaction to individuals who desire considerable freedom of action, responsibility, and authority.

CHOICE OF AN ORGANIZATIONAL DESIGN

Whether you choose traditional, human relations, or contingency organization theory—and whether you opt for a centralized or decentralized structure—you will need to choose between three basic organizational designs: the functional organization, the goal-oriented organization, and the matrix organization. Basically, the functional organization tends to be traditional while the goal-oriented organization tends to be based on human relations theory. But there are elements of human relations theory that can be incorporated into the functional organization, and the goal-oriented organization can have aspects of traditional theory. A matrix organization attempts to secure the best of both worlds, and it too can have underpinnings of both theories in its construction.

The Functional Organization

The functional organization utilizes a traditional organizational structure, with division of labor built around various operating functions, activities, or processes. For example, operating functions in a manufacturing company might be engineering, marketing/sales, and production as shown in Figure 3.

A functional technical organization is shown in Figure 4. In this example, the functions are design, quality control, mock up/prototype laboratory, engineering drawing, and research and development. Functional organizations tend to work better with centralized types of structures in which the head of the technical organization is making most of the policy and important day-to-day decisions. In fact, a functional

FIGURE 3. A functionally organized company.

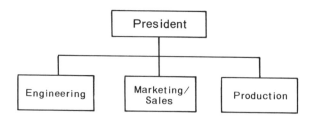

FIGURE 4. A functionally organized technical organization.

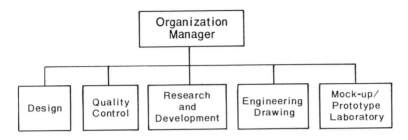

design usually has all the advantages and disadvantages of the centralized type of organization discussed previously.

But it has other characteristics that may assist or hinder you in accomplishing your objectives within the unique circumstances that your organization faces. These include:

o The division of labor in a functional organization often leads to greater efficiencies than would be possible in a goal-oriented organization. For example, a human factors engineering department servicing a corporation at two different locations may consist of a psychologist and a design engineer. However, if instead each geographic area was responsible for its own human engineering support, the corporation would require four professionals or one professional possessing skills in both psychology and design engineering.

o There is a greater likelihood that personnel resources will be utilized efficiently in a functional organization. This is because an engineer or scientist who runs out of work can be directed to do work in other organizations within the company with no change in supervision or of organization.

o There is more professional synergism in a functional organization, since professionals of one specialty interact with one another. Thus a new person will be more easily trained in his or her specialty, and all members will tend to increase their knowledge of their specialties and improve their technical skills. However, this is a two-edged sword. A member of a functional organization will understand less of other specialties in the overall organization and may tend to focus more on his or her profession than on the goals of the larger organization to which the functional organization belongs.

o Performance evaluation is likely to be more accurate in a functional organization, since the organization is generally supervised by a specialist qualified in that function.

○ Functional organizations have more difficulty coordinating, scheduling, and integrating their activities with other functional organizations in the company. This is because of conflict and competition between different organizations as well as the lack of an overall manager—except at the highest level—who can resolve these problems. Consider a special project within engineering that requires a limited production run. That production run is in competition with the normal production requirements of the company. Further, the manufacturing manager is judged not on his ability to support engineering by turning out a limited production run, but on his ability to meet daily production requirements. Since the project will be viewed as an "engineering project" rather than a "company project," the manufacturing manager may favor his normal production work over the special work even when this is not in the best interests of the company.

○ Functional organizations tend to be more formal and less flexible. Conflicts may be more difficult to resolve because of the rigid relation between levels of authority within the organization and between different organizations. New tasks or activities that fall outside the domain of the established functional organization generally require new organizations to be established, since the old organization will tend to resist taking on new responsibilities.

The Goal-Oriented Organization

A goal-oriented organization may have elements of the traditional organization as well as those of human relations concepts. As the name implies, the organization is designed around the organization's goal—most often according to different products, different geographical areas, different categories of customers, or different projects. For example, an energy company, as shown in Figure 5, may be organized around different operating divisions for each product: petroleum, gas, and coal. A company selling consumer products might organize according to customer: retail sales, wholesale sales, and institutional sales. Or a company might organize according to geographical areas: Northwest sales division, Eastern sales division, and so on. A sample technical organization built around goals is shown in Figure 6.

Each division of a goal-oriented organization is more or less self-contained and can operate relatively independently. The petroleum division of the energy company, for example, will probably have its own engineering, production, and sales divisions. Goal-oriented organizations, being self-contained, permit informal contact between different special-

FIGURE 5. A company with a goal-oriented organization.

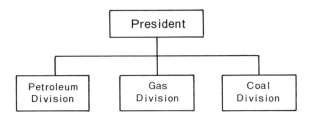

ties with a resulting reduced need to refer conflicts to higher authority for decisions.

In this independence, however, also lies the goal-oriented organization's greatest weakness: duplication. There may be duplication of personnel, of skills, and of equipment, whereas one set of everything could be sufficient to support the same level of effort in a functional organization. In addition, the goal-oriented organization has other drawbacks, which are in some cases the mirror images of the advantages of the functional organization. There is less likelihood that personnel resources will be utilized effectively. This is because the area of work in a goal-oriented organization is more limited in size as a result of the focus on the goal. When there is no work within the goal-oriented organization, the engineer or scientist cannot easily be directed elsewhere without a change of supervision or change in organization. There is also less professional synergism and less likelihood of accurate performance evaluation of specialists.

However, the goal-oriented organization has one major advantage that can outweigh all else: the organization is focused on achieving the goal rather than on the day-to-day work routines of the functional organization. Schedules and coordinating and integrating work to ac-

FIGURE 6. A goal-oriented technical organization.

complish a specific goal are far more effective when the end goal is within the organization itself.

Accordingly, when the emphasis is on the satisfactory accomplishment of a project or task, when schedules absolutely must be met, when a unique service is being offered, or when unique problems are to be solved, the goal-oriented design generally works better in reaching the goal than a functional design.

The Matrix Organization

The matrix organization was developed over the last 15 years in an attempt to make use of the best features of both the functional and goal-oriented organizations. Whether the matrix organization formed is permanent or temporary, it is comprised of individuals who are assigned to one or more other suborganizations within the overall organization. Thus, supervision comes from more than one source. This is illustrated in Figure 7, in which Project A and Project B form matrix organizations within an overall functional organization. Note that all the engineers have at least two supervisors. Engineers E and I have three. Both report to their functional supervisor as well as to the chiefs of Projects A and B. The project chiefs may also have other functional jobs. The chief of Project A, for example, may be the head of the mechanical engineering department.

Before a matrix organization can be adopted, certain preconditions must be met:

○ There must be a sufficiently large functional organization to serve as a reservoir of technical personnel to be assigned to the matrix organization.
○ There must be a need for multiple projects.
○ As with the goal-oriented organization, the overriding objectives must be task accomplishment and meeting of time constraints, as opposed to economic efficiency.

Also, the matrix organization must get its power from somewhere. The mere establishment of the matrix organization does not provide it with enough authority to stand against and win out over a functional department. Unlike the manager of a typical functional department, the head of a matrix organization has no formal authority over the personnel he has "matrixed" from other organizations; his authority is over the

FIGURE 7. A matrix organization.

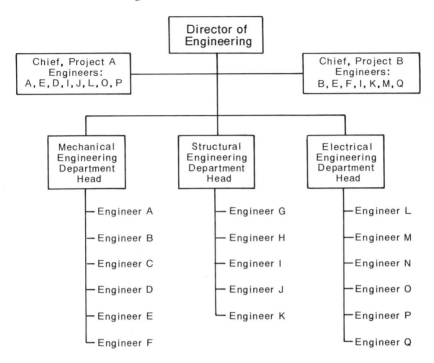

project only. The most common method of providing this authority is through project funding. Funds are allotted to the head of the matrix organization, who in turn "buys" engineering services from the functional departments. In this way the functional organizations are made dependent on project funds from the various matrix organizations for their existence.

One other point should be considered when deciding for or against the matrix organization. Organizational esprit de corps—the common spirit of organizational oneness that can inspire great enthusiasm and devotion to group goals—is much more difficult to foster in an organization that is only one of several to which an individual belongs.

The advantages of the matrix organization are the goal-oriented organization's advantages of flexibility and focus on objectives. But unlike the goal-oriented organization, the matrix organization does not suffer from duplication of effort, since the same individual may be a member of more than one matrix organization.

ADDITIONAL FACTORS TO CONSIDER IN ORGANIZATIONAL DESIGN

We have talked about general concepts of organization, different organizational structures, and their advantages and disadvantages. Still, there are additional factors you must consider that will affect the sort of organization you want to evolve. These are:

> The authority level at which you are managing.
> The individual capabilities of the people in your organization.
> The company environment and its philosophy.
> The stage of development of your organization.

The Authority Level at Which You Are Managing

The authority level at which you are operating will determine not only what kinds of organizational structures you are free to select but also whether you can change the organizational structure at all. If you are at the top—perhaps the president—of a small to medium-size company, or the divisional general manager of a larger company, you probably have the greatest freedom to organize as you wish. You may still have to convince someone that the organizational structure you have decided on is proper. But you probably have the authority to change from a functional structure to a goal-oriented one or vice versa, or to establish a matrix organization.

A lower-level manager may not have this authority. For example, if you are a first-line supervisor, your organization's structure may be a "given," either because the size of your organization dictates that it be organized functionally; because your boss doesn't want four functional organizations and one goal-oriented one, or four goal-oriented and one functional organization reporting to him; or just because your boss doesn't want you to tamper with something that's been the same way for a long time.

The Individual Capabilities of Your People

Individual capabilities are important. You should not design a job or construct the organization to suit a particular individual. On the other hand, you must have (or be able to get) qualified individuals to fill the organization you have constructed. This makes it rather poor judgment to establish matrix or project organizations in your functional organization if you have no one in your organization capable of handling this kind of job, and cannot get anyone from outside the organization. One must be a realist.

The Company Environment and Its Philosophy

Every company is different—different not only in industry, personnel, and products or services offered, but also in environment and philosophy. If your company's philosophy is loose and freewheeling, with much decentralized decision-making, it's going to be extremely difficult and probably a mistake to establish your organization as a highly centralized, formalized organization. Similarly, even when a matrix management appears to be called for, if you can't get authority over the project funds it may be better to prepare some other structure for getting the job done. In this case it's preferable to do the best you can with a nonoptimal organizational structure rather than to have a theoretically optimal structure yet be stymied by not being able to do very much with it.

The Stage of Your Organization's Development

A technical organization progresses through three stages in its development, at any one of which it can remain indefinitely. This means not only that you need to apply the principles of organization in a general fashion, but that you are aiming essentially at a moving target. In order to apply the principles, you must see exactly where that target is and you must realize that if you are going to continue to hit the target, you must stay with it as it moves.

An organization should not be changed without very good reasons. But one such reason may be that the organization is coming into or has already passed into a new stage of its development. The three stages of the technical organization are the start-up stage, the functional orientation stage, and the diversification stage.

1. *The start-up stage.* This is the initial stage of a technical organization. It is generally characterized by direct influence by the new organization's manager, a limited "product line" or service, and limited expertise in functional areas, both technical and nontechnical, that are covered. Accordingly, in the start-up stage, members of the organization may wear several hats. The manager himself may do technical work in addition to his managerial functions.

The start-up stage organization lends itself to a goal-oriented structure because:

- ○ There are insufficient members for a functional structure.
- ○ The small size of the organization can foster a project or goal flavor.
- ○ The size permits maximum impact by the manager's personality on all personnel in the organization.

Many technical organizations, even those that are years old, do not progress out of the start-up stage. This is not necessarily a bad thing. This stage may be where the organization should be in order to do its job. It is not necessary that the organization get any larger or in any way increase its responsibilities. For other organizations, the start-up stage is only that—a starting point for additional growth.

2. *The functional orientation stage.* In this second stage of the developing technical organization, the responsibilities of the organization have increased. Additional personnel are brought into the organization. It is more difficult for the manager to exert his personality over and control the number of people reporting to him directly. It is no longer necessary for the manager or other members of the organization to be responsible for more than one function. Indeed, it is more efficient to organize along the lines of a division of labor by specialty. During this stage, a technical organization tends to be functionally oriented because:

- ○ The increasing depth of responsibilities of the organization cannot be handled easily by a nonspecialized staff, and there are too many different responsibilities for the members to perform multiple functions.
- ○ The increasing number of specialized personnel available permits a functional organization.
- ○ The size of the organization no longer allows the manager to derive much advantage from one-on-one contacts with all his personnel.

Again, many technical organizations attain the functional orientation stage and then grow no further.

3. *The diversification stage.* This is the final stage of the technical organization. Here the responsibilities of the organization have become even more diverse. The manager who is still operating with a functional organization finds he must make general decisions cutting across functional organizational lines. The number of decisions he must make has increased to the point where he feels he is losing control. He may then decentralize by going back into a goal-oriented organization in which he

delegates some general decision-making to submanagers in charge of semi-autonomous units.

The diversification stage of the technical organization is once again goal-oriented because:

- It permits delegation of some general decision-making authority to submanagers, giving the manager of the overall organization more time and greater control over increased responsibilities.
- It enables a return to an entrepreneurial flavor, in that each of the suborganizations may now be viewed as being in the start-up stage.

Note that the stages of a technical organization imply a cycle: goal-oriented—functional—goal-oriented. A matrix organization might also be introduced, during either the functional orientation stage or the diversification stage. Sometimes a matrix is used as an alternative to the goal-oriented structure in the diversification stage.

In summary, building an organization for efficiency and effectiveness requires (1) establishing or confirming your main objectives, (2) breaking your main objectives down into tasks and subtasks, and (3) considering alternative organizational structures in terms of objectives, tasks and subtasks, and other factors—including the authority level at which you are managing, the individual capabilities of the people in your organization, and the company environment and its philosophy. The final step is to make a selection and design your organization.

CHAPTER 3

How to Staff and Recruit for Your Technical Organizatization

It may be that you have always considered staffing and recruiting to be strictly the purview of someone in personnel work, and not the responsibility of a technical manager. It is true that personnel departments exist and that the twin functions of staffing and recruiting are two of their most important activities. But as the manager who in the end must reap the benefits of good staffing and recruiting or must suffer the results of poor work in this area, it is you who must be primarily concerned. A personnel expert can assist you greatly in helping you to design the specifications for a position, or in finding a suitable engineer or scientist to fill it. But the position is not his personal concern. He cannot successfully guess at your requirements, and he cannot fill the need once established by simply recruiting for a "mechanical engineer" or some other title with which you have furnished him. In the end, it is not the personnel manager's organization that will suffer from mistakes or shortcomings during the process of staffing or recruiting—it is your organization. Since staffing and recruiting can have a major impact on the future effectiveness and efficiency of your organization, these activities are among the most important to which you can devote your time as a technical manager.

ESTABLISHING PERSONNEL REQUIREMENTS

The first step in the recruitment process is not to begin to recruit, but to plan ahead for your organization's future needs. To do this you should pick a fixed period of time—say, a year from now. What will be your organization's objectives during this period? Do you plan to develop a new product? Will a current program require additional expansion at some point in time? Will other activities in your company require expansion of your organization in order to provide proper support?

Personnel requirements must start with the planning process covered in Chapter 8. Each activity in the plan is made up of a number of tasks, and each task will be performed by a professional who will staff your organization. Therefore, for every project and task, write down what type of professional you will need to fill the job and an estimate of how many manhours during the year will be required of that person, expressed by month. Also indicate whether the position will be filled by someone already in your organization or whether an addition to your staff will be necessary. Much of this information can be obtained from other planning documents. A manpower requirements worksheet such as the one shown in Figure 8 may be used for this purpose. The figure is illustrative only, and is not meant to be accurately descriptive of the number of tasks or type of tasks in a real project. The numbers in the worksheet indicate the number of manhours required per month.

In this example, the organization has need of a mechanical engineer beginning in February and continuing through most of the year; for one electronics engineer beginning in January, increasing to two electronics engineers in April and going back to one in October; and for one-half of a materials engineer beginning in June and continuing through November. An analysis of these requirements must consider:

1. Can the same engineer perform different tasks that are required, or are the requirements of each task sufficiently different that different engineers must be used? An example of this type of decision could be the case of the electronics engineer required for headset integration of Widget A until July and the electronics engineer needed for prototype testing of Widget A in August. Could this be the same engineer?

2. What should be done about "partial" engineers that are needed? For example, consider the one-half of a materials engineer required for June through November for exploratory testing on Project X. Should the task be altered to enable another category of engineer to do the job? If a materials engineer is hired, can other tasks be done by this type of engineer instead of the type originally envisioned? Is the

FIGURE 8.

PROJECT/TASK	REQUIREMENT/ADDITION	JAN.	FEB.	MAR.	APR.
Widget A Project management	Mech. Eng. on staff	165	165	165	165
Widget A Design facepiece	Mech. Eng. addition		165	165	165
Widget A Headset integration	Elec. Eng. addition				165
Widget A Prototype construction	Mech. Eng. addition				
Widget A Prototype testing	Mech. Eng. on staff				
Widget A Prototype testing	Elec. Eng. addition				
Project X Project management	Materials Eng. on staff	165	165	165	165
Project X Exploratory research	Elec. Eng. addition	165	165	165	
Project X Exploratory testing	Elec. Eng. addition				165
Project X Exploratory testing	Materials Eng. addition				
Total requirements		1 mat. 1 mech. 1 E&E	1 mat. 2 mech. 1 E&E	1 mat. 2 mech. 1 E&E	1 mat. 2 mech. 2 E&E
Total additions to staff		1 E&E	1 mech. 1 E&E	1 mech. 1 E&E	1 mech. 2 E&E

task sufficiently unique and/or important that a special engineer must be obtained if the person will be used only 25 percent of the time?

3. There is a learning process involved, and few if any of the professionals you hire will be fully effective in the jobs you will want them to do at the time of hiring. This period of learning must be allowed for in your planning, or you will not be able to accomplish your goals within the budget and schedule that you develop.

Obviously all of these factors will affect your thinking about what kind of engineers or scientists you want to hire for different tasks. Because of this, your job specifications will begin to deviate from what you thought they were initially. This is entirely normal, and this process of change in job specifications will continue to a greater or lesser degree right up to the time you hire someone.

Manpower requirements worksheet.

MAY	JUNE	JULY	AUG.	SEP.	OCT.	NOV.	DEC.
165	165	165	165	165	165	165	165
165							
165	165	165					
		165	165	165	165		
				165	165	165	165
			165	165	165	165	165
165	165	165	165	165	165	165	165
165	165	165	165	165			
	85	85	85	85	85	85	
1 mat.	1½ mat.	1½ mat.	1½ mat.	1½ mat.	1½ mat.	1½ mat.	1 mat.
2 mech.	1 mech.	2 mech.	2 mech.	3 mech.	3 mech.	2 mech.	2 mech.
2 E&E	2 E&E	2 E&E	2 E&E	2 E&E	1 E&E	1 E&E	1 E&E
	½ mat.	½ mat.	½ mat.	½ mat.	½ mat.	½ mat.	
1 mech.		1 mech.	1 mech.	1 mech.	1 mech.		
2 E&E	2 E&E	2 E&E	2 E&E	2 E&E	1 E&E	1 E&E	1 E&E

ESTABLISHING JOB SPECIFICATIONS

At this point, your initial analysis should be complete, and you should
have a preliminary list of professional personnel requirements and when
you need each person. Let us assume that after considering the tradeoffs,
you arrive at the following list:

January	1	Electronics engineer
February	1	Mechanical engineer
March	1	Electronics engineer
April	1	Materials engineer

Note that these dates do not match perfectly the need dates indicated in
Figure 8. This is because of the learning process and other factors you
have considered as outlined above.

FIGURE 9. The job specification form.

JOB TITLE   Project Engineer, Mechanical

REPORTING TO   Project Manager, Oxygen Breathing Mask

BACKGROUND

A new project is being established to develop an advanced lightweight oxygen breathing mask for use by pilots of high-performance aircraft such as the F-15. The development of this mask is planned as a private venture and is expected to take 24 months and cost $2 million, with a planned professional staff of ten full-time engineers. This project has been approved by top management, and the necessary funds have been allocated. However, except for the Project Manager, who has already been selected, the professional staff has not been identified within the engineering division. The Project Engineer, Mechanical, must be hired no later than October of this calendar year. He will be hired by the Director of Engineering Projects with the approval of the Project Manager.

REQUIRED TASKS

This engineer will be responsible for all mechanical design work on the project and specifically will design the facepiece, attachments to the masks, and all valves. He will be responsible for all nonelectronic developmental and prototyped testing. He will also advise the Project Manager and other engineers on the project on matters having to do with mechanical design. It may be that this engineer will be assigned additional duties as Deputy Project Manager, but this decision has not yet been finalized. He will have other engineers and technicians reporting to him on a temporary, task basis.

DESIRED PRIOR EXPERIENCE

Ideally this engineer should have at least ten years experience, but five years would also be acceptable, if the decision is made not to assign him additional duties as Deputy Project Manager. Also, ideally he should have design experience with oxygen breathing masks. However, barring this he should have experience with some type of valve design, and experience in working with materials such as silicon or rubber. He should also have project experience, with prior responsibility for scheduling and cost, as well as design work considered a definite plus.

EDUCATION

This individual must have a B.S. in mechanical engineering, or a B.S. in some other engineering field with the desired design experience. An M.S. is better. An M.B.A. is okay, but not necessarily an advantage for this job. A Ph.D. would over-qualify the engineer for this job.

SPECIAL PROBLEMS

The Project Manager has a very demanding personality and cannot get along with all subordinates. This problem tends to be more acute with young engineers in their early 20s. It is essential that the engineer hired have the confidence of the Project Manager and be able to get along with him.

FACTORS THAT WOULD DEFINITELY EXCLUDE A CANDIDATE FROM CONSIDERATION
REGARDLESS OF OTHER QUALIFICATIONS OR ACCOMPLISHMENTS

(1) Having less than a B.S. degree. (2) Being unwilling to travel. (3) Being unable to get along with the Project Manager. (4) Being in any way averse to working on military-type projects.

TRAVEL REQUIREMENTS

About 5–10% per year.

SALARY RANGE

$25,000–35,000/year

OTHER COMPENSATION

Standard retirement plan, insurance, company savings plan (company puts in $1 for $1 up to 6% of salary). Could include use of company car under special circumstances.

WHY SHOULD SOMEONE TAKE THIS JOB?

(1) Professional growth—job may include Deputy Project Manager assignment. (2) Expansion in engineering division has been 300% over last five years. Current Project Manager was hired for similar job four years ago. (3) Program is important—to company and to U.S. air force. (4) Stability. There have been no layoffs since 1963.

For each requirement you would now write a detailed description of what exactly you want the person to do and other factors considered important. For this purpose Figure 9, the job specification form, can be used.

Note that even in the job specification form, the requirements are still not cast in iron. The job title can be changed at any time, and tasks can be added to or reduced in number or scope. Prior experience and education should be very flexible, since it's what the engineer or scientist is going to do, not what he or she has done already, that is critical. Past experience and education are important only as indicators of the individual's potential to perform future work. For this reason, number of years of experience should always be loose. Salary should be stated as a range, and even this range should be considered only a guideline. You can establish a more accurate upward limit by writing down a first-cut figure and then asking yourself whether you would pay 20 percent more for someone exceptional. If you would, keep adding increments of 5 percent until there is no way, under any circumstances, that you would be willing to pay the figure you have written last. If you couldn't pay the initial 20 percent more for a superstar, start increasing your original estimate by 5 percent until you find an exact maximum figure.

Don't forget to write down why someone should take the job. Put yourself in the candidate's shoes. Why should he or she go to work for you? If your only reason is that no one else is willing to make an offer, you're going to have a pretty weak staff. If you want good people, you should know the reasons why a candidate should come to work for you rather than going somewhere else or staying where he or she is now.

When you have completed the job specification forms for your staffing requirements, you should have a pretty good idea of what you want and what you're willing to pay. Even if you don't do the recruiting yourself, your surrogate in the form of a personnel manager should be able to do a much better job for you.

SHOULD YOU RECRUIT FROM WITHIN OR GO OUTSIDE?

Recruiting internally has advantages and disadvantages; so does recruiting outside your organization or the company. Whether it is better to do one or the other depends on your unique circumstances. You should consider both alternatives.

Recruiting from Within Your Organization or Company

Staffing from within is a good idea when personnel for the tasks required are currently available. Choosing this alternative is generally less expensive than recruiting an outsider. Also, the individual recruited internally is already familiar with people, procedures, policies, and special characteristics of your organization. Therefore, he will usually require less time to become operationally "up to speed" for the tasks to which you assign him. Staffing from within also gives you an opportunity to select individuals for future increased responsibilities. Nothing beats seeing an "up-and-comer" in action for making a realistic assessment of his or her ability and future potential for your organization and the company. Staffing from inside your organization can also provide a fringe benefit: if the assignment is perceived as an earned promotion, it will motivate not only the "recruit" but also other ambitious members of your organization.

Recruiting from Outside

The obvious time to recruit from outside is when an available candidate doesn't exist inside. If the people currently available are not already trained or do not have the necessary prior experience for the job, recruitment from outside the firm can reduce the expense of training new employees and lower the risk of failure. For example, if you have a critical R&D job to be managed, it may be cheaper and less risky to hire someone from outside who has successfully done this type of thing before rather than to promote someone from within and hope the person can grow into the job. Some firms are overzealous about promoting from within and will go to the extreme of attempting to structure the organization around the person they are grooming. The only trouble is that this sets off a chain reaction. You will soon find yourself changing not only this person's job but your entire organization as well. Should this individual ever leave the job, you can plan on making all these changes all over again.

Organizations that never hire above entry-level professionals tend to suffer from narrowness and stereotyped thinking. Such organizations never receive an infusion of new ideas from people coming in from other organizations. No one with the objectivity or perspective of a senior outsider is ever around to challenge or question the standard ways of doing things.

The disadvantages of recruiting from outside your organization are the other side of the coin: additional expense, lack of familiarity with your organizational situation, and possible demotivation in members of your organization who may get the idea that they cannot be promoted to a higher position.

In summary, you should staff from outside:

1. When no one is available to do the job who is already in the organization.
2. When using your current people would mean too extensive a training period or too high a risk of failure.
3. When your present organization is overstaffed with people who have grown up within it.

SOURCES OF PROFESSIONAL TALENT

You may need people at a time when there is a great demand for technical people or a time when there is an actual glut of technical professionals on the market. In either case, good people exist, and they are available. The trick is to locate them and attract them to your organization. Some of the sources of personnel we have already touched on; others we have not. In any event, here are six places to look for professional talent for your organization:

In your own organization.
Not in your organization but in your company.
In someone else's company.
Newly graduated or about to graduate.
Unemployed.
Probable layoffs due to cutbacks, project completions, and so on.
Job shops.

All of these people fall into one of two general classes: happy or unhappy. Regardless of source, a potential recruit should be approached and treated with the courtesy and tact due him as an individual and as a professional.

People in Your Own Organization

If the individual is currently in your own organization and is fit for the job you have in mind, you must consider three other aspects of his recruitment. First, what will happen as a result of his leaving the position he has held? While you obviously cannot indefinitely block a promotion because a person has been doing a good job, you cannot allow his area to fall apart because of his transfer either. The second thing you must consider is the impact on the candidate. How does he perceive the transfer, and does he want the new job? Finally, the impact on the rest of your organization must be taken into account. If the appointment is an obvious promotion, it is important that the promotion be deserved. If the appointment is more ambiguous, it is important that it not be seen as a demotion.

Paul G. was the manager of research and development in a small engineering company. He had five project engineers reporting to him and, because of expansion, needed an additional project engineer. Paul's problems were several. He wanted to build a professional organization in which all of his engineers had at least a bachelor's degree. There were no other engineers within the company who were available for transfer to Paul's organization. However, Paul's organization included an engineering drawing group. One of these draftsmen had, on several occasions, done work far and above that normally required of him. In fact, his work was on a par with the work required of any of Paul's engineers.

In deciding whether or not to appoint this man to an engineering position, Paul had to consider the following:

o How would the man relate to his former associates and vice versa?

o Would the fact that he had no degree create serious problems with the other project engineers, with other members of Paul's organization, or with members of other organizations?

o What could be done about the salary differential, considering that there would be limitations on how fast the new engineer's salary could be increased and how long it might take before anything approaching equity with the other project engineers could be achieved?

o What advantages would this individual bring to the job as an engineer in Paul's organization? He has had experience as a draftsman and is already familiar with general routines and procedures, both in the organization and the company. This would save some of the start-up time that would be required with an engineer hired from outside the company.

o A promotion to engineer from draftsman could be a motivating factor and might raise the expectations of other draftsmen. Is this desirable or not?

o People with this type of product experience are extremely difficult to find. It would be not only expensive but time-consuming to find an engineer outside the company who had experience with the product.

o What would be the impact on the organization and the draftsman if he failed in his transition to engineer?

In this particular case, Paul decided to promote the man into the engineering position. There were some minor problems with members of other organizations in the company, and some other small problems in adjustment that were worked out, but within a short period, this new engineer was doing better-quality work than most of his degreed counterparts. And because he worked longer and harder, he was promoted to even more responsible technical positions as time went on.

The point here is not that a draftsman should always be given the opportunity to be an engineer. Rather, it is that the technical manager should weigh all the tradeoffs before deciding whether or not to go outside his own organization in filling a position.

People Not in Your Organization but in Your Company

Here you have to be extremely careful in your recruiting so that you are not, rightly or wrongly, accused of raiding. The key to obtaining highly qualified personnel from other organizations in your company is good connections with the managers of the organizations in which the candidates currently serve. Although it is sometimes possible to get a key professional without the approval of the individual's manager, this is generally a very poor policy that can result in poor relations and problems with the manager of that organization in the future. Therefore, no matter what happens, keep in close contact with the candidate's current manager.

Sometimes an individual will come to you. This implies he is not fully happy in his present circumstances, or at least sees a better opportunity in your organization. At other times you identify the candidate. In either case, your action should be to approach the candidate's current manager, explain the need, and ask if you can speak officially to the candidate about a transfer. Obviously you will not always get approval. Without this manager's agreement, unless your need is desperate, it's best to leave the situation alone and look elsewhere. If the candidate is extremely unhappy and has come to you, it might be better if he approached his boss about permission to talk to you officially about a transfer. If you have a desperate need for the individual and the candidate's manager refuses to consider a transfer, bring this need out into the open. Make the request through your chain of command, letting your own boss and the candidate's manager know how serious the situation is.

This type of recruitment situation should be handled with extreme tact, and a confrontation with the candidate's manager should be avoided if possible. When the need for this individual is critical, however, you will have little choice. Recognize that this is no small thing, and don't expect very cordial relations with this individual in the future. Think twice before demanding the person and ask yourself which is more important to your organization—the person, or good relations with the other organization?

People in Someone Else's Company

Here you needn't worry about relationships with the other organization so much. It is generally accepted that if you can offer a better opportunity, an individual should be free to go and the other organization free to hire him.

In this situation you should find out whether the individual is currently unhappy or not. This will affect the candidate's readiness to move and will influence how you should handle the interview. Perhaps the classic faux pas made by an interviewer is asking a carefully recruited (by an executive recruiter) and happy-on-the-job candidate why he wants to move. If you retain an executive recruiter or head-hunter to find candidates for a certain professional position, it may well be that the most promising candidates are currently happily employed and really don't want to move—but they are ambitious enough to be willing to look at a better opportunity, if it is truly better. With this type of candidate, you need to present the job situation in its best light and make it sufficiently attractive in terms of compensation to motivate the candidate to switch.

People Who Are Newly Graduated or about to Graduate

If you are a large company you are probably already familiar with this potential source of employees. Large companies send recruiters out all over the country in search of suitable new hires. If you are in a small company, this source of candidates is much more difficult to exploit. This is because large companies make very extensive recruiting efforts, and most new graduates are attracted by the name and salary that large companies are able to offer. However, smaller companies can offer the new graduate the advantages of more rapid advancement, better visibility to top management, and more responsibility at all levels.

If you are in a smaller company and want to hire new graduates, call the placement offices of colleges or universities in your geographic area. You can compete with larger companies by emphasizing what *you* can offer, and you can do this without an extensive budget or having to travel all over the country.

Unemployed People

A candidate is unemployed because he was fired, quit, or was laid off from his former position. The reasons behind each of these actions are many and varied and need not reflect unfavorably on a candidate. Find out as much as you can about the reasons for unemployment, simply as part of your routine analysis of the candidate's suitability for the position.

Sometimes an unemployed candidate is not considered as good a prospect as one currently holding down a job, but the reasons for this are often more psychological than real. The candidate may be somewhat more apprehensive than an employed candidate due to his or her situation and may communicate this discomfort in an interview. Or the potential employer may feel employed candidates are more desirable because they may be harder to get.

Probable Layoffs

In some cases a candidate is on the verge of being laid off because of a cutback, project completion, project cancelation, a merger, or an acquisition. In this case whether the candidate is happy or unhappy with his current job is irrelevant. Like it or not, he may soon be in the unemployed category.

The key to this source of candidates is to get there first. You may, of course, be lucky and place an advertisement at the time that a pending reduction in force is announced. But to exploit this source of candidates effectively you need to take more initiative. Keep your eyes and ears open. If you read or hear about a pending cutback, project completion or cancelation, merger, or acquisition, call the company's personnel department and let the manager know you are hiring and what exactly you are looking for. Ask for résumés of suitable candidates, if available.

Very large companies, especially aerospace, are always facing these situations periodically. Within one day 2,000 previously employed engineers could become available. Most of these companies have established offices specifically to assist their former employees in finding new jobs. If you are generally in an expanding mode, it wouldn't hurt to talk with these offices in all the large companies in your area. Again, tell them what you are looking for and ask if they will call you first should excess technical personnel become available.

Job Shops

Job shops, also known as "body shops" and by other names—some less complimentary than others—are a source of temporary professional help, even though this "temporary" help could be for a year or even longer. Essentially the job shop hires the engineer and pays his or her fringe benefits. The person is then rented out to various companies such as your own on an "as needed" basis. The advantage to the individual is twofold: he is paid at a slightly higher rate than he would receive if he were working for any one company, and he is guaranteed continual employment with less chance of a layoff from work than might otherwise be the case. The job shop, of course, makes a profit.

For you, the advantage is that you do not have to retain excess personnel for jobs that require peaks of labor that will not be maintained. One disadvantage of using job shoppers is that it is more difficult to make them a part of your organization. As mercenaries of the professional world they are not likely to be as fully committed to your goals as permanent employees would be. It is also more difficult to control proprietary information with them than with the permanent members of your staff.

METHODS OF RECRUITING

Now that we know where your candidates are going to come from, let's consider ways of recruiting them. These methods include word of mouth, advertising, government employment agencies, executive recruiters and personnel agencies, schools, and professional associations.

Word-of-Mouth Recruiting

This is the easiest way of recruiting, but it is inefficient and somewhat catch-as-catch-can. You simply call around to likely sources such as friends and professional associates, asking them if they would be interested or know someone who might be.

This method of acquiring candidates has several advantages. It doesn't cost anything, or costs very little. It is easy and informal; anyone can do it. And you will probably know more about the candidate before hiring than you would if you located candidates in other ways.

The biggest disadvantage of a word-of-mouth campaign is that you will not reach as many potential candidates as you would otherwise. In addition, friendship commitments may lead you to waste your time interviewing candidates you know you don't want to hire. And if there is a need to keep the knowledge of your search quiet, it is almost impossible to do so once you have initiated a word-of-mouth campaign.

Advertising

Advertising is more expensive, but it will reach likely candidates and, if your advertisement is reasonably well written, you will get sufficient responses to make a selection. If you are in a hurry, advertising in newspapers, both classified and display ads in the business section, is usually best. If you have more time, the technical and professional magazines are good. They require a month or more lead time before the ad can appear.

Advertising can be of two types, open or blind. An open advertisement is one in which you make no attempt to conceal the name of your company and the fact that you are searching. However, there may be reasons why you would not want your competitors, your customers, or even your own people to know that you are hiring. In this case you place a blind advertisement, using either a post office box number or a box number provided by the advertising medium you have chosen, and do not reveal the name of your company. The problem with a blind ad is that it will significantly decrease the number of responses. You must therefore weigh your need for secrecy against the quantity of responses you want to receive.

If you do decide to advertise, remember that you are seeking to convince top-quality candidates for your job to respond and to send you their résumés. In other words, you are selling, and your product is the position for which you are recruiting. Study some advertisements appearing now in your newspapers or technical journals. Note that those that attract your interest are written to sell by presenting the position in its best light. Note also the eye-stopping headlines. If you are going to write the ad and place it yourself, go to the library and consult a good book on mail order advertising. Ask yourself whether you would bother responding yourself to an ad that made a technical position sound dull, underpaid, or unimportant.

If you are advertising in local or big-city papers, advertise on Saturday and Sunday only. Potential professional candidates who read the daily papers are not numerous enough to make it worth the added expense.

One advantage of the advertising method of recruitment is that you can locate candidates to be interviewed fairly rapidly. The method is sure: unless you write a really bad ad or are looking for someone extremely specialized, you're going to get responses. You can keep your recruitment secret by using blind ads. And short-term advertising is not overly expensive. While continuous and extended advertising can be costly, usually recruitment for a single technical professional can be completed through advertising for less than $1,000.

One major disadvantage of advertising is that you will normally only reach candidates who are actually looking for this type of position during the period that you advertise. This means they are either unhappy with their present jobs or out of work. You will rarely reach potential candidates who are the fair-haired performers in their current organization. In addition, if you are looking for a specialty that doesn't exist in large numbers, you may not be able to find potential candidates through advertising.

Government Employment Agencies

Government employment agencies *can* be of help in finding someone, but frankly, they usually are not. Why? Most professional people don't go to government employment agencies until they have tried other means of finding employment. Therefore, if you are being selective in your hiring, you will discover that candidates from a government employment agency usually possess some negative factor that limits their desirability in comparison with candidates from other sources.

I once interviewed a candidate from a local government employment agency for an entry-level engineer's job. At a time when newly graduated engineers were being paid $12,000 a year, this individual was asking $9,000–10,000. Yet, he had a unique background that included a series of progressively more responsible positions until in one company, as a director of engineering, he had been earning $35,000 a year. At that point, as a result of a merger, he was dumped right into the recession of 1971. After two years of poor self-marketing techniques he was depressed, still out of work, and desperate. Not only was he unsuited for a permanent starting engineer's position, but I perceived that at the first chance he got for a director of engineering position elsewhere, he would naturally leave.

I advised him to take stock of his accomplishments (which were not insignificant) and seek only top-level management engineering jobs. A year and a half later I ran into him. What a change! He was no longer desperate. From a poor, out-of-work reject, he had transformed himself and had been hired as vice president of engineering for a rather large N.Y.S.E.-listed company. I think he made *me* a job offer.

It may not be a bad idea to routinely check with government employment agencies, but the chances of finding what you are looking for are frankly slim.

Executive Recruiters and Personnel Agencies

I've listed these two types of "head-hunters" together because they operate in a similar, sometimes identical fashion, and today there is a lot of difficulty in knowing exactly what you're dealing with anyway.

In theory, an executive recruiter or search firm is paid by you to go out and find the types of candidates you are looking for. A fairly large number of candidates are prescreened and interviewed, and you're presented with a final list of three to six candidates to interview and narrow down to one. For this service you generally pay a commission for a successful hiring, from 20 to 35 percent of the hired individual's annual salary. You also receive some sort of guarantee that the person is going to work out, usually for up to one year.

Personnel agencies, at least originally, worked for job applicants rather than the company seeking candidates. The applicant would register at an agency and leave his or her résumé on file. A company with a need would contact the personnel agency and receive a number of unscreened résumés. Upon being hired, the successful job applicant would pay a percentage of his or her first year's salary to the agency. The agency gave no guarantee, and it was the hiring company's responsibility to check the applicant's background and references.

Today these distinctions between the search firm and the personnel agency are becoming blurred. Most professionals do not pay personnel agencies for finding them a job. The hiring company pays. Many agencies do screen candidates, check background and references, and even offer a guarantee. Many, if not all, search firms collect and file résumés and many, if not all, personnel agencies go out and actively recruit among currently employed personnel to find candidates who meet the job specifications of hiring companies.

Some search firms maintain that the difference between themselves and agencies are that the search firms recruit for higher-paid positions, work on retainer only, and get paid whether or not a hire is made, while agencies recruit for lower-paid positions and get paid only if the person is hired. But even this is not strictly true, for executive search firms do sometimes recruit for lower-paid positions, and some will recruit on a contingency-of-hire basis. At the same time, many personnel agencies have successfully recruited and placed individuals earning $75,000 a year or more, and some work on a retainer rather than a contingency basis.

Many states now require a firm to secure an agency license if it recruits candidates in a certain salary range. For example, if a firm recruits for or places candidates earning $20,000 a year or less, it may be required to maintain an agency license. Search firms are not wildly enthusiastic about such laws, and have little desire to be identified with "agencies." But many search firms are required to maintain an agency license because on occasion they recruit for more junior management positions. To legally meet such a recruitment without the stigma of the agency label, some executive recruiters resort to maintaining an agency subsidiary.

When done properly, recruiting through an agency or search firm has a number of advantages. You can be much more precise in the requirements you set for potential candidates. You can save much time that might otherwise be wasted on interviewing and screening. There is probably a greater chance of the hire succeeding, and if it doesn't succeed you can usually get your money back or have the search firm recruit for you until you find another suitable candidate. And finally, if you recruit from a competitor, you are probably off the hook legally.

One major disadvantage is high cost. You will pay about 30 percent of the hired professional's annual salary. For a $30,000-a-year engineer, that works out to be about $9,000. Further, this means of recruiting is not necessarily fast. If a firm is working for you on a contingency basis, it is going to go after the easy jobs first. If yours isn't easy, it might not get worked on. When you have someone on retainer, you should get some idea of how fast he or she is going to work before you start.

One organization that fits (although not perfectly) into the category of the agency is a national organization known as Forty Plus. This organization is really a self-help personnel agency comprised of members who have reached the age of 40 or older and are unemployed. The members, all of whom are temporary, run the organization themselves, and their contributions in time and money make it work. As a result, the hiring company generally pays nothing. While it is foolish to rely solely on an organization like Forty Plus for candidates simply because it's free, it is equally foolish to ignore the possibility that good candidates may be available from this source.

Schools

School recruiting was mentioned previously during our discussion of new graduates as a source of candidates. For a large firm, school recruiting of one sort or another is a must, since so many younger engineers are needed that they cannot be obtained by any other means. Schools are also a source of candidates who may not graduate in June, or older graduates who have called the school in the chance that a firm like yours has called in with a need. To check out this source call the placement offices of colleges and universities in your area.

This type of school recruiting can be quite inexpensive. But here

again, you probably won't get a large number of candidates and you will
need to be more than a little lucky to find the right individual from this
single source.

Professional Associations

Many professional associations will place your recruiting advertisement in their newsletter or act as a clearinghouse of job openings as a
service to their members. As with other low-cost methods, the problem
is that you cannot rely solely on this method with any surety of success.
However, it is worthwhile when used as an adjunct to other recruiting
means.

Clearly, which method or combination of methods is best for recruiting for your organization depends on your specific need and the
unique situation you are facing.

HOW THE HIRING PROCESS WORKS

So far, we've talked generally about the recruiting of candidates. In specific terms, the hiring process consists of three important steps: screening, interviewing, and making the offer.

Screening

If you used a search firm or a personnel agency, your recruiting has
probably already been accomplished for you, and you will be presented
with three to six candidates who all meet the qualifications set forth in
your job specifications. If you receive résumés from other sources, the
screening must be done by you or someone else in your company.

The purpose of screening is to reduce the number of job candidates
to manageable proportions for interviewing. Some types of recruitment,
especially advertising, will net 200 résumés or more, so you obviously
can't interview everyone. You should first screen for candidates who
meet those of your job specifications that are absolutely essential. Occasionally your specifications are too high and no candidate meets them
all. When that happens you should go back over your specifications and
loosen up on those you feel are of less importance. Then screen again.

Your second screening should take in all of your specifications,
both essential and merely desirable. Again, if no one meets all the
"desirable" requirements, screen for the most important ones.

The number of candidates you should actually interview should probably not exceed six. Therefore, continue to screen until you have about ten good candidates. The extra candidates are needed because some really good candidates may accept another position by the time you start interviewing. Also, if the candidates have provided references, it is worthwhile checking them by telephone before the interview. While a candidate will not usually provide a reference unless it is a good one, you may learn something about a candidate that will cause you to decide not to interview him or her.

Often it is in the candidate's interest not to provide references for you to check until mutual interest has been established. This saves the person's references from being overworked by the time he or she is actually hired. If the candidate provides references but requests that you not check them prior to his approval, you should respect that request. However, if references are provided with no restrictions, then it is in your interest to check them prior to the interview. You might learn something about the individual that would lead you to decide not to interview him or her, which saves you both time and money. For example, one technical manager learned from a reference that the candidate was on a two year's leave of absence from an academic appointment. Further, even if you learn nothing that would cause you to change your mind about inviting the candidate in for an interview, a reference check can reveal things that it would be important for you to ask about during the interview.

When you call for a reference check tell the individual exactly why you are calling (that Janet X is a candidate for a position as a _____ and that she has listed the individual as someone who might be checked as a reference) and ask the individual if he or she would mind answering a few questions to help out. You should ask:

o How long the reference has known the candidate.
o Under what circumstances he or she has known the candidate.
o About the candidate's personal qualities: honesty, reliability, dependability, and so on.
o About the candidate's background.
o About specific things that you feel are relevant to the job. For example, how many years did the candidate spend in computer work? What kind of managerial experience has he or she had, if any? What jobs has the person worked on, and what exactly did he or she do in them?

Do not tell the reference anything about the job. You still may not interview the candidate, and the reference may well get back to the candidate to report the conversation. You don't want him coming in for the interview with more intelligence on you than you have on him.

Don't be surprised if out of three references one actually turns out to be bad, even though the candidate furnished all three. People are a funny lot, and it is not infrequent that for some strange or obscure motive such as jealousy, an individual will give what amounts to a bad reference. Watch the pattern. If two references are outstanding and one is bad, I would probably interview the person but ask for some additional references. If two out of three references are bad you're probably dealing with a turkey, and I'd drop him.

Reference checks can substantially narrow down the field. Once you have ten good candidates, sit down and pick your six best. At this point it's your personal judgment that makes the difference, rather than what the specifications say. Even if someone else in the company does the initial screening for you, you should do the final selection of six candidates for the interview yourself.

Interviewing the Candidate

You should prepare ahead for an interview. First, if you have the time, mail out an employment form about a week before the interview and require the candidate to complete the form and return it to you. The reason for the employment form is that it forces the candidate to list complete information in some sort of chronological order. A clever candidate will structure his résumé around your requirements. It is to his advantage to keep extraneous information that may negatively affect his chances out of your hands, whereas it is to your advantage to learn everything you can. Use the information you have obtained about the person, as well as your job requirements, to develop a series of questions that you will ask this specific candidate.

Arrange for the candidate to be interviewed by at least two other people in your organization or company besides yourself. Select individuals who have a good understanding of what the job will require as you have structured it. Multiple interviewing has several advantages. It brings in opinions besides your own. Sometimes others will pick up things that you do not, and visa versa. It allows the candidate to meet other members of the company and gives him a better idea of what the company is like, what its people are like, and what's going to be required of him. If he's not going to like it, it's better for him to learn that now rather than after he has been hired and it's too late. Finally, you may be able to use the multiple interview to your advantage politically by getting someone inside or outside of your organization who will be working closely with the new employee to commit himself favorably to the individual who is ultimately hired.

It is generally wise to have the candidate relax as much as possible. Don't put him under pressure and give him a trial by fire unless that environment is to be part of the job. Rather, you want him relaxed and talking so that you can learn everything possible about him in order to assess what kind of performance he would be able to turn out on the job. During the interview, you should also endeavor to find out as much as you can about the candidate's current or former compensation and what salary figure he has in mind.

A skilled interviewee will have done his homework on your company and learned everything possible about the job. He may also have made up a mental list of questions to ask you. One purpose of the questions is to exhibit his alertness and interest in the job. Another purpose is to learn what you want so that he can slant his answers to your questions to best support your needs. Therefore, do not allow yourself to be drawn into answering questions in detail until you have your own questions answered.

No matter how good the candidate seems, do not make an offer during the interview, even if you've already seen all the other candidates. Always wait to think it over and compare notes with the other interviewers.

To let a candidate know that you are interested, tell him more about the job and its importance, the company, fringe benefits, and so forth. Promise that you will get back to him as soon as a decision is made.

Making the Offer

Once the decision to hire has been made, state your offer either by telephone or in person. You should open 10–15 percent lower than what you think the person will accept, so long as this figure is in line with what is paid for similar work in your organization. Many candidates will state a minimum figure that is really the maximum amount they feel they can get. They may be perfectly willing to accept 10–15 percent less if that is not lower than the approximate going rate for the work. If the person is inflexible and you really want him or her, you can always allow yourself to be negotiated up to the top figures in your predetermined range.

A few candidates will ask for an unreasonably high figure. Explain to such candidates that while you want to hire them, the salary they want is high. Offer them what you think the job is worth and emphasize the positive: promotion opportunities and fringe benefits.

Your object in negotiation is *not* to hire the person at the cheapest salary you possibly can. Even if you succeed, he will probably leave you when he learns that he has been taken advantage of. Rather, you want to hire your scientist or engineer at the lowest fair price for the work—and you have already determined what that figure is.

ABOUT PSYCHOLOGICAL TESTING

In the 1950s and 1960s, psychological testing was very popular as a part of the interview process for a wide variety of jobs. Today its use is much more limited, and it is probably not appropriate for most professional personnel.

Perhaps the most successful of psychological tests has been the general testing of aircrew candidates. Since World War II, almost 200,000 candidates for flying training have been tested. Yet this test, the most successful one known, is only valid 64 percent of the time. In fact, if those candidates who failed the test had been admitted into flight training anyway, statistics show that 56 percent would still have passed the course. The test was and is used because it isn't cost-effective to have 44 percent of a flight training class fail after partial training.

If your company gives one kind of test or another by policy, make certain that the criteria for evaluating the results have not been set by amateurs. I once worked with a company that had a tremendous turnover in its sales force. It had bought a popular psychological test and had given it to almost 100 candidates over a period of three years. Testing of all salespeople was accomplished, and a certain minimum passing score was arbitrarily established. Those who fell below that score were judged to have failed the test and weren't hired. Those who scored at or above the arbitrary requirement were judged to have passed the test, and, all else being equal, they were hired. However, my analysis showed that the most successful salespeople in this organization—who had been around before the testing was instigated—had scored slightly below the score established as passing. Therefore, had they been subjected to testing during the hiring process, they would have been eliminated! It was also obvious that a disproportionate number of candidates scoring above the cutoff point were sure to fail. Successful salespeople in this industry scored above a certain minimum value but also *below* a ceiling value.

What this firm had been doing was eliminating its good candidates and hiring from a group that would have a high percentage of failures.

For many professional employees, testing is not recommended. If you do use testing as part of the interview procedure, make certain it's done by professionals. Don't try to do it yourself.

There is yet another type of psychological testing that should be noted. This is the so-called assessment center, which originated with the OSS during World War II. Groups of individuals were isolated and assessed by trained evaluators as to their ability to perform tasks similar to those they would be required to perform in combat. Today's assessment centers do the same type of work in assessing executives for industry. The advantage of assessment centers over testing or interviewing is that the assessment is based on evaluation of performance in situations similar to those with which the executive will be confronted on the job. With other types of testing or interviews, the evaluator is required to imagine what a candidate would do.

WHAT THE PERSONNEL DEPARTMENT CAN AND CANNOT DO FOR YOU

If your company has a personnel or employment department, many of the above tasks, beginning with recruitment, can be done for you. You furnish the job specifications and other details, and the personnel department furnishes you with candidates. The department may screen candidates, make reference checks, have the candidates complete application forms, and even negotiate salary for you if you decide to make an offer.

It is wise to make maximum use of the personnel department. In the normal course of events, a personnel department will see and deal with considerably more people in the hiring situation than you will. Personnel people can therefore handle many of the tasks associated with the hiring process more quickly and efficiently than you can. They can also make recommendations and give you opinions based on no small amount of experience. On the other hand, you must not forget that the responsibility for the hire is yours, not that of someone in the personnel department. Should the hire not work out, you will be the one to suffer. Therefore, you must involve yourself very closely in the critical stages of hiring: selecting candidates, interviewing them, negotiating salary, and making the offer.

CHAPTER 4

How to Train Your Technical Staff

An important factor in achieving effectiveness and efficiency in your organization is how well the members of your organization are trained. Even if the personnel reporting to you were trained at some time before they joined your group, old skills will be forgotten or will become irrelevant to current tasks and responsibilities. New techniques and tools are continually being developed that may at first be merely beneficial to your operations but eventually are absolutely required in order to maintain technical competence and keep up with your competitors. For example, technical management tools such as PERT, data processing, and zero-base budgeting have today become required knowledge in many areas where once simple charts were considered state-of-the-art for management control. Individuals who have not been trained to use such tools certainly cannot be expected to be able to employ them effectively in their area of responsibility. Depending on the circumstances, lack of knowledge of some of these management instruments could result in a critical failure or could at the very least mean that your organization is performing at something less than optimum levels. A lack of up-to-date knowledge in any technical discipline can have similar results. Therefore, training prescribed and controlled by you as the technical manager is both an opportunity and a necessity. It is an opportunity because if training is done properly, good results will be achieved and your organization will enjoy an advantage over competing technical organizations in other companies. It is a necessity because without the training, your organization will suffer technological obsolescence and, in the end, will fail.

WHY TRAINING MUST BE A CONTINUOUS PROCESS

Training must be a continuous process in your organization for several reasons. First, it is needed to equip all personnel in your organization, both new and old, to do the general type of work that is assigned to them. Second, it is needed to train your personnel to do specific tasks that may be required. And finally, it is needed to update the skills and knowledge of your personnel in order to prevent technical obsolescence.

Accordingly, training of one sort or another should always be going on and should continue throughout the life of your organization and throughout the individual professional lives of all of its members—including yourself. Such training may be either formal or informal, and includes on-the-job training to qualify technical personnel to work in new positions, training to update skills in current areas of responsibility, orientation training for personnel new to the organization, and training intended to qualify individuals to use a new instrument, procedure, or technique.

THE PSYCHOLOGICAL ROLE OF TRAINING

In your organization, training will play an important psychological role that—although it may be crucial—is frequently neither understood nor appreciated. Depending on how the fact of pending training is presented to the intended recipient, and how this fact is perceived by him and others in your organization, it may:

- ○ Raise his expectations for future promotion.
- ○ Create an image of the selectee as a "crown prince" and have an upsetting effect on those not selected for training.
- ○ Create the impression that you have a low opinion of the current capabilities of the selectee.

Let us see how and why this is so. Say you send a nonsupervisor to a training course intended primarily for supervisors. One interpretation your people may come up with, if no other is given, is that you intend to make this individual a supervisor. If it is not felt that this "promotion" has been earned, your selectee will be thought of as a personal favorite. It may be your long-run intention to send all technical people to a course for supervisors. But by sending one person without any explanation, you can cause some definitely upsetting effects in your organization. In exactly the same way, if you send an individual who is currently a supervisor to a training course for supervisors without any explanation, you may find that members of your organization, including the supervisor in question, may believe you do not have a very high opinion of his current supervisory skills.

The key to using this psychological role of training to your advantage is to keep your people informed about your intentions. If you have decided to establish a policy of having all your personnel, or certain classes of them, take certain training, let them know. If you have decided to create a pool of potential supervisors by sending nonsupervisors for training, it is generally better to let everyone know this fact and know the criteria for selection to this pool.

Yes, there may be dissatisfaction among those not selected. But at least you'll be able to explain why an individual was or was not selected. Otherwise people may make inaccurate assumptions about your motives in sending or not sending certain people for training. 'It is difficult to convince people that their assumptions are incorrect, and in some cases you may not even realize that such views are held or are causing problems in your organization. It is therefore extremely important that an individual selected for a course of instruction know why he had been selected, and that everyone else in your organization be kept informed about your training selection policies.

TRAINING OBJECTIVES AND SELECTION OF INDIVIDUALS FOR TRAINING

The reasons why you want a certain individual to receive training may or may not be identical to the reasons he desires the training. This similarity or lack of similarity of training objectives may either help or hurt your organization.

For example, an individual's training objectives may be the following, in order of priority:

1. To acquire the skills he would need for a higher-level or different job.
2. To enable him to perform better on his present job.
3. To avoid technical or professional obsolescence.

The organization's training objectives may be almost identical but may have a different priority:

1. To increase effectiveness, efficiency, and productivity on the present job.

2. To prepare him for future promotion and higher responsibilities.
3. To retrain him for a new job at the same level or new tasks on the present job.

The important difference is that the individual may see his primary training objective as acquiring the skills necessary for a higher-level job or a different job, while the organization's main objective may be to improve his performance on the present job. Frequently the objectives of the individual and the organization will be less clear-cut and somewhat mixed, and naturally they will vary depending on the situation.

Conceptually, the organization's versus the individual's training objectives can be visualized as shown in Figure 10. In Situation I, the two objectives barely overlap and mutual objectives almost do not exist. Situation II is the opposite. Here individual and organizational objec-

FIGURE 10. An individual's training objectives and those of the organization do not always coincide.

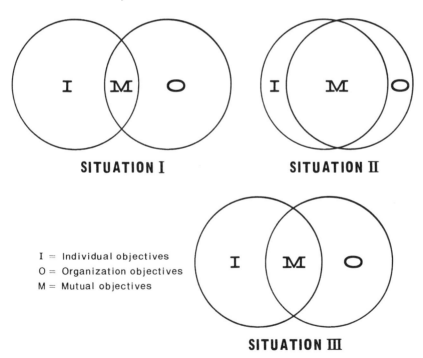

I = Individual objectives
O = Organization objectives
M = Mutual objectives

tives are nearly identical. Finally, Situation III illustrates a case where there is a mixture of identical and nonidentical training objectives. Ideally, we would always like to be in Situation II. Realistically, most training situations will be more accurately depicted by Situation III. Stiuation I is extremely dangerous for your organization. If you have any choice at all, you should avoid sending individuals into Situation I training. Here's why:

- o The training may set up expectations that the organization does not intend to fulfill.
- o The training and organizational resources may be wasted because the individual is not motivated to learn what the organization wants him to learn.
- o The acquired training may actually enable or encourage the trainee to leave the organization.

As the manager of a technical organization, what should you do when you face a potential Training Situation I? First, it is imperative that you interview every potential trainee before sending him or her for training. This will help you to identify individuals who would be in Training Situation I. Try to gain a thorough understanding of the individual's personal and professional goals, and state the organization's goals and training objectives quite clearly. Sometimes a potential Situation I can be converted into a Situation III if you and the potential trainee reach an understanding that his objectives and the objectives of the organization will be identical at some time in the future. At other times, such preselection counseling will convince you or the individual that the training should proceed with significantly changed objectives on the part of either the individual, the organization, or both. At times, the solution may be to alter the type of training given. Still another alternative that must be clearly faced is not to send the individual for training at all. This decision might be reached if other alternatives would create a greater negative impact on the organization.

In summary, before sending anyone for training, analyze the situation and determine which type of training situation you are in. If you are in Situation I, give careful consideration to all the facts as they affect the individual and the organization before making a decision.

MAKING THE TRAINING PROGRAM A SUCCESS

A successful training program is one that accomplishes the intended objectives of the organization. In order for any training program to be a success it must have a good content, be well organized, enjoy your support, and be well taught.

Good Content

A training course must not be a "square filler"—that is, a course which accomplishes little besides filling squares on a chart. A training course must fulfill an organization's objectives, or it is a misallocation of the organization's resources, a waste of money, a bad investment.

Whether the objectives you set for a course are fulfilled depends to a significant degree on what's in the course. As manager of the organization whose members attend the course, you are always ultimately responsible for the resources expended in conducting it and for the performance of those who attend it. Whether the course is given by someone within your organization or company or by an outsider makes no difference. You, as technical manager, must ultimately bear responsibility for the content of the course.

Good Organization

Even if the content of the course is good, it will not be assimilated very well by the students unless the course is well organized. Good organization means that the material is presented in a logical sequence, that administratively what is intended to happen during the course happens when it should, and that the students' time is well utilized. Here again, as the organization's leader, you have a vital interest in the course's efficiency because it will impact directly on your organization's resources: time, money, and people.

Support of the Training

No course given to members of your organization can succeed without your support and the support of other technical managers reporting to you. Support for a training program can manifest itself in many ways. It can mean allowing attendees freedom from their normal job duties in order to attend. In the case of part-time attendance at a full-time university, it can mean allowing your personnel sufficient time to study. If you establish the course, it definitely means actively encouraging participation and ensuring that the student has an opportunity to use his newly acquired knowledge once he returns to his full-time position in the organization. It is counterproductive and wasteful to send your people to any type of training if the training does not have your support. Again, it is your responsibility as a manager to follow through.

Good Teaching

The training to which you send your people must be well taught, or all your support and all your efforts to ensure the content and organization of the training will have been wasted. Indeed, a poor teacher is worse than no teacher or instructor at all. If you have control over who teaches the training course, select top-flight leaders for your instructors. Yes, you will lose them from other important duties. But it is an investment. A good teacher will multiply the value of your training program to your organization many times over. A poor one will cause you to lose your entire training investment.

TYPES OF TRAINING PROGRAMS

Your organization can benefit from the following types of training programs: (1) an orientation program, designed to increase the effectiveness of new organizational members from the first day; (2) specific task training, designed to increase the capabilities and better the performance of your personnel; (3) a master training plan for your organization; and (4) an effective off-duty training program.

Orientation Training

Research has shown that providing new personnel with training to orient them to the organization can greatly reduce the length of time it will take them to begin performing at their maximum potential. Indeed, the right orientation training can get the new member producing on the first day, and certainly that should be the goal, if not the actual realization, of all orientation training.

An orientation training program has the objective of orienting a new member to his or her job within the organization. This may include familiarizing the person with his required duties, conveying that he is welcome, introducing him to key contacts in the organization, and indoctrinating him in the organization's goals, procedures, and objectives. Such an orientation program should be developed in three phases: basic orientation briefings, facility tour and introductions, and assignment of a sponsor.

BASIC ORIENTATION BRIEFINGS

Basic orientation briefings should provide general information about the company and your technical organization, including managers, products, general and specific objectives, goals and current progress toward them, and how and where the newcomer's job fits into the overall picture. At the end of these briefings, which can last from several hours to several weeks depending on the level and complexity of the job, the new professional should have a basic understanding of what is expected of the organization and what will be expected of him or her.

FACILITY TOUR AND INTRODUCTIONS

A facility tour and formal introductions to key people can greatly speed up the ability of the new professional to begin effective performance of his job. Remember that for a new person, where to go to get a report or an engineering drawing, who to see about conducting certain required experiments, or even where to go for secretarial support is an obstacle to job performance. It is far better to anticipate these problems by showing the new professional around and introducing him to the people whom he must work with to accomplish his job. In this way:

○ The new professional will have an idea of where things are and where to go to get certain types of work done.

○ He will have a better idea of what types of services are available to him and with what groups he must coordinate the work he is doing.

○ He will have met most of the key people already and won't have to meet them at a time when he is knee-deep in a problem and the pressures of time, resources, and performance associated with it.

○ Key people within the organization and company will be familiarized with the new professional's function, so that when he does contact them with work, he won't have to explain himself with such basics as who he is and what he does.

If the new technical employee reports to you, you should conduct this facility tour and make the introductions if at all possible. If not, his assigned supervisor should do so. During the tour, the individual conducting him should be certain to explain the titles and functions of the various people to whom he is introduced, as well as stating the duties and title of the new employee.

A layout map such as the one shown in Figure 11 will be of considerable help to the new professional in learning who does what and is

Figure 11. A sample layout and function map.

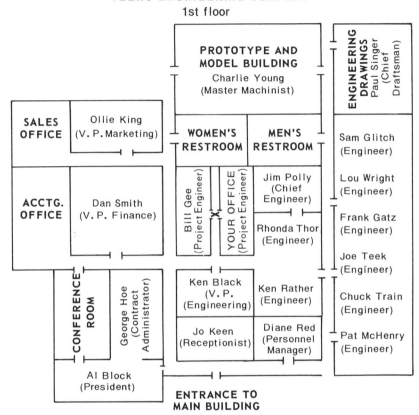

located where. While it may take only five minutes for you or one of the members of your organization to draw such a map, it can save hours in time and needless questions over the first few weeks of a new professional's employment in your organization.

ASSIGNMENT OF A SPONSOR

Assignment of a sponsor should be a key part of any orientation program. Yet this technique, which can be of tremendous value, is rarely used. What is a sponsor, and what does he or she do?

A sponsor is an individual who has already been in your organization a while and knows the ropes. He or she should be at approximately the same technical or management level as the new employee, and should be involved in duties similar to those anticipated for the new person. Usually he should have the same boss as the new employee. His duty is to accept responsibility for the new employee's smooth and easy integration into the organization. He makes those introductions which you didn't realize were important. He shows the new person ways of getting things done that are faster and more efficient than the formally established way and that you and many of your managers didn't even know existed. He helps the new person solve problems, both personal and professional, that you couldn't have anticipated. And he helps the new person with the peripheral problems that must be solved in order for him to do his job, until he understands the organization better and can do this on his own.

Clearly, duties of this nature cannot be assigned to just anyone. This special responsibility should only be given to a proven and trusted professional, an individual who has both technical and leadership abilities. The person assigned duties as a sponsor should be well briefed as to exactly what you want him to do before he starts. The new employee should be similarly briefed as to the functions of his sponsor.

How long should a member of your technical staff serve as a sponsor for a new member? Usually three to six months is ideal to derive maximum benefit from such a program. Sometimes it is best to set no fixed time period, but to allow the sponsor to serve in a semi-official status to help the new employee as long as help is requested. You might vary your approach, sometimes assigning fixed periods of responsibility and sometimes assigning indefinite periods, to see which works best for your organization.

In summary, sponsor assignment can benefit your organization in three ways:

- It can help your organization in getting earlier production from the new professional.
- It can help your new professional over the rough spots of becoming one of your team and can ease the trauma of organizational change.
- It can help train your sponsor for technical management and leadership responsibilities.

Specific Task Training

A specific task training program is given to members of your organization:

To qualify them to perform some special task.
To qualify them to operate some type of equipment.
To develop their skills in some area.
To update their knowledge in some area of their technical or managerial work.

Examples of this type of training are: training in how to make technical presentations, a course in writing proposals to the government, a training program in negotiating, or a course on the latest techniques of advanced composite manufacturing.

It is well to establish an annual budget for this type of training and to lay out the types of training you want your personnel to receive over the coming year. Usually, unless all of the individuals reporting to you are in the same specialty, you will plan different training requirements for different professional specialties. Managers will take certain types of courses, and other of your straight technical people will take other courses, depending on organizational needs or their specialties. This should be laid out carefully a year in advance along with your annual budget.

A Master Training Plan

Few technical organizations attempt to anticipate their future training requirements. Most respond passively, waiting for specific training opportunities to arise rather than actively pressing toward training goals. For example, if the company is very large, a separate training organization may inform all departments that a course is available in, say, leadership. Perhaps the training director thought the company ripe for such a course, or perhaps a company officer observed that leadership skills throughout the company were not quite up to snuff. You as a technical manager may be offered the opportunity to send some of your people to such a course. Alternatively, you or one of your people may receive a brochure about a certain course taught by an outside organization. You decide that a certain individual or individuals should attend such a course, or perhaps the individual himself thinks it's a good idea and requests permission to go.

The point is, both of these situations are reactive rather than active. You are responding to a training opportunity rather than planning your training requirements ahead. As a result, the training given in your organization will be rather spotty. In some cases, individuals who need the training offered will be too heavily engaged in their jobs to break loose at the time the training is offered. In other cases, vacations, work travel, or personal problems will interfere. Without planning, you may fail to allocate sufficient budget funds for training. Every individual case that arises will take time and effort away from other management duties. Therefore, for maximum benefit, it is essential that a master training plan be developed on an annual basis.

A master training plan will give the following information: what training will be given, who will receive the training, how the training will be given, and when the training will be given.

WHAT TRAINING WILL BE GIVEN, AND TO WHOM?

To answer the first question, you must again look to your organization's objectives and what you intend your organization to be doing during the coming year. You must also consider the needs of individual personnel and whether training will be needed for people who will be assuming new positions within your organization. Sometimes deciding what training will be given is easier if it is divided into different categories, such as preparing individuals for new positions, upgrading skills, information updating, and so forth.

The question of who will receive the training is dependent on the training offered, or sometimes the training offered will depend on whom you have in mind to train. Therefore, these two questions should be considered together.

HOW WILL THE TRAINING BE GIVEN?

The how question is more important than it may first appear. You will usually have several options. Sometimes the training is of such a nature that it is better for someone in your organization to conduct it. If a training organization exists within the company, this organization may be able to supply the training. Or you may be able to send your people to a course held outside the company, usually at a motel or hotel location. If you have a number of people destined to receive the identical training, you may want to bring someone to your facility to conduct the training.

Each option will have advantages and disadvantages associated with it, depending on your unique circumstances. One factor to consider is cost. Each different method of training will have a different price tag. Since your budget for training will not be unlimited, this will be of no small importance to you. Any advantages and disadvantages should be considered in the light of your overall training budget before making your final decision as to how to conduct the training.

FIGURE 12. Master training plan worksheet.

TRAINING	TRAINEE	ALTERNATIVE METHODS TRAINING	COST*	POTENTIAL DATES
Project management	Smith, A. M. Able, J. R.	Course, J. R. & Associates	$500/person $3,000 total	April 1–5, Aug. 20–24, Nov. 16–20
	Jones, T. H. Buckle, C. R.	J. R. & Associates in-house	$5,000, but can send ten trainees	Any date if two months notice
	Allen, L. M. James, A. A.			
Marketing for engineers	Tuck, R. A.	Course, Marketing Training Company	$300	Jan. 17–19, March 3–5, July 7–9, Oct. 17–19
Basic computer programming	Ray, J. P. Land, P. O.	Course, Computrain, Inc.	$1,000/person $2,000 total	Aug. 15–31
		Course by company training division	No cost to organization	July 11–18 and Aug. 1–8
		Part-time course by organization	Estimate $1,500	5 days, ½ day any time

Topic	Attendees	Source	Cost	Dates
Advanced methods of plastic forming	George, W. A. Hart, R. J.	Course, A. P. Bocker & Associates	$300/person $2,700 total	Febr. 1–2, April 27–28, June 4–5
	Cramer, F. M. Shine, R. A.	In-house course, A. P. Bocker & Assoc.	$2,000	March, July, or Nov. (2 days)
	Kinding, G. W. Pop, I. R.			
	Weedle, S. O. Fit, B. C.			
	High, D. F.			
Leadership	Smith, A. M. Buckle, C. R.	Course, J. R. & Associates	$500/person $1,500 total	April 7–11, Aug. 11–15
	James, A. A.	In-house seminar by company training div.	No cost to organization	Febr. 1–7, Nov. 1–7, ½ day only
		Seminar by organization	Estimate $1,500	5 days, ½ day any time
Technical writing	George, W. A. Fit, B. C.	Course, U.C.L.A.	$500/person $2,000 total	Aug. 1–5
	Ray, J. P. Land, P. O.	Course, Cavanaugh Associates	$500/person $2,000 total	Febr. 7–11, March 10–14, Sept. 20–24

*Excludes cost of trainee manhours.

WHEN WILL THE TRAINING BE GIVEN?

Certain types of training are only available at certain times. This is the last input to your worksheet, as discussed below.

A master training plan worksheet such as the one shown in Figure 12 can assist you in making these decisions. Several things should be noted about the worksheet. First, you should list all potential training programs on the sheet, even when the cost of the training is outside your budget. This can be helpful if last-minute changes necessitate certain training for individuals who are delayed or dropped. Other training options, which you otherwise would prefer not to use due to budget restrictions, can be immediately substituted. The worksheet may also come in handy when you develop your master training plan for the following year. If a training method that you desire is not possible as planned, or must be changed for the following year because of unforeseen circumstances, you will have this information immediately available.

Once your budgetary constraints for training have been established, use your worksheet to determine the training to be conducted. Then draw up a master training plan, as shown in Figure 13. Remember that transportation and living allowance costs must also be considered and that sometimes a higher-cost method must be selected for various reasons.

An Off-Duty Training Program

It is generally in your interest to encourage off-duty training. Such training can greatly increase the capabilities of your personnel at little cost. But you should exercise care here, for though it is generally in your organization's interest to have members attend off-duty training of one sort or another, there are specific instances where the goals of such training deviate greatly from your organization's goals. In such cases you may wish to actively discourage the training or at least be aware of its potential consequences. Examples of such training may be legal training or training for an M.B.A. when neither your organization nor your company has a need for someone with these specialties. If there is no possibility for employment, completion of these or any courses of instruction will raise expectations that cannot be fulfilled, leading to frustration and possibly the individual's resignation. Therefore, you should be fully aware of what courses individuals in your organization are taking. In fact, it's a good idea to counsel with them, so that if possible the train-

FIGURE 13. Master training plan.

DATE	TRAINEE	TRAINING	TRAINING METHOD	COST
Jan. 17–19	Tuck, R. A.	Marketing for managers	Course, Marketing Training Company	$300
Jan. 20–24	Ray, J. P.	Basic computer programming	Part-time course by organization	$1,500
Febr. 1–7	Smith, A. M.	Leadership	In-house seminar by company training division	No cost to organization
Febr. 1–7	Buckle, C. R.	Leadership	In-house seminar by company training division	No cost to organization
March 5–6	George, W. A.	Advanced methods of plastic forming	In-house course, A. P. Bocker & Associates	
March 5–6	Hart, R. J.	Advanced methods of plastic forming	In-house course, A. P. Bocker & Associates	$2,000
March 5–6	Cramer, F. M.	Advanced methods of plastic forming	In-house course, A. P. Bocker & Associates	
March 5–6	Pop, I. R.	Advanced methods of plastic forming	In-house course, A. P. Bocker & Associates	
April 7–11	James, A. A.	Leadership	Course, J. R. & Associates	$500
April 27–28	Fit, B. C.	Advanced methods of plastic forming	Course, A. P. Bocker & Associates	$300
April 27–28	High, D. F.	Advanced methods of plastic forming	Course, A. P. Bocker & Associates	$300
Aug. 20–24	Smith, A. M.	Project management	Course, J. R. & Associates	$500
Aug. 20–24	Able, J. R.	Project management	Course, J. R. & Associates	$500
Nov. 16–20	Jones, T. H.	Project management	Course, J. R. & Associates	$500
Nov. 16–20	Allen, L. M.	Project management	Course, J. R. & Associates	$500
			Total	$6,900
			Total Training Budget	$7,000

ing they take matches present organizational needs or needs anticipated in the future.

Many organizations fund off-duty training in whole or in part. Unless you are the president of your company, you probably will not have the authority to decide whether this option will be offered. However, as a technical manager, you will be in line to approve or deny company expenditures for this purpose. You may well be in a position to encourage off-duty training by authorizing early departure to make class times, or even use of company time to accomplish work that can both benefit the company and fulfill academic requirements. However, to encourage off-duty training means more than to merely act in a passive role. If in general your policy is to encourage your personnel to take such training, you should announce it as policy, as well as outline the advantages to the individual, the company, and the organization. Give public recognition to those members of your organization who successfully complete their courses of instruction. Depending on the circumstances in your company and the importance of this training to your organization, you may want to consider a more tangible form of reward—such as a nominal increase in compensation—for an individual who has completed a more significant program such as an advanced degree.

APPLYING LEARNING THEORY TO YOUR TRAINING PROGRAM

Considerable research has been done concerning learning, and you can apply some of this body of knowledge directly to your training program to greatly increase the results you can expect.

Motivation and Learning

One of the things researchers have discovered about learning is that without motivation, little or no learning will take place. For one reason or another, a certain small percentage of the personnel you desire to train will be self-motivated. These people will not need to be motivated by you; they will apply themselves to the training you give, and with very little effort on your part, they will learn. Unfortunately, for the vast majority of trainees motivation isn't optional—it is required if your training objectives are to be achieved.

Note, incidentally, that the degree of external motivation required for an individual says nothing about how he performs on the job, whether he is a self-starter, or what his potential is for promotion. It simply says that you must motivate him for the training you desire to give. With some other type of training, the situation might be reversed. The small percentage of self-motivated might join the majority requiring motivation, while a former member of the group requiring motivation becomes one of the self-motivated.

How can you motivate your personnel for the training you have decided to give? There are two key things you must do to accomplish this. First, going along with the general philosophy of keeping your personnel well informed, you must explain the general reasons why the training will be given and the specific reasons why you will be sending this individual to the training. Here is an example of how you might explain this to a potential trainee: "The overall win rate for engineering proposals in our organization is only 50 percent. As a result, we're spending too much money to acquire the business we're getting. I'm going to send all the section managers to a course on how to write engineering proposals. You are the first. When you get back, I want you to spend some time educating your people on how to do it. Also, I'll want your ideas on what we've been doing wrong, and your recommendations on what we can do to improve our situation and better our win rate."

The second way of motivating the trainee is to explain the benefits of the training to him. What new skills will he learn, and how will this help him in his job? What advantages will he get from the training that he might otherwise not have? How will the training help him in his career?

One word of caution: you must be careful not to overmotivate the trainee. An example of overmotivation might be if you threatened an individual with loss of his job if he didn't complete a course of training successfully. If the motivation you give the trainee is extreme, it can inhibit rather than assist in learning.

Reinforcement and Learning

A trainee needs to know whether he is doing something correctly or incorrectly. Therefore, both positive and negative feedback are required.

You can deepen learning by reinforcing it with some kind of reward. The reward need not be valuable in a materialistic sense. For example, a certificate of training completion is worth almost nothing in material terms. Yet the recognition it affords provides a positive reward and reinforcement for the training given. Even public congratulations for completing the training—along with a few appropriate words regarding the efforts the individual has made and the contributions of the training toward the organization's objectives—can function as a reward.

Should you ever link training with punishment, as in the old carrot and stick approach? Punishment should *not* be used with learning, for it can cause the person to exhibit a type of behavior known as fixation. With fixation, the learning failure is punished, the person repeats it, and he or she is punished again. The would-be trainee becomes fixed on the learning *failure* rather than the learning. In effect, the trainee learns what not to do rather than what to do. Therefore, concentrate your efforts on positive reinforcement (reward) rather than negative reinforcement (punishment).

How do you handle negative feedback if you're not going to use punishment? One of the best examples I've ever heard of appeared in Dale Carnegie's famous book, *How to Win Friends and Influence People.* Carnegie told a story about Charles Schwab, giant of the steel industry during the first part of the century and one of the first men in history to be paid a salary of $1 million a year. Schwab was passing through one of his steel mills when he saw some of his employees smoking directly under a "No Smoking" sign. Striding over, he handed each man a cigar and said, "Boys, I'll appreciate it if you smoke these outside."

When you must give negative feedback, try to turn the situation around so that it becomes a positive learning situation. Charles Schwab wasn't paid $1 million a year without reason.

Involvement and Learning

Learning is more effective if the trainee is involved in the learning experience rather than merely being subjected to lectures. This is one reason for the success of case-study and simulation approaches in modern instruction: the trainee or student becomes more involved in what he is supposed to be learning. This is also the reason on-the-job training can be both important and successful.

Try to structure your training so that it involves a mix of formal training and involvement on the job. Perhaps recent graduates of a formal course of instruction can be given practical experience by putting their training to immediate use (under appropriate supervision) on their job. Or, possibly they can be assigned the duty of instructing others in what they have learned. For effective training, get the trainee involved in the training!

CHAPTER 5

How to Compensate the Technical Professional

Compensation is measured in more than dollars. Lack of awareness of this fact is the biggest cause of failure in compensation programs developed for technical employees. In the 1880s, Congress, in one of its more serious cost-reduction efforts, failed to appropriate money for the salaries of military officers. Thus, in one step all officers on active service had their incomes reduced to zero, able to support their families at the subsistence level only because they lived in government quarters and were able to eat at government facilities. Clearly, the compensation that these officers received was other than in dollars. How many of your professional people would be willing to work without pay, the only material compensation being subsistence for themselves and their families? Yet, these officers worked without salaries, with little hope of ever receiving back pay, for almost two years.

Peter Drucker, in his book *The Effective Executive*,* tells the story of the problem the military had had in retaining its physicians since World War II. Dozens of studies had been carried out, and an equal number of remedies proposed. Yet all recommendations had failed because all studies had begun with the erroneous assumption that the basic problem was pay, whereas in fact it was something entirely different. Today, thirteen years after *The Effective Executive* was published, the military still has trouble holding onto its doctors. Yet physicians in the military are more highly paid than ever before.

*New York: Harper & Row, 1967.

NONSALARY ELEMENTS OF THE COMPENSATION PACKAGE

From the above example it is clear that compensation consists of numerous elements, of which salary is only one. Other aspects of compensation are bonuses, fringe benefits, working environment, and terms of employment.

Bonuses

A bonus is given in addition to the salary promised. It should be tied in some way to the performance of the individual and the organization. You must be as careful with the bonus as with the basic salary. Used correctly, a bonus element of compensation can help motivate performance and be an important part of the compensation package that you offer. Used incorrectly, it can cause intense frustration and actually hurt the morale of your personnel, with resulting damage to the performance of your organization.

One small company that I am familiar with established a bonus system with the announced intention of rewarding significant contributions by individuals toward the profitability of the company. However, the selection of who were to receive bonuses and the decision on the amounts to be awarded were made not by the technical manager but by the president and financial vice president of the company. Since the technical manager had no control over—or even input into—the bonus system, it performed no motivational function. In fact, it served only to create frustration among those who received no bonuses, and suspicion about the relative sizes of bonuses among those who did. In addition, it disrupted the normal chain of command since the bonus decision was made by people other than those responsible for technical output. Since bonuses, like salaries, will probably not be equal throughout the organization, great care must be taken in administering this element of the compensation program.

Fringe Benefits

There are two kinds of fringe benefits: those that everyone gets, and those that are reserved for key personnel. Certain basic fringe benefits have become very common with many companies. These include life insurance policies, retirement plans, and medical and hospital insurance. Such supplements to salary will be expected, and if you are trying to hire someone who now has one or more of these benefits at his current place of employment, you will find that if you cannot duplicate this benefit, you will be expected to compensate through raising some other element in the compensation package. Similarly, those fringe benefits unique to your organization will be of interest to a potential new hire and can be used as substitutes for other compensation elements, such as salary.

Fringe benefits for key personnel are stock options, use of a car, living quarters, and so forth. At very high levels of management, the fringe benefits can be structured in such a way that this element is larger than the salary element. This helps keep the executive's salary from serving as a conduit of cash from the corporation directly to the Internal Revenue Service.

Working Environment

The working environment is an extremely important element that encompasses a wide range of factors. What are the working conditions? Does your organization have new buildings, air-conditioned offices, the latest equipment? Or are your facilities dated, must you drive five miles to use someone else's equipment, and is there no decent place to eat lunch? In what part of the country is your firm located? Working environment also includes such factors as the kind of reputation your company has and the esprit de corps that you, as the organization's leader, have developed in the group you manage.

For example, the reputation of the Green Bay Packers in professional football, of Lockheed's "Skunk Works" or McDonnell-Douglas's fighters in aerospace, of IBM in computers, or of MGM in the motion picture industry will continue to function as an important part of the compensation package for anyone considering joining such an organization. You as technical manager should recognize and allow for this fact in considering the overall compensation package that you offer.

Terms of Employment

Terms of employment include many items, both tangible and intangible, that cannot accurately be described as fringe benefits. Terms of employment as a part of compensation can include security offered, hours of work, and number of holidays and vacation days permitted. For example, both the military and academia have traditionally offered unusually good job security while providing rather lower salary compensation. Academia also offers a good example of how hours of work can indirectly influence an instructor's compensation. Most colleges and universities have fixed annual salaries offered for different ranks of appointment, but the effective hourly rate can be increased by simply lowering the hours of teaching required. Similarly, the amount of annual vacation allowed—from two weeks to four weeks or more—is a term of employment that is also a part of the compensation package.

Title or position can also be a term of employment. Do you think the differences in the titles "engineer," "engineering manager," and "director of engineering" are of importance as terms of employment if the salaries are all identical? You bet they are! More than one engineer has changed jobs, stayed on in the same job, or accepted transfer mainly because of the title. As Joe B., an engineer from Philadelphia, once told me, "I took this job not because it pays more than my former one; it actually pays less. But it has a much better title. Before I was only an engineer. Now I'm an 'engineering manager,' even if my job is still basically the same."

Freedom of action is also a term of employment. For example, "hobbying"—allowing a research scientist time and facilities to accomplish his own, rather than company, research—should generally be avoided, as was pointed out earlier. But as a term of employment, hobbying may on some occasions be desirable to attract certain talent and may therefore be made a part of planned freedom of action. Sometimes direct access to you may be a desirable term of employment.

Such terms of employment should be thought through very carefully before they are offered, since they cannot fail to have an impact on the older members of your organization. If you offer such terms to obtain an Einstein for your organization, your action will probably be understood and accepted. To secure someone of lesser stature, offering excessive freedom of action may not be appropriate.

THE IMPORTANCE OF SALARY

So far in this chapter, I've said little about compensating your employee through salary and instead have concentrated on other means of compensation. The organization of this presentation has been intentional, since most discussions of compensation place excessive emphasis on salary and downplay the fact that other elements are a very significant part of compensation, especially with knowledge workers who will derive much of their satisfaction from the work environment. Still, it is salary that must be the major compensation element for most people. In terms of Maslow's hierarchy of needs, money satisfies both lower-level psychological needs, such as those for sustenance and security, and higher-level needs, such as those for job satisfaction and recognition. Therefore, regardless of how it is structured, the compensation package must be built around the salary element.

DEVELOPING AN EFFECTIVE COMPENSATION PACKAGE

The first step in developing a compensation package is to select a basic compensation strategy. There are three possibilities:

1. Offer competitive compensation approximately equal to that offered by similar firms in your industry in your geographic area.
2. Offer higher compensation than that offered by similar firms in your industry in your geographic area.
3. Offer lower compensation than that offered by similar firms in your industry in your geographic area.

Companies offering competitive compensation feel that they can attract the necessary personnel while keeping their technical labor costs at reasonable levels. Companies that offer higher compensation are generally seeking better technical labor. They feel they can keep labor costs down through higher productivity and reduced turnover. Companies offering lower compensation control their costs by trying to get by on the minimal acceptable technical labor. Excessive turnover and lower technical productivity are accepted as costs of doing business. Any one of these strategies may be acceptable for your technical organization. The main criterion is whether the strategy contributes to the accomplishment of your organization's objectives as discussed in Chapters 1 and 2. If it does, the strategy is a good one for your organization. If it does not, it should be changed.

Quantifying the Elements of Your Compensation Package

Frequently the elements of a compensation package can be traded off, one for another. But before compensation tradeoffs can be considered, the various elements must be quantified. The first step in doing this is to find out what compensation other firms are paying for similar work. Such data are available from professional organizations and associations, industrial organizations, local chambers of commerce, the U.S.

Bureau of Labor Statistics, and management consultants (especially executive recruiters).

Frequently it is best to compare several sources of compensation data, since compensation surveys will vary in completeness and in applicability to your specific technical work, and since no technical job is perfectly comparable to one in another company. For example, the job of mechanical engineer, nonsupervisor, may differ significantly according to industry and function, and salaries for this position will vary depending on geographic area, size of company, and other factors.

Once you have found out what other firms are paying for similar work, you can list these data on a form such as the one in Figure 14. If the technical people you will require are reasonably mobile, you will need to consider other geographic locations and apply such factors as cost of living, weather, and what your location has to offer. For example, if all other factors are equal, southern California may be more attractive than New York to many people because of the weather, lifestyle, and lower cost of living. Quantify in dollars those factors that are quantifiable. Do not attempt to quantify intangibles such as stability of employment or reputation of your organization or firm, but do list them. Note that the final result for the work you are analyzing should be a range of quantitative compensation figures along with a list of intangibles important as a part of the compensation package.

Since you may or may not be able to make significant changes (or any changes at all) in the current policies regarding compensation in your company, you should adapt the form shown in Figure 14 to your particular situation. For example, even if all other companies have retirement plans, there is little point in considering such plans on the form if your company does not provide them. Note, however, that if you have some ability to alter the current policy of your company, such an analysis with its results and conclusions could form part of a staff study to your company management recommending such an alteration.

In the Figure 14 example, the study of 300 firms has been used simply to check the basic salaries of the three local firms for which full information on compensation has been obtained. In the compensation package to be offered, the minimum salary figure has been significantly increased to compensate for the fact that a retirement plan is not offered. The quantitative range of the package to be offered is 23.2–39.2K, which is roughly comparable to the total quantitative compensation offered by Firms B and C. Firm A is able to keep its maximum compensation very low, probably due to its reputation and its provision of stable employment. Such a profile might also occur in a firm that has few

FIGURE 14. Form for compensation comparisons.

JOB: Mechanical Engineer, Nonsupervisor

COMPANY	SALARY	BONUS	LIFE INS.	HEALTH INS.	RETIREMENT PLAN	OTHER QUANTITATIVE	TOTAL QUANTITATIVE	NONQUANTIFIABLE
A	16–26K	—	1K	1K	1.5K	2 weeks vacation: .6–1K	20.1–30.5K	Very stable employment; best engineering reputation in area.
B	17–32K	—	1K	1K	1.5K	Auto provided for senior engineers: 2K / 2 weeks vacation: .7–1.2K	21.2–38.7K	Frequent layoffs.
C	17–30K	5–10% base salary	1K	1K	2K	Company-funded savings plan: 5% of salary / 2 weeks vacation: .7–1.1K	23.4–39.6K	Advanced education 100% funded for technical personnel.
Study, 300 firms in industry	15.5–35K	?	?	?	?	?	?	—

Salary range: 15.5–35K

Total quantitative range, 3 firms: 20.1–39.6K

Compensation strategy: Be competitive with firms in local area

Compensation package to be offered:

Salary range: 18–33K

Life insurance, health insurance, 2 weeks vacation, retirement plan, salary savings plan (5% of salary)

Total quantitative range: 23.2–39.2K

senior engineers and depends primarily on younger technical people to accomplish its objectives. In drawing up your comparison, take care to analyze all factors, both quantifiable and nonquantifiable, and make sure the package to be offered is competitive, high, or low, consistent with the strategy selected to accomplish the firm's or organization's objectives.

A compensation package must be developed for every position in your organization, for until all positions have been analyzed none of the compensation packages proposed can be finalized. You must now ensure that the whole system you have put together makes sense. Some positions will be of lesser or greater importance than other positions with the same title, and will have greater or lesser responsibilities. For example, the project manager of a $50,000 project has less responsibility than the project manager of a $2 million project. All other things being equal, the manager of the smaller project should probably be given less compensation. Yet such differences cannot always be picked up in surveys, and the compensation range for a given job title may or may not allow for these differences. Therefore, your entire range of positions must be analyzed to ensure appropriate compensation relationships among all positions in your organization.

Determining the Compensation Relationships among the Professional Positions in Your Organization

In some cases, especially if your organization is small, it will not be necessary to determine the compensation relationships that exist in a formalized fashion. Say, for example, your organization consists of several project engineers who manage similar-size projects, and engineers of similar responsibility reporting to the project engineers. In this case it is clear that your staff consists of a compensation group of project engineers and a compensation group of engineers of various specialities, and that the project engineers should be given higher compensation than the general engineers. However, compensation relationships are not always this easy to resolve. For more difficult situations, a formalized method is required in order to bring your whole compensation system into correct perspective. One such method is the point system. The point system consists of the following four steps.

1. SELECT THE RELEVANT FACTORS

The factors selected depend on conditions in your organization, your objectives, the type of work being accomplished, and other elements. Each factor should represent a characteristic of the work that you feel is both relevant and important. For example, factors for rating engineering supervisory positions in your organization might be as follows: education required, experience required, technical ability required, leadership ability required, level of responsibility of job, and number of individuals supervised.

2. DEFINE THE FACTORS BY POINTS

Each of these factors must now be defined by points. For example, if we used 100 points as a maximum, the education factor might be point-defined as follows:

No degree required	25 points
Bachelor's degree required	50 points
Master's degree required	75 points
Doctorate required	100 points

Other factors might be point-defined as shown in Figure 15.

3. WEIGHT THE FACTORS

The next step is to decide on the relative importance of each of these factors in doing the work. No matter how many factors are considered, the total must equal 100 percent. Thus, with the factors selected above, you might decide on a weighting such as this:

Education required	10%
Experience required	20
Technical ability required	15
Leadership ability required	25
Level of responsibility of job	25
Number of people supervised	5
	100%

Perhaps number of individuals supervised was not one of the factors you selected for this particular type of work. The five remaining factors must still have weightings totaling 100 percent.

4. PERFORM THE NECESSARY CALCULATIONS

Our fourth step is to make the necessary calculations for each position. This is accomplished by reviewing the job specifications developed earlier (see Chapter 3), applying points for each factor, and multiplying the number of points by the factor weighting. For example, let us assume that the job specifications require:

FIGURE 15. Factor/point assignment for determining compensation relationships.

	POINTS		POINTS
EDUCATION REQUIRED		LEADERSHIP ABILITY	
No degree required	25	REQUIRED	
Bachelor's degree required	50	No leadership ability required	25
Master's degree required	75	Little leadership ability	
Doctorate required	100	required	50
		Some leadership ability	
EXPERIENCE REQUIRED		required	75
Less than 5 years required	20	Much leadership ability	
Less than 10 years required	40	required	100
Less than 15 years required	60	LEVEL OF RESPONSIBILITY	
Less than 20 years required	80	OF JOB	
20 or more years required	100	Responsible for less than	
		$1 million/year	25
TECHNICAL ABILITY REQUIRED		Responsible for less than	
No technical ability required	25	$5 million/year	50
Little technical ability required	50	Responsible for less than	
Some technical ability required	75	$10 million/year	75
Much technical ability required	100	Responsible for more than	
		$10 million/year	100
		NUMBER OF INDIVIDUALS	
		SUPERVISED	
		No personnel supervised	20
		1–10 supervised	40
		11–50 supervised	60
		51–100 supervised	80
		More than 100 supervised	100

1. A bachelor's degree
2. Less than five years' experience
3. Much technical ability
4. Little leadership ability
5. Responsible for less than $5 million/year
6. No personnel supervised

From Figure 15, the point value for these specifications are:

1. 50 points
2. 20 points
3. 100 points
4. 50 points

5. 50 points
6. 20 points

If we assume the factor weighting is as per the previous example, we multiply each point value by the percentage weighting as follows:

1. 50 points × 10% = 5
2. 20 points × 20% = 4
3. 100 points × 15% = 15
4. 50 points × 25% = 12.5
5. 50 points × 25% = 12.5
6. 20 points × 5% = 1
                    ───── ─────
                    100%   50 points

This would be considered a 50-point position. This total is recorded and compared with totals for other positions. The final step is to make adjustments, if necessary, in the proposed compensation packages.

Setting the Salary Offer for a New Hire

You will now have the finalized compensation package for the position, which includes a salary range that has been adjusted for compensation relationships within your organization. The tactics of making the offer and negotiating were discussed previously, in the chapter on staffing and recruiting. The exact salary figure you offer will depend on the following:

○ The experience level and years of experience of the potential employee.
○ The current salary levels of individuals who are doing the same or approximately the same job in your organization.
○ The education level of the potential employee.
○ Particular skills possessed by the potential employee, and how badly you need them.
○ Demonstrated past performance of the potential employee.

Note that you can sometimes switch around elements of the compensation package, or introduce new elements, to maximize the attractiveness of the offer while ensuring that it is consistent with your overall strategy and compensation policies. For example, it may be possible to promise an initial salary review after six months rather than one year (if the one year is standard in your company) in lieu of a higher starting salary that would be inconsistent with the salaries paid other individuals in your organization.

MAKING THE COMPENSATION PROGRAM WORK TO YOUR ORGANIZATION'S BENEFIT

As a technical manager you will probably not have responsibility for administering the compensation program in any official sense. This will usually be the responsibility of the personnel manager. However, as with everything else contributing to technical performance, you will benefit or suffer from the administration of this program. Therefore it is essential to understand how it operates, or can operate, so that within the constraints that prevail in your company, you can work within, change, or manipulate the system as necessary in order to promote achievement of your organization's objectives.

First, accept the fact that you will never have the perfect compensation system, whether you create or administer it or whether this is done by someone else. There will always be some unfairness in the way compensation is apportioned among the members of your technical organization. You may find that:

- New engineers or scientists hired directly out of school are being paid only slightly less than older, much more experienced engineers or scientists.
- New technical personnel with substantial experience are being hired at higher salaries than those currently earned by similarly qualified personnel on your technical staff.
- Salaries paid some of your present staff members are outside the planned ranges for their positions.
- Some employees are being paid more than other employees in similar jobs who are performing better and are of greater value to your organization.

You cannot eradicate all inequitable compensation situations in your organization. But you can minimize them through knowledgeable control of an appropriate compensation system. The full compensation system includes not just the compensation package we've been talking about but also a mechanism for making future compensation adjustments.

How Compensation Administration Works

The method for administering compensation in your company will fall into one or more of the following categories:

Negotiated increases.
Administered increases.
Increases based on replacement cost.
Increases based on performance ratings.
Increases based on the maturity curve.

NEGOTIATED INCREASES

Negotiated increases mean no increases at all until such time as the employee approaches his or her boss and asks for a raise. The two then begin to negotiate whether there will be an increase and, assuming that there will be, how large the increase will be. The theory behind the negotiated increase is to put the burden on the technical employee. The manager takes the attitude that, after all, who better knows what he is worth in the present market, or when he deserves an increase?

The negotiated increase method of salary administration is really no administration at all. It is rarely used today. Few professionals are enthusiastic about being at the boss's mercy and having to initiate a salary review in order to get a raise. True, the technical employee frequently finds it worthwhile to determine what he is worth in the marketplace, but rather than put up with the hassle of an indeterminate number of future salary negotiations, he is more likely to get his just due by switching jobs.

ADMINISTERED INCREASES

Administered increases involve a periodic review of the current salary. Typically the review is made once a year, but some companies have six-month reviews and other companies have scheduled reviews every other year. The point is, salaries aren't just allowed to drift; they are reviewed and adjusted in accordance with performance, inflation, and/or the current market for the technical specialty involved. A variation of the administered increase is the automatic administered increase. With this method, automatic increases may be conferred based on years of service or, in some cases, may even be linked directly to the cost of living on a yearly basis.

INCREASES BASED ON REPLACEMENT COST

Replacement cost is something of a ruthless system in which the company adjusts salary on the basis of what it would cost to replace the engineer or scientist in question. The employee is not given an increase until it is demonstrated that it would cost more to replace him than it is currently costing to retain him. This system seems on first glance to have a ring of perverted fairness about it. Presumably, as market demand for a certain skill rises, replacement cost would rise as well. Inflation would be taken care of in similar fashion. Good performance and increased experience would be seen as factors that raise the person's replacement cost.

In practice the system breaks down for two reasons. First, there is a time lag between measurement of replacement cost and what that cost actually is at any given time. It takes time to do salary surveys; meanwhile employees are not being paid what they're worth. Usually this problem can be handled through some type of administered increases —raises based on inflation, years of service, or whatever. But when the cost of replacement can be determined only after a survey, there is no intermediate increase to take up the slack. Thus, even if replacement cost could always be determined perfectly on an ongoing basis, it will always be behind real replacement cost. How far behind it is will correlate with morale and labor turnover.

The second problem with this system is the difficulty of expressing job performance as a replacement cost. Real replacement cost is almost impossible to calculate, since one of its primary characteristics, performance, cannot be cranked into the formula easily. How, for example, does outstanding job performance affect the replacement cost of an engineer or scientist? Clearly it should go up, but how much?

INCREASES BASED ON PERFORMANCE RATINGS

Performance ratings are standard in almost every company employing technical personnel today, and well they should be. The performance rating does a number of good things for the organization, such as identifying individuals with potential for more responsible positions and providing feedback on how bosses feel their employees are doing. This system is the basis of so-called merit increases. During these times of high inflation, it has become the practice in many companies to give a combined merit and cost-of-living increase. Thus almost everyone gets an increase of some kind or another. Performance ratings will be discussed in some detail in a later chapter dealing with performance appraisal. At this point it is just important to recognize that while a routine "merit" increase is the norm, poor performance does not and should not require an increase.

INCREASES BASED ON THE MATURITY CURVE

Maturity curves came into being because of a perceived difficulty in making judgments about the quality and quantity of technical output. The idea here is to make salary conform mainly to known facts of education and seniority. Curves based on these factors are published by many engineering associations, and companies, depending on their compensation strategy, may endeavor to base their salaries on some part of these curves. Some large companies develop their own maturity curves.

The main problem with maturity curves is that seniority and education probably are not the primary factors in the successful technical output of your organization. Performance, which usually *is* a primary factor, is relegated to a secondary role. The curve places a psychological limit on the amount of salary that can be given, since a significant deviation from the average will stand out dramatically and, if not considered in conjunction with other factors, may seem inappropriate. Actually, a salary outside the usual range may be perfectly appropriate in light of the entire compensation package.

Some companies attempt to integrate performance into the equation by bringing top performers above the median through larger-than-average increases and dropping individuals performing poorly below the median through smaller increases or no increases at all.

How to Succeed with Whatever Compensation System You Have

Whatever compensation system exists in your company, there will be four keys to success:

Knowledge of how the system works.
Fairness.
Communication of the system to your personnel.
Manipulation of the system to your organization's advantage.

If you employ these keys, you can make compensation work for you in your organization. If you fail to employ them, you will encounter problems that can be traced directly back to compensation, regardless of whether you personally are responsible for the administration of the compensation system in your company.

Consider the first point. You now have a head start on knowledge of how the system works, or is intended to work. You should make an effort to understand the finer points that will be peculiar to your company. Apply the system to your organization with the utmost fairness that is within your power to provide. And make sure that all the personnel reporting to you understand exactly how the system works, including what causes a salary increase and what can retard one. In an idealized sense, it might be desirable to go so far as to communicate all salaries to all your personnel, so that everyone knows exactly where he or she stands. Lest you think such an approach totally radical, there are many sales organizations and organizations such as the military, academia, and civil service in which each member has exact information regarding the incomes and other compensation of every other member of the organization. This provides each professional with important feedback about how well he or she is doing and ends uncertainty about whether the system is being administered fairly. Of course, with no secrecy, the system must be scrupulously fair.

The biggest impediment to immediately unveiling salary information that was formerly secret is probably a fear by top management that doing this will lead to uncontrollable bad feeling. So strong is this attitude in most companies that unless you are running the company yourself, it is unlikely that you will in any way be able to change the policy. But if you have any hesitancy about communicating other information regarding the compensation system, keep in mind that numerous organizations go so far as to communicate actual compensation and suffer few ill effects in the process.

Manipulation of the system to your organization's advantage can be described more tactfully as working within the system to reap the maximum benefit from it. This does not mean that you are out to rip off the company for the benefit of your technical organization. It just means you are aware that the compensation system is there to support *you*, not vice versa.

What does manipulating the system mean in practice? John F. and Ken B. were both technical managers in the same company. Their technical organizations did approximately the same kind of work and had the same kinds of engineers in terms of both specialty and quality. Yet John's engineers were frequently refused the full salary increases he recommended for them, whereas almost every request for a salary increase turned in by Ken was approved. What was Ken's secret?

Ken had learned how to manipulate the compensation system successfully. All salary increases were based on annual performance ratings for which a special form was used. This form required the evaluator to rate various individual factors of performance such as job knowledge, judgment, and quality of work. Three lines were provided at the bottom for remarks. John gave the highest ratings possible to the engineers whose salaries he wanted to raise. In the three lines provided for remarks, he would say something like: "This person has done top-notch work on every occasion."

Ken did about the same thing with the rating form. But he also did something else. The final decision for salary increases was made by the president, who based his decision on a published company policy stating that salary raises for merit would be based solely on documented performance. The president interpreted this statement literally. Since the form used for performance rating did not allow for documented examples, the president did not feel that the recommended engineers had really done anything to desire a merit raise under the company's policy. As a matter of fact, he usually had little knowledge of what they had done at all. When Ken had come to understand how the system worked, he instructed each engineer to keep track of his or her specific accomplishments during the year. When Ken turned in the rating form along with his recommendation for a raise, a separate page was attached that documented everything the engineer had done during the year to deserve the raise.

Ken had learned to manipulate the system for the benefit of his organization. John followed every rule he was supposed to to secure a raise for deserving individuals in his organization, but his engineers usually failed to get the full raise. Which engineering manager do you think was more successful? Which organization do you think had the highest morale? Which organization do you think had the greatest productivity? It is definitely worthwhile to learn how to manipulate the compensation system to make the system work for, rather than against, your organization.

CHAPTER 6

How to Be a Successful Leader of Your Technical Organization

Leadership means different things to different people. According to one old source in the Armed Forces, leadership is "the art of influencing people to progress with cooperation and enthusiasm toward the accomplishment of a mission." But another source in the Armed Forces defines leadership not as an art but as "the quality, power, or ability to lead others; specifically, a function of command to provide sound concepts of action and inspire others to carry out a mission with energy and spirit." In his book *Group Leadership for Self-Realization,** Taylor McConnell defines leadership quite simply as "the way you handle power"; while management professor Elmer Burack, writing in his book *Organizational Analysis: Theory and Applications,†* says: "Leadership consists of such action by group members as those which aid in setting group goals, moving the group toward its goals, improving the quality of the interaction among its members, building the cohesiveness of the group, or making resources available to the group."

Whatever leadership is, it is crucial to your organization, because with it the mediocre can be transformed into the outstanding. History is full of examples of this amazing transformation. During World War I, the young and recently promoted Brigadier General Douglas MacArthur stood viewing a battalion of his troops shortly before they were

---

*New York: Petrocelli Books, 1974.
†New York: Dryden Press, 1975.

scheduled to go roaring over a front-line trench in a deadly daylight charge directly into the German lines. These troops had never fought before, and their battalion commander, though completely trusted by his men, had himself never before been in combat. The 38-year-old brigadier general beckoned the even younger colonel: "Colonel, when the signal comes to go, I want you to climb up over the parapet ahead of your men and lead the charge. If you do this, your men will follow you, and I will see that you are awarded the Distinguished Service Cross." Standing back, MacArthur stared intently at the younger officer. Stepping forward again, MacArthur said, "I see that you are going to do it. You shall have the Distinguished Service Cross now." And so saying, MacArthur took one of his own Distinguished Service Crosses from his tunic and pinned it on the battalion commander's uniform. Do you think this unit probably acquitted itself fairly well in its first combat action? The difference was all in the leadership.

A young Ph.D. in mechanical engineering took over as manager of a failing organization whose business it was to conduct funded research and development for the military service. Slippages were common, and every program was overrun in cost. Not a single project had resulted in a technical success. The young manager was advised by his boss, the vice president of engineering, that the engineers in the group were incompetent, the military customers with which the organization did business made unreasonable demands, newer defense contracts could not be won because salaries in the group were too high, and costs could not be made competitive. Within weeks, the organization seemed to take on a new spirit. Within nine months, four major defense contracts bid by the young Ph.D.'s organization had all been won. During the next three years, as these contracts were completed, not only was technical success achieved but every contract was completed on time and within the costs budgeted. The personnel were the same as before. The facilities hadn't changed. What was the secret? Leadership! Today, the young Ph.D. is the vice president of engineering.

Jason C. won a multimillion-dollar contract for development of a new pump almost solely on the strength of his leadership abilities. Jason headed up an engineering company specializing in the development of oil pumping equipment. One day he unexpectedly received a request for proposal from an agency of the U.S. government to develop a *water* pump. Jason didn't know anything about water pumps, and his first inclination was to throw the request away. Fortunately, he read the request for proposal. Though he knew next to nothing about the type of pump desired, he had some vague ideas about how the job might be done, and, and, as he admitted later, the size of the contract attracted him. Calling his key people together, he said, "I know we don't know anything about water pumps, and I would be a fool to tell you that we're definitely going to win this thing. However, I've read the request for proposal, and it's possible for us to win it if we can satisfy all requirements at the minimum cost. Anyway, if *any* outfit can win it under these circumstances, I believe we can—and I think it would be a hell of a challenge and fun to try. But I'm not going to bid this contract unless every single one of you people agrees, because if we're going to have any chance of winning, we'll all have to work nights and weekends over the next month. I don't want to do that much work myself, or have anybody else in this company do it, unless we're going to go all out." Jason got unanimous approval from his subordinates for the bid, and everyone put in a lot of noncompensated overtime during the following month. The result was that Jason's company won the development contract over six companies that were experienced in water pump development. Leadership got Jason's company into an entirely new business.

Regardless of what definition you choose, it should be clear from these examples that leadership has one basic function: to induce one's subordinates to perform to their maximum abilities and capacities.

WHAT RESEARCH TELLS US ABOUT LEADERSHIP

With a subject as important as leadership, one would expect that a considerable amount of study of the topic has been accomplished, and that is exactly right. There has been no shortage of research on leadership, especially since World War II. In general, the theories of leadership can be categorized as being based on personal traits, leader behavior, leadership situations, or some combination of these factors.

Personal Traits

The trait idea is that successful leaders must have certain common traits that account for their success, or that leaders must have certain traits in common as compared with nonleaders. Traits that have been considered are intelligence, physical strength, enthusiasm, good health, responsibility, and so on. While some correlations have been found among certain traits and leadership, not enough correlation was found to explain leadership results in many situations. Accordingly, in their attempts to develop a leadership equation, social scientists next focused on leader behavior.

Leader Behavior

Some theorists divide leaders' behavior patterns into four categories: autocratic, participative, instrumental, and instrumental-participative. An autocratic leader is a leader who leads primarily by his ability to give or withhold reward and punishment. The general concept of participatory leadership is that the individuals who are led participate in the decision-making. The leader encourages his subordinates to use their own initiative in accomplishing a task. Instrumental leadership sees the leader as mainly a manager acting in a rational fashion in executing the functions of his office.

Many researchers thought at first that participatory leadership would lead to great breakthroughs in the way leaders approached their job, and, in fact, some initial work seemed to support the theory that participatory leadership was far more effective than autocratic leadership. But as traditional research was carried out, the results were less clear-cut. In fact, in some situations autocratic leadership was shown to be both more effective and more efficient. Searching for a reason for this lack of consistency, some leadership theorists turned to a combination of instrumental and participatory theories combined as an explanation. One of the most famous of the participatory-instrumental theories that evolved was the Managerial Grid® developed by R. R. Blake and J. S. Mouton. The Managerial Grid, which is illustrated in Figure 16, is a chart consisting of nine divisions on the horizontal and vertical axes. The horizontal axis is labeled "Concern for Production," and the vertical axis "Concern for People." Various points on the grid, representing different combinations of concern for production or people, indicate different types of leadership behavior combinations.

Leadership Situations

Since a universal model for leadership could not be developed from either leader traits or leader behavior, researchers began to focus on the situation of leadership. Here increasing evidence was found that leadership success depends not only on the leader but also on such situational factors as his or her subordinates, the organizational climate, and the leadership task. The implications of this research are that any given

FIGURE 16. The Blake-Mouton Managerial Grid.

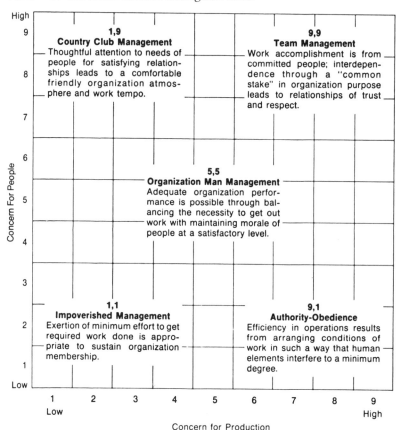

From *The New Managerial Grid* by Robert R. Blake and Jane Srygley Mouton. Houston: Gulf Publishing Company, © 1978, page 11. Reproduced by permission.

leader may be ineffective in one situation, effective in another; that organizational environments must be constructed so that leaders can perform most effectively; and that leaders must alter their behavior to suit the situation if they want to achieve maximum effectiveness.

For example, scientists Paul Hersey and Kenneth Blanchard* see leadership of any organization in terms of an organizational life cycle. In their research they noticed that many conditions affect the way in which the most appropriate leadership is provided. They compared these condi-

---

* As described in Taylor McConnell, op. cit.

tions with the conditions existing in the rearing of a child. When the child is very small, the parents provide a highly structured environment in which almost all decisions are made by them, with very little consideration of the child's personal preferences or desires. As the child grows older, more emphasis is placed on what the child prefers to do. The parents provide high structure but also high consideration. As the child progresses into his mid- and late teens, he takes increasingly more responsibilities for his actions, while the parents now provide much consideration and much less structure. Finally the child matures into an adult, and the parents respond by taking a position of both low consideration and low structure.

Hersey and Blanchard suggested a similar life cycle for organizations and advocated that the leader respond in his leadership style according to what part of the life cycle the organization was in. If an organization is proceeding along effectively and efficiently with a task that is well understood, then, as with the child grown into an adult, very little direction or support is needed from the leader. However, if a new task comes along that is imperfectly understood, the group cycles back to an earlier position on the life cycle in which a more highly structured, lower-consideration leadership style will be most effective.

Combination of Factors

Today, many researchers and leadership theorists take a contingency approach, saying that all of these theories—traits, behavior, and situation—have some truth in them, and each (or some combination of the three) may be a governing theory in a particular situation. Thus, a manager who would be a leader must draw on all basic approaches that attempt to explain the leadership process.

HOW TO DEVELOP YOUR OWN LEADERSHIP ABILITIES

An old saying would have us believe that leaders are born, not made. But this proverb has been disproved a thousand times over. Any person of reasonable intelligence can learn to be a leader. Below are some suggestions on how you can develop yourself into an outstanding technical leader. Note that you must decide for yourself how to apply these general principles to your own leadership circumstances. Good leadership goes beyond motivational theories and basic leadership knowledge—it is an art as well as a science.

Know Yourself

You are the most important part of the leadership equation. Accordingly, knowing your own strengths and weaknesses is essential.

Know Your Job

During World War II, thousands of GIs fresh out of combat were surveyed regarding their views of leadership and their leaders. Among other questions, these GIs were asked to rank attributes that they wanted their leaders to have. "High intelligence," said many. "Courage," said others. "Physical strength and endurance," "good judgment," "a sense of fairness," and "being understanding" were all ranked on many lists. But one trait was on everybody's list, and of all the attributes listed, it came out as number 1 with none other being even a close second. This attribute was, of course, job knowledge.

Those who follow you will expect you to know what you are doing professionally. This does not mean that because you are an engineering manager you will be expected to be the best engineer in the organization. You don't need to know everything about engineering, but your people would like you to be the best engineering manager possible. You owe it to them, your organization, and your superiors to be at least competent in this field. Reading books such as this one is a start in the right direction. Above and beyond any reading, you must make it your business to learn everything you can about your job and ways to do it better.

Know Your People

It is amazing how little most engineering managers know about the people who work for them and on whose shoulders the organization's well-being depends to a significant degree. It is your business to know everything of a nonprivate nature about individuals who report to you, and it is well to know as much as you can about every individual in your organization. It is for this reason that you as a supervisor are permitted access to the personnel records of your engineers or scientists. How few managers take advantage of this privilege! Yet how many benefits might be reaped if every engineering manager simply took the time to look at the personnel records of the people in his organization.

Ned Z. was an engineering manager who did take the time to learn about his engineers. He was vice president of a medium-size engineering company in southern Illinois that develops and produces braking devices for the automotive industry. Ned realized that an offshoot of one program seemed applicable to the racing industry, which no one in the company apparently knew much about. The device seemed to have as many problems as potentials, however. Then Ned remembered that Bob P., one of his engineers, had once driven cars in competition. Bob solved the problem in a matter of days, and in addition he had the contacts in the racing industry to assist with the marketing. As Ned Z. said, "If we had had to pay for the expertise to work out these final problems it would have cost us a bundle, and if we had tried to do it without any help, we would have thrown away what has turned out to be a very profitable product."

In the same way, Bill A. discovered that one of his engineers was fluent in German and used this fact to good effect when some important visitors came from abroad; Dick I. learned that a senior chemist had a background in finance and immediately used him for a special assignment; Gordon I. found out that one of his technical people was qualified to personally test the diving gear that the company had been developing.

It is also important to know how your people are likely to respond to your behavior. In your dealings with others, keep in mind that people may respond totally differently to an identical action if it is performed by different individuals, and people may respond totally differently to identical actions performed by the same individual at different times.

Different stimuli—anger, friendliness, intimidation, cheerfulness, and so forth—all elicit different responses from different people at different times. It is essential that you sort out these various responses of those who report to you so you can use the correct technique to obtain the response desired, while avoiding actions that will result in negative or unwanted responses.

Some managers have an aversion to the study of responses to stimuli that they themselves inititate. They argue that this technique is too manipulative and that leadership should be "natural." This is nonsense. If a manager by his actions or words tends to irritate others to the extent that it damages his effectiveness, isn't it far better to know this and correct the problem rather than allow something that hurts the organization to continue? Whether it is manipulative or not is irrelevant.

Take Responsibility for Your Actions

As a manager, as well as a leader, you are responsible for everything that the members of your organization do or fail to do. This means that if your organization is successful, you will be given the credit, but if your organization fails in something, you must also accept the blame. If you really want to be a leader, you will go one step beyond this. When your organization is successful, you will give credit to those of your personnel who are primarily responsible for that success, both when speaking to them and to your boss. And when your organization stumbles, as it occasionally will, you will accept the full responsibility for the mishap.

Many technical managers do the exact opposite of this. They take credit for the labor of those reporting to them, and are quick to blame these same people when something goes wrong. It doesn't take long before superiors and subordinates alike understand precisely what is going on. How much respect would you have for an individual who does this? The engineers or scientists working in the organization of such a manager will not have much respect for this sort of person either.

Understand What Motivates Your People

Understanding what motivates your people is really a part of complete understanding of your people, but many managers who go so far as to try to understand the background of those reporting to them stop short and do not attempt to think through what motivates each person.

I have noted previously that motivations differ among different people. One of the most common mistakes you can make as a technical manager and leader is to assume that the same things that motivate you will automatically motivate your engineers and scientists as well. The only thing that is certain is that these motivations will not be identical.

You will find some engineers and scientists who are motivated primarily by the task itself. That is, the job itself provides its own intrinsic motivation, whether this involves the discovery of a new phenomenon, a new invention, or some relatively mundane engineering calculation. But all technical people are not like this. Other of your subordinates will be motivated primarily by ambition, material reward, recognition, appreciation, or even the desire for friendship—to name just a few of many possible motivators. Usually more than one motivating factor will be present, although one motivator will probably be primary. If you do not *know* what motivates your people, you will obviously not be able to motivate them. It is clearly foolish to attempt to motivate someone primarily through financial gain when, for all you know, he may be financially independent and relatively uninterested in the salary component of compensation.

Herman P. worked for a small engineering development company. Herman was called in to explain why he wasn't paying one of his project engineers overtime, when company rules said that engineers making less than $25,000 per year could be paid overtime with the approval of the engineering manager. Herman said, "All of my project engineers work overtime, but none of them get overtime pay because they're all—except for this one engineer—making more than $25,000 a year. As a matter of fact, my project engineers are the highest-paid engineers in my department. Accordingly, it's something of a status symbol that they *don't* get paid overtime for their work. Now this engineer is making less than $25,000 because he was promoted over the heads of many other engineers, and he's doing a marvelous job. If he continues to perform as he has, he will be making more than $25,000 per year within two years. But this engineer doesn't need the money, and money isn't his primary motivation. His status as a project engineer is. If I recommend that he be paid overtime, this will give him additional money that he doesn't need but it will take away from his status, which he *does* need. Therefore, I don't recommend that he be paid overtime."

Protect Your People

If you are to be a leader as well as manager, you must protect your people. A study done on research and development in the Air Force looked for characteristics that were indicative of successful Air Force program managers. Two characteristics stood out: the ability of the program manager to get money for his program, and his ability to protect his people.

What does it mean to protect your people? Earlier in this book I spoke of the manager's primary requirement being accomplishment of his objectives, with his secondary need being to take care of his people. To protect your people means to look out for their well-being with regard to compensation, layoffs, working conditions, and so forth. How can you do this when as a company manager you must look out primarily for the company's interests in accomplishing your objectives?

Let's look at the example of layoffs. Few managers enjoy discharging loyal company employees, especially professionals. Still, business conditions sometimes necessitate this for the company's well-being or even survival. It is your duty as a company manager to support a retrenchment program if it becomes necessary. But it is also your duty to your company, as well as to the people who work for you, to ensure that top management has all the facts before requiring you to make cutbacks.

Sometimes cutbacks not only hurt individuals in the short run but hurt the company in the long run.

During the 1974 recession, the managers of two of the engineering departments of a large company in Massachusetts were called in and told that they would each be required to lay off five engineers. Both had contracts pending with the government. The manager of the first department pointed out that his pending contract, which was expected to be awarded within two months, would require all of the engineering expertise of his department and more. He requested that the layoffs be postponed for two months until this contract either was awarded (in which case the layoffs would be unnecessary) or was definitely lost. He made recommendations about how part of the money could be cut from his budget in other ways.

The other engineering manager also had a contract pending with the government, but he reacted in a very different fashion. This manager assumed that he could do nothing about the order to lay off five of his engineers. He gave no thought at all to protecting his people. He did make some sort of a mild protest to his superior, but he let it go at that. He laid five of his engineers off. Top management decided to retain the five engineers in the first department, and then cast about for ways to reduce overhead elsewhere. Since the second engineering manager had made no firm protest, top management assumed that the cut was not creating any serious difficulties for him. He was therefore instructed to lay off two more engineers. This he did also with minimum protest. Within two months, both departments had been awarded the contracts pending with the government. The first department hired the few additional engineers required for the program, but the second department was short seven engineers to begin with. New engineers were hired, but a period of time was required before they were fully up to speed and producing to capacity. As a result, the second program was in trouble from the beginning and was completed only after a serious slippage. The engineering manager could have avoided this slippage by simply following the basic guideline of protecting his people.

Similarly, you should protect your people in their problems with other organizations, other managers, and even top management. Against top management, you say? Perhaps it seems no engineer would be worth that much.

But a good engineer or scientist *is* worth that much. An engineer or scientist not worth protecting shouldn't be in your organization anyway. Philip G. was a great scientist who was terribly disorganized. He continually frustrated top management whenever documentation was required of his inventions or discoveries. He rarely kept any organized notes at all, and he usually misplaced those he did keep. One day Philip's boss was called in by the president of the company and instructed to fire Philip. "I can't put up with him anymore," he said. "I've told him a thousand times to keep organized notes of his work, and he has yet to obey me." Philip's manager refused to discharge him. "Boss," he rejoined, "Philip is the most creative scientist we have. That he won't or can't keep organized notes is irrelevant to this fact. Firing him would be a loss to the company that I cannot agree to and still accept responsibility for doing my job." Philip stayed because his manager protected him. If you want to be a true leader of your organization, you must protect your people as well.

Practice Self-Discipline

You cannot indulge yourself emotionally and remain a leader. You must observe, analyze, and make your decisions without allowing those decisions to be influenced by emotional factors. Strive to do the harder right rather than the easier wrong.* To accomplish this requires a great deal of self-discipline. In many instances, no one is going to tell you what to do except you yourself.

Dan R. was a director of research for a cosmetics company. The retirement of one of Dan's chemists left a senior managerial opening for one of his two product managers. George S. had been a classmate of Dan's in college. He had known George and his family for more than twenty years. George was a good chemist and had done reasonably well as a product manager. Chuck S. was a younger man. But where George was good, Chuck was fantastic. He had worked extremely hard, and the product for which he was responsible was more profitable than any other similar product in the history of the company. Something that no one but Dan knew was that on two occasions Dan had reversed decisions made by George, decisions of such magnitude that they could have caused the ruination of his program. Although Dan had spoken frankly to George about these mistakes, George had not seemed to realize their importance and had regarded Dan's intervention as merely minor help from a friend.

No one would have criticized Dan if he had selected George for promotion. George had been with the company a long time and had per-

---

*This phrase is from the West Point Cadet prayer, which says in part: "Make us to choose the harder right instead of the easier wrong."

formed well and faithfully. Chuck's ability was recognized, but he was regarded as still a little young for a senior position. On one side stood a twenty-year friendship and the knowledge that the decision to promote George would be criticized by no one. On the other side stood only the doubt that George might unknowingly make a decision that could hurt the organization, and the confidence that Dan had in Chuck's ability to succeed in the job. The harder right was for Dan to choose Chuck for promotion, and this is the decision that Dan made.

George left the job to go to another company and never spoke to Dan again. Chuck went on to do an outsanding job, and eventually replaced Dan as director of research when Dan himself was promoted. George also eventually was promoted to a position as director of research with his new company. He continued in this position for several years, and then made a serious error in judgment that caused his firm to suffer—and eventually lose—a multimillion-dollar lawsuit, whereupon he took early retirement.

Listen to the Opinions of Your Subordinates

No matter how intelligent and talented you are, you are occasionally going to be wrong, one or more of your subordinates are going to see a solution where you do not, or you are just not going to understand the problem. Therefore it is imperative to keep communications open between you and the technical people reporting to you and to listen to what they say.

One research and development manager I knew used to say this to his people: "There will be times when in your presence I'm going to say something stupid, or be about to make a decision that in your opinion is clearly wrong, or just fail to understand something important that I should. If you don't say something, I'm going to assume that you agree with me one hundred percent. Therefore, unless you do totally agree with me (in which case I *will* suspect that something is wrong), I want you to say something about it. And I want you to say something about your views in the loudest possible terms, even if you have to pound on my desk or grab me by the coat lapels, until you're sure that I'm listening and understand the point you're trying to make. I won't punish anyone for doing this. However, it's your duty to me and to the organization to do this up until the time I make a decision, even if I *were* to punish you. This doesn't mean I'm abdicating my decision-making authority. I may still go ahead and do the very thing you think is stupid.

That's my right, and my responsibility. But I want to hear what you have to say in every instance."

Needless to say, this manager was a successful and competent leader.

Be Inspirational

People are not rocks. Even if you are dealing with the greatest engineering and scientific talent in the nation, these people can be inspired to do better than they have done in the past or would do under other circumstances without your leadership.

During the battle of Fort Donelson in the Civil War, subordinates of General Grant allowed Southern troops to penetrate on Grant's outnumbered right flank. The flank was soon crushed, endangering the entire Union line and thus the battle, which until then Grant had been winning. Though the predicament had occurred through the fault of others, Grant wasted no time in blaming subordinates, but jumped on his horse and dashed up and down his own line shouting, "Fill your cartridge cases quick; the enemy is trying to escape and he must not be permitted to do so." Grant's inspirational action turned what could have been a defeat into a Confederate rout.

Robert B. was called back to take charge of an engineering company for which he had formerly worked as vice president of engineering. The company had gone into Chapter 11, which means that it had staved off bankruptcy only by resorting to the law, and was being administered by a bank. Ninety percent of the work force had been discharged. Others, including engineers and managers, had deserted the company. Everything was in disarray. The only glimmer of hope was some backlog orders for which full material was on hand for production, but insufficient workers were on hand to do the job. Robert called what was left of the company together and explained the predicament. He outlined his plan for working the company out of its financial problems and explained the importance of the first step of getting production started again. So inspirational was Robert's talk that the employees agreed to work for two weeks without wages and with no compensation for overtime. The production was accomplished by secretaries, engineers, managers, and even the president himself under the guidance of what remained of the labor force. Through Robert B.'s inspirational efforts, his company was saved and is still in business today, 15 years after the events described.

Build a Team

As a leader, it is your duty and responsibility to build a team—a technical team that is every bit as cohesive and has the same esprit de corps and morale as a winning football team or an elite military unit. Your goal must be to build an organization of such drive and spirit that any performance less than outstanding is viewed not only as a failure but as an outcome worse than anything else that could happen to someone in the work environment. You can build such a team, but you can build it in one way, and in one way only. You must be not only your organization's manager. You must be the *leader*.

CHAPTER 7

How to Appraise the Performance of Your Personnel Accurately and Successfully

If your company doesn't have a personnel performance appraisal system, it should have. If necessary, you should start one yourself. Performance appraisal does too many good things for your organization for you to lose out because a system is not currently in use. Accurate and successful performance appraisal will:

- Enable you to select individuals for promotion wisely and fairly.
- Help you to determine merit raises fairly.
- Help you identify individual needs for special training.
- Provide an opportunity for a full discussion with each of your engineers or scientists regarding career goals, progress, organizational policies, and many other subjects that might not otherwise be discussed with you.
- Help you to think through how each of your engineers or scientists is performing his job.
- Provide feedback that can help your engineers or scientists to improve their performance.

The first step in achieving accurate and successful performance appraisal of your personnel is to choose the type of appraisal method that is most suitable for the objectives you would like to emphasize.

METHODS OF PERFORMANCE APPRAISAL

There are several basic methods of performance appraisal that will enable you to evaluate the personnel in your organization. Each has its own advantages and disadvantages as well as suitability to your organization and objectives. The seven basic methods of performance appraisal are the graphic rating scale, forced distribution, forced choice, critical incidents, ranking method, essay appraisals, and management by objectives.

The Graphic Rating Scale

The graphic rating scale is a scale, either numerical or descriptive, in which an individual is rated on a variety of different factors. This method allows for a total score and thus permits easy comparison of large numbers of personnel. The individual score on each separate factor also permits identification of those areas where the rated individual is doing well or needs to improve. An example of a graphic scale is shown in Figure 17. The disadvantages of the graphic scale are that:

- It implicitly assumes that each rated factor is of equal importance for the job rated.
- It implicitly assumes that the same factors are applicable to all job positions rated.
- It fails to provide specific evidence as a reason for each rating chosen.
- It is highly prone to rating errors of various types (which will be discussed later in this chapter).
- Excessive emphasis is placed on traits rather than demonstrated performance.

In order to get around the problems with the graphic rating scale, various solutions have been proposed and used. Some firms use the scale only as a worksheet to support some other type of evaluation, such as forced choice or forced distribution. In this case a separate overall evaluation is made, and the graphic rating scale points are not totaled. Some firms require that the graphic scale be supplemented by an essay appraisal in order to provide a more complete picture and document demonstrated performance.

Forced Distribution

With the forced distribution method, the rater is required to rate a certain number of individuals and place each in a number of percentage groups. Typically, the individuals are rated on just one overall factor rather than a number of different factors. For example, a forced distribution type rating once used at the U.S. Military Academy at West Point required each cadet to distribute his fellows into groups comprising the upper 25 percent, middle 50 percent, and lower 25 percent according to the criterion: "The ability to lead an organization in combat and accomplish all assigned objectives while maintaining the highest standards of leadership, morale and esprit de corps."

One advantage of the forced distribution system is that it eliminates the danger that the rater will be either too severe or too lenient. Further, there is a greatly reduced chance that the criterion standard will be interpreted in different ways by different raters. Finally, the forced distribution system is fairly easy to administer.

The main disadvantage of forced distribution is that it assumes all groups have identical percentages of poor, fair, and outstanding performers, a situation that is highly unlikely to be true. Therefore, if the method is to work at all, a reasonably large number of people must be rated. Along these lines, how does a supervisor of a small number of people distribute them into percentage groups to be accurately and fairly compared with a larger group of people who have been rated in the same fashion? The answer is that it can't be done very well. The U.S. Air Force adopted a forced distribution system for ratings several years ago, and finally dropped it in 1978 when it proved to be unworkable mainly due to the small number of people rated by most raters.

Forced Choice

The forced choice rating method forces the rater to choose a most descriptive and least descriptive statement out of several statements that are listed together in the same group. A number of these groups make up the rating form. A typical forced choice group might be as follows:

	Most	Least
1. Exhibits a high degree of job knowledge	( )	( )
2. Carries out assignment reliably	( )	( )
3. Fails to demonstrate good judgment	( )	( )
4. Is not always dependable	( )	( )

FIGURE 17. A graphic rating scale used by the U.S. Air Force.

IDENTIFICATION DATA (Read AFM 36-10 carefully before filling out any item.)

1. LAST NAME—FIRST NAME—MIDDLE INITIAL	2. AFSN	3. ACTIVE DUTY GRADE	4. PERMANENT GRADE
5. ORGANIZATION, COMMAND AND LOCATION	6. AERO RATING : CODE	7. PERIOD OF REPORT FROM: THRU:	
	8. PERIOD OF SUPERVISION	9. REASON FOR REPORT	

II. DUTIES—

III. RATING FACTORS (Consider how this officer is performing on his job.)

1. KNOWLEDGE OF DUTIES

NOT OBSERVED	SERIOUS GAPS IN HIS KNOWLEDGE OF FUNDAMENTALS OF HIS JOB.	SATISFACTORY KNOWLEDGE OF ROUTINE PHASES OF HIS JOB.	WELL INFORMED ON MOST PHASES OF HIS JOB.	EXCELLENT KNOWLEDGE OF ALL PHASES OF HIS JOB	EXCEPTIONAL UNDERSTANDING OF HIS JOB. EXTREMELY WELL INFORMED ON ALL PHASES.
○	☐	☐	☐	☐	☒

2. PERFORMANCE OF DUTIES

NOT OBSERVED	QUALITY OR QUANTITY OF WORK OFTEN FAILS TO MEET JOB REQUIREMENTS.	PERFORMANCE MEETS ONLY MINIMUM JOB REQUIREMENTS.	QUANTITY AND QUALITY OF WORK ARE VERY SATISFACTORY.	PRODUCES VERY HIGH QUANTITY AND QUALITY OF WORK. MEETS ALL SUSPENSES.	QUALITY AND QUANTITY OF WORK ARE CLEARLY SUPERIOR AND TIMELY.
○	☐	☐	☐	☐	☒

3. EFFECTIVENESS IN WORKING WITH OTHERS

NOT OBSERVED				
INEFFECTIVE IN WORKING WITH OTHERS. DOES NOT COOPERATE.	SOMETIMES HAS DIFFICULTY IN GETTING ALONG WITH OTHERS.	GETS ALONG WELL WITH PEOPLE UNDER NORMAL CIRCUMSTANCES.	WORKS IN HARMONY WITH OTHERS. A VERY GOOD TEAM WORKER.	EXTREMELY SUCCESSFUL IN WORKING WITH OTHERS. ACTIVELY PROMOTES HARMONY. [X]

4. LEADERSHIP CHARACTERISTICS

NOT OBSERVED				
OFTEN WEAK. FAILS TO SHOW INITIATIVE AND ACCEPT RESPONSIBILITY.	INITIATIVE AND ACCEPTANCE OF RESPONSIBILITY ADEQUATE IN MOST SITUATIONS.	SATISFACTORILY DEMONSTRATES INITIATIVE AND ACCEPTS RESPONSIBILITY.	DEMONSTRATES A HIGH DEGREE OF INITIATIVE AND ACCEPTANCE OF RESPONSIBILITY.	ALWAYS DEMONSTRATES OUTSTANDING INITIATIVE AND ACCEPTANCE OF RESPONSIBILITY [X]

5. JUDGEMENT

NOT OBSERVED				
DECISIONS AND RECOMMENDATIONS OFTEN WRONG OR INEFFECTIVE.	JUDGEMENT IS USUALLY SOUND BUT MAKES OCCASIONAL ERRORS.	SHOWS GOOD JUDGEMENT RESULTING FROM SOUND EVALUATION OF FACTORS.	SOUND, LOGICAL THINKER. CONSIDERS ALL FACTORS TO REACH ACCURATE DECISIONS.	CONSISTENTLY ARRIVES AT RIGHT DECISION EVEN ON HIGHLY COMPLEX MATTERS [X]

6. ADAPTABILITY

NOT OBSERVED				
UNABLE TO PERFORM ADEQUATELY IN OTHER THAN ROUTINE SITUATIONS	PERFORMANCE DECLINES UNDER STRESS OR IN OTHER THAN ROUTINE SITUATIONS.	PERFORMS WELL UNDER STRESS OR IN UNUSUAL SITUATIONS.	PERFORMANCE EXCELLENT EVEN UNDER PRESSURE OR IN DIFFICULT SITUATIONS. [X]	OUTSTANDING PERFORMANCE UNDER EXTREME STRESS. MEETS THE CHALLENGE OF DIFFICULT SITUATIONS.

7. USE OF RESOURCES (M) (P)

NOT OBSERVED				
INEFFECTIVE IN CONSERVATION OF RESOURCES. [MATERIEL] [PERSONNEL]	USES RESOURCES IN A BARELY SATISFACTORY MANNER. [MATERIEL] [PERSONNEL]	CONSERVES BY USING ROUTINE PROCEDURES. [MATERIEL] [PERSONNEL]	EFFECTIVELY ACCOMPLISHES SAVINGS BY DEVELOPING IMPROVED PROCEDURES. [MATERIEL] [PERSONNEL]	EXCEPTIONALLY EFFECTIVE IN USING RESOURCES [MATERIEL X] [PERSONNEL X]

8. WRITING ABILITY AND ORAL EXPRESSION (W) (S)

NOT OBSERVED				
UNABLE TO EXPRESS THOUGHTS CLEARLY. LACKS ORGANIZATION. [WRITE] [SPEAK]	EXPRESSES THOUGHTS SATISFACTORILY ON ROUTINE MATTERS. [WRITE] [SPEAK]	USUALLY ORGANIZES AND EXPRESSES THOUGHTS CLEARLY AND CONCISELY. [WRITE] [SPEAK]	CONSISTENTLY ABLE TO EXPRESS IDEAS CLEARLY. [WRITE] [SPEAK]	OUTSTANDING ABILITY TO COMMUNICATE IDEAS TO OTHERS. [WRITE X] [SPEAK X]

IV. MILITARY QUALITIES (Consider how this officer meets Air Force standards.)

NOT OBSERVED				
BEARING OR BEHAVIOR INTERFERE SERIOUSLY WITH HIS EFFECTIVENESS.	CARELESS BEARING AND BEHAVIOR DETRACT FROM HIS EFFECTIVENESS.	BEARING AND BEHAVIOR CREATE A GOOD IMPRESSION.	ESPECIALLY GOOD BEHAVIOR AND BEARING. CREATES A VERY FAVORABLE IMPRESSION.	BEARING AND BEHAVIOR ARE OUTSTANDING. HE EXEMPLIFIES TOP MILITARY STANDARDS. [X]

AF FORM 77 NOV 66   PREVIOUS EDITION OF THIS FORM WILL UNTIL STOCK IS EXHAUSTED.

COMPANY GRADE OFFICER EFFECTIVENESS REPORT

With the forced rating method, some of the rater's choices are disregarded by the person analyzing the results. For instance, let us say that in the example given above, tests have previously shown that factors 2 and 4—"Carries out assignment reliably" and "Is not always dependable"—are not highly relevant to job performance. In this case, if the rater marked one of these factors as most or least descriptive, the choice would be ignored. The rater doesn't know which statements will influence the score and which will not.

The main advantage of the forced choice rating is that it minimizes rater bias. There is also evidence that the forced choice rating correlates better with productivity than other forms of rating. However, forced choice suffers from some serious drawbacks. First, it is a very expensive method, since the forms and scoring must be specially prepared and administered. More than any other method, it implies that the rater cannot be trusted to give an unbiased rating. Finally, in an evaluation interview, the forced choice method provides almost no basis for feedback to improve the performance of the engineer or scientist being rated.

Critical Incidents

With this method of performance appraisal, you begin by drawing up a list of requirements considered critical to the performance of the job. For example, your list for an armor development engineer might include:

- Solves engineering problems pertaining to armor development.
- Tests and supervises the testing of potential engineering solutions.
- Writes technical reports and specifications.
- Makes recommendations pertaining to the application of materials, both metallic and nonmetallic, to the development of armor.

Once the list has been prepared, you as manager would be responsible for noting incidents, both positive and negative, pertaining to each of the critical requirements listed. For example, your notes concerning the "Writes technical reports and specifications" requirement might read:

6 July 80   Wrote technical report for development of aircraft armor that customer commented was "the best he'd ever seen."

20 August 80   Prepared specifications for XP-1 armor. Production

noted numerous errors, and specifications had to be returned for reworking.

1 Oct 80   Completed specifications for XF-2, XF-3, and XF-5 armor on emergency basis within two weeks by voluntarily working nights and weekends.

6 November 80   Was one week late in preparing technical report for the XV passive defense system.

The obvious advantage of the critical incidents method of rating is that it provides specific examples of performance rather than generalities. It is excellent for counseling during an evaluation interview. Its disadvantages include problems of comparing results among a number of different engineers or scientists being rated, as well as a danger that the manager will begin to supervise in detail rather than manage.

Ranking Method

This method is extremely easy to administer and accomplish. The manager simply ranks the individuals reporting to him, starting with his top person and proceeding down to his worst. Ranking has a number of uses, such as deciding on priorities for promotion, layoff, or training. However, it is of little use in an evaluation interview and of no use whatsoever when your rated technical personnel must be compared with rated technical personnel in another organization in your company.

Essay Appraisals

Descriptive essays on subordinate performance go far back in history. Examples of essay appraisals of officers of the Continental Army are on file in the National Archives. These descriptions include: "This man is a blackguard and a scoundrel" and "This officer is more fit to carry the hod than the epaulet."

Essays permit a more thorough description of performance than might otherwise be possible. They frequently make use of critical incidents. Essays can be very useful for the evaluation interview and for documenting recommendations and observations of the rater that are outside the normal focus of evaluation rating questions. The problem with descriptive essays is that they make comparisons among numbers of technical people very difficult and are time-consuming to accomplish. For this reason, essay appraisals are usually coupled with some other form of evaluation.

Management by Objectives

Management by objectives, or MBO, can be viewed not only as a performance evaluation system but as a style of management. This approach involves specific, quantifiable performance goals that are usually set jointly by the engineer or scientist and his manager.

Typically, the subordinate will be requested to establish short-term, quantifiable performance goals. For example, a subordinate may set a goal of accomplishing an engineering development within a six-month period, or completing a certain engineering job within a given period, or even getting a certain number of professional papers published. The subordinate and the manager discuss these goals together and adjust them as required to make them consistent with the organization's objectives and the goals of other individuals in it. At the end of a fixed period, the subordinate and the manager meet together again to discuss progress, evaluate what has been accomplished, and determine how results might be improved in the future. Herein lies a basic difference between traditional performance appraisal methods and MBO: with the latter, it is not the manager who writes the appraisal report, but the subordinate. In effect, the subordinate is his own rater.

There are many important advantages in using MBO:

o The manager-subordinate relationship is reviewed, developed, and strengthened.
o The subordinate has an opportunity to discuss problems with his manager that he might not otherwise bring up.
o The standards used for performance evaluation are unique to the characteristics of the particular job.
o The focus is on the future, not the past. The rating procedure is not a historical analysis but a working procedure for solving organizational problems and accomplishing organizational objectives.
o The method is consistent with psychological research which shows that individuals perform better when given clear-cut goals over specified periods.
o MBO encourages detailed feedback by the manager and thus permits the subordinate engineer or scientist to know exactly where he stands.
o Since the procedure permits the subordinate to set and strive toward his own goals, it encourages self-motivation and initiative.

○ MBO concentrates on what is relevant to the job rather than what is not.

○ MBO acts as a system of instruction as well as a system of evaluation, training the subordinate in a number of desirable activities.

MBO also has a number of limitations that must be considered before it is used. First, since the subordinate realizes that he will be judged on his ability to meet the goal he has set for himself (or helped set), there is a danger that he will set the goal too low so he can accomplish it easily. Also, MBO stresses the quantifiable, and many aspects of technical performance are very difficult to measure. This leads to two undesirable tendencies: stressing what can be measured, which may not be anywhere near as important as the unmeasurable (for instance, creativity); and emphasizing quantity, when quality may be far more important. Further, in any rating system in which the subordinate rated provides the input for his own rating, there is a risk that the facts will be covered up or manipulated. In addition, under some circumstances, the revelance of certain goals set for MBO can change very rapidly. But the MBO evaluation system does not adapt readily to changing goals. Thus MBO may encourage work toward obsolescent goals while ignoring current objectives that require emphasis. Finally, it is difficult to make MBO meaningful for promotion purposes. An MBO evaluation says little about how a person would do when pursuing different goals, and it is not easy to compare MBO ratings among different subordinates.

HUMAN ERRORS THAT CAN RUIN YOUR PERFORMANCE APPRAISAL SYSTEM

All forms of performance appraisal are applied by human beings. As such, they are subject to human error—and error in performance ratings not only may invalidate the appraisal system you have decided to use but may cause undeserved or unwise promotions and create havoc in the organizational team you are trying to build. The primary errors that creep into rating systems are:

Failure to discuss shortcomings with subordinates until regularly scheduled rating periods.

Failure to discuss ratings with subordinates at all.

The halo effect.
Lack of standardization in ratings.
Insufficient and distorted data for evaluation.
A tendency to rate to the extremes.
A tendency to rate average.
Distortion related to level of job.
The rich-get-richer and poor-get-poorer syndrome.

Failure to Discuss Shortcomings with Subordinates until Regularly Scheduled Rating Periods

Some managers mistakenly believe that the intent of the evaluation interview is to save all of an individual's performance problems to be discussed at the same time. Or they may put off such discussions because of laziness or fear of confrontation. They wait until the rating is due, write down all the individual's problems with performance, and then, in the vernacular of the day, "lay it on him" all at once.

This is wrong for several reasons. First, the shortcomings in performance will not get corrected until after the evaluation interview. This hurts the organization. The individual, who might otherwise get an opportunity to improve himself prior to a bad rating, has no such chance. And hitting a subordinate all at once with every performance fault can be psychologically devastating. For all these reasons, it's best to make suggestions and corrections pertaining to individual performance as events occur, not once a year or once every six months. Then give examples of the subordinate's desirable and undesirable performance during the evaluation interview.

Failure to Discuss Ratings with Subordinates at All

Managers, being human, tend to dislike discussing unpleasant facts. Thus, some managers fail to discuss bad ratings with their subordinates at all. This is clearly wrong. The manager is paid to do unpleasant things as well as pleasant ones. Recall that his credo must be: "Do the harder right rather than the easier wrong." Failing to discuss a bad rating with a subordinate is bad for the organization, since the person will continue to perform in the same manner, and it is unfair to the individual since he will not get the feedback he needs in order to improve. Intentional failure to discuss performance ratings with subordinates is a sign of poor leadership.

The Halo Effect

The halo effect occurs when a rater has to rate an individual on multiple factors, as with, for example, a graphic rating scale form. The rater may tend to rate the remaining factors according to how he rated the first few. If the first few factors were rated high, he tends to rate the following factors high also; if they were rated low, he may tend to rate succeeding factors low as well, even though a higher rating is warranted. Keep the existence of the halo effect in mind and be on guard against it. You can also minimize the halo effect when you are rating several subordinates if you go through and rate all subordinates on one factor of performance before proceeding to the next.

Lack of Standardization in Ratings

One person's definition of "good" is another person's definition of "fair" and yet another's definition of "excellent." Managers differ in their standards of judgment and in their conscious and unconscious prejudices. Part of the solution to the lack-of-standardization problem is in the system, and part is in the hands of the rater. The system must provide very precise definitions of what is meant by good, bad, or indifferent and should not leave it up to the rater to supply his own definitions. You, as an individual rater, should focus on the subordinate's accomplishments or lack of accomplishments rather than on trait or behavior patterns that you may disagree with but that are irrelevant to performance of the job. For example, an aggressive, hard-driving manager may have difficulty empathizing with a somewhat lethargic, easygoing person. But if that individual is doing the job he is supposed to do, what difference does it make that he is doing it in a manner more suited to his personality than to yours? Prejudice of any kind has no place at all if you are to have a successful performance assessment program or if you are to succeed as a technical manager.

Insufficient and Distorted Data for Evaluation

Technical people come in all shapes, sizes, personalities, and abilities. Any rating system is prejudiced in favor of the subordinate who can communicate his accomplishments best and present his performance in the best light. As a result, every manager, through his own observations, gets insufficient and distorted data that hinder his ability to accomplish an accurate and fair rating.

Again, there is no way to completely negate this human error of evaluation. One can only attempt to minimize its impact. In one study to determine the reasons for a major business failure, a researcher studied the career of the man whose decisions were primarily responsible for the defeat. Amazingly, in a thirty-year career, this man had gone from one failure to another. In his entire career, he had never had a major success! Only the magnitude of his last failure brought the publicity that provided the impetus for these astounding facts to emerge. Therefore, again you should focus not on how a subordinate does something but on the final results of what he or she does.

Another technique that will assist you in making fair evaluations that overcome insufficient and distorted data is to do what Ken B. did, as described in Chapter 5, and require your subordinates to keep their own records of their accomplishments. You will learn more things about your organization, its members, and what they consider important than you ever thought possible.

A Tendency to Rate to the Extremes

Some raters tend to be extremely lenient in their ratings. They may fear that the effect of a bad rating will be to demotivate the subordinate and make him perform worse. They may be afraid that a bad rating will reflect unfavorably on their own ability to manage. They may harbor a desire to be popular among their subordinates. Or, an overly lenient rating may be the only way to ensure that the individual rated will ever get promoted. This latter approach leads to gross inflation of the ratings and makes the whole system much less fair and effective. In the early 1960s, the U.S. Air Force had a system for rating officer effectiveness that tended to produce many over-inflated ratings. So bad was the system that it was found that an officer discharged for incompetence carried an overall rating of "very fine officer."

At the same time that many raters tend to be overly lenient, others rate too strictly. In some cases this stems from a desire to "really make the person work for a good rating." Some managers feel that it is wise and in the subordinate's own best interest to begin with low ratings and gradually rate the person higher as he or she acquires more experience. According to this theory, the ratings show that the subordinate is making progress and thus should increase his chances for promotion; the subordinate is generally pleased, since his ratings are always rising; and the rater looks good as a trainer and leader. In real life, the subordinate may lose out on a promotion to someone who is being rated more fairly or leniently, so his feeling of well-being may be relatively short-lived. The manager's abilities as a trainer will also be called into question when it is realized that all of his subordinates are showing gradually and progressively higher ratings.

The solution to the problem of the tendency to rate to extremes is to compare the averages of your ratings with the overall averages of other raters. Compiling these data and computing these averages should be done by someone outside of any one single technical organization. Probably this job is best accomplished by the personnel department.

A Tendency to Rate Average

Here we have a human error due to the manager-rater's desire not to stick his neck out too far in any direction. All of his ratings tend to congregate about the mean or average description of performance. A comparison of ratings is usually not too helpful in solving this problem, since the very averageness of the ratings tends to conceal the problem. One solution that seems to work well is to drop "average" from the form. Instead of having an odd number of descriptors on the rating form, use an even number. For example, instead of having a graphic scale that reads "excellent," "above average," "average," "below average," and "poor," have one that reads "excellent," "above average," "below average," and "poor." This forces the evaluator to pick a term other than "average."

Distortion Related to Level of Job

How can a senior scientist do a poor job? The answer, according to research on the evaluation of senior people, is that he apparently can't. The higher the job, the higher the rating tends to be. Complicating this problem is the fact that the higher the job, the fewer other individuals there are whose ratings can be compared with that person's. There may be hundreds of engineers, but there is only one vice president of engineering.

One solution to this problem is to make rating comparisons not by job function (engineering) but by job rank (vice president). Another is to accept the fact that ratings will be higher for the more senior job positions and to use a different rating form from that used to rate subordinates occupying junior-level positions. Since the rating is going to be good, there should be an increased number of descriptions of good on this form: perhaps "superior," "excellent," "very good," and "good."

Even these description might be broken down into subdivisions, with, for example, three or more "superior" categories. Naturally, for decorative purposes you must include a similar number of divisions on the bad side, which no one will ever use. This rather obvious deception will allow all senior people to receive "good" ratings while still allowing for discrimination among performance levels.

The Rich-Get-Richer and the Poor-Get-Poorer Syndrome

There is inertia in every performance appraisal system, with the result that individuals who have had good performance reports in the past tend to get good ones again and individuals who have had bad reports in the past tend to continue along these lines regardless of actual performance. This syndrome finds its roots in psychological research which shows that we tend to expect good performance from past good performers, and something less from those subordinates who have not done well previously. Unfortunately, we tend to rate according to these expectations.

A large company in Washington, D.C., once actually refused a salary increase recommended by a manager based on an excellent performance report because "this engineer has never received an excellent performance report in the past, and we therefore feel that this rating is inflated." I won't go into the enormous implications of such a philosophy. You should endeavor to carry out every appraisal as if it were the first, and remind yourself that you are not rating a person's reputation—only his performance and what he has actually done during the rating period.

HOW TO CONDUCT THE PERFORMANCE RATING INTERVIEW FOR MAXIMUM POSITIVE RESULTS

The performance rating interview, or evaluation interview, is the meeting during which you discuss the rating you have given with the subordinate you have evaluated. First, it is crucial not to make this important meeting a catch-as-catch-can encounter. The performance rating interview is important to your organization as well as the individual being interviewed. Since how well you conduct the meeting will have an impact on what the subordinate thinks of you as his manager and leader in the future, you also have a direct investment in the outcome of the meeting. For all of these reasons, schedule a definite time for the interview when nothing else is likely to disturb you, and make certain you have allowed enough time so you can conduct the meeting without being rushed.

Open the interview by stating its purpose. For example: "Joe, the purpose of this meeting is to go over the performance rating I've given you for the last period so that the evaluation can help you to do a better job."

Before presenting your evaluation to your subordinate, ask him how he thinks he has done in each of the areas evaluated. Make it clear that his comments are not going to affect your already completed evaluation rating one way or the other. The advantage of this approach is that it is easier to accept criticism from oneself than it is from someone else. Once you present the evaluation, your subordinate is going to be on the defensive, and it will be much harder for you to get him to accept failures in his performance. You will sometimes be surprised by (and sometimes not surprised by) the very critical evaluation that your subordinate will make of his own performance.

Having given your subordinate the chance to present his own evaluation of himself, you should proceed to go over your evaluation. Always present the strong points first. Regardless of what rating form you are using, you must deal in specifics and not generalities. If you have rated the person low because he lacks cost-consciousness, be sure to give some "for instances" so he knows what you're talking about. Don't bring up every single occasion on which he failed to adequately control costs. One or two examples should be sufficient.

After you have gone over your entire evaluation, ask your subordinate for comments. Expect the worst. Your purpose in asking for comments here is simply to defuse—under controlled conditions—the psychological bomb that you have built by your criticisms. Let your subordinate have his say with minimum comment, and do not argue with him. Of course, you may receive explanations you might consider acting on, but at this point such questions are secondary to defusion.

You will be able to sense when your subordinate has unloaded sufficiently so that you can proceed into the final stage of the interview, in which you should help him come up with concrete actions for overcoming the performance problems you have identified. Begin by asking him how he sees his progress and problems. Get him to suggest ways of solving these problems. If you don't think a proposed solution would work, say so and state why. Work with your subordinate to develop a course of action that you and he both agree on. Conclude the interview in such a fashion that your subordinate knows exactly where he stands and exactly what he must do to improve his performance.

Be sure that any criticism you make is relevant to the job. Never try to create the perfect person—or the perfect engineer, scientist, chemist, or whatever—through the performance appraisal process. Perfection will not solve your technical problems. Competence at what is relevant to the job will.

WHAT TO DO IF A PERSON CONTINUALLY PERFORMS POORLY

With few exceptions, there is nothing you can do with the habitually poor performer except get rid of him or get him out of a responsible position. Retaining a loser is unfair to the other members of your organization, since by his actions he hurts the organization and retards its ability to reach its objectives. For this reason alone, you should never get rid of a poor performer by having him transferred to another organization unless the person's new boss knows what he or she is getting and agrees to the transfer.

On the chance that the individual can be salvaged, as well as in fairness, you should first give a warning. But you need not wait until performance appraisal time before either warning the person or taking some other action. For both warnings and firings, the best course to take is tactful forthrightness. One thing that is certain is that the person you fire will work again. Maybe the work he is doing is wrong for him. Maybe the problem has something to do with the environment of your organization or company. At any rate, if you are giving a warning, you should make it clear exactly why the warning is being given, indicate what your subordinate needs to do to improve, and indicate that you will fire him if he does not improve. For a firing, you need to be just as forthright but you should be more tactful, suggesting that you don't feel that he is a bad professional in general but only that he has not done well enough at the particular work he has been assigned in your particular organization.

There are alternatives to firing that you can consider when someone is a poor performer but special circumstances surround his employment, such as past exceptional service to the company or seniority. You can request that the person resign, or you can retain him until a period of layoffs and then lay him off. Either action removes the stigma of firing. You can also transfer him from a position of responsibility to a dead-end job with no responsibility and no opportunity for a pay increase or promotion. This is a humiliation, though, and unless the subordinate is close to retirement, he will probably end up resigning anyway.

Unless the person himself desires to be retained because he is close to retirement or some other special circumstances exist, the best alternative for everyone concerned is usually dismissal. However, with good leadership, continual poor performance will be rare in your organization and so you won't need to struggle with these problems very often.

A good performance appraisal system will have a positive effect on your employees, which will contribute to good performance in your organization by enabling you to select individuals for promotion and merit raises on a fair basis, identifying the needs for training, and providing the opportunities for two-way communication that you might not otherwise have.

CHAPTER 8

How to Budget and Control Costs

Any discussion of budgeting must begin with the term "planning." Planning is bound up in all other functions of management. It is one of the basic functions that you must perform as a technical manager, since it involves decision-making and selection from among alternative courses of action. We have already looked at some types of planning in our discussions of organizing, staffing, recruiting, and training. In this chapter we'll look at perhaps the most conspicuous type of planning the technical manager carries out—that having to do with money.

As with all types of planning, your organization's financial plan, or budget, must be based on objectives. You can't decide how to get anywhere until you decide where you're going. Once you have developed your budget, cost-control procedures are needed to ensure that you keep to that budget.

THE USE OF ORGANIZATIONAL OBJECTIVES
IN FINANCIAL PLANNING

Organizational objectives may come from many sources and from many combinations of sources. As the organization's manager, you sometimes will participate in setting them and sometimes will not. For example, objectives for your organization may come from top management, your immediate superior, yourself, or managers of other organizations that your organization is doing supporting work for.

Regardless of where they originate, all objectives have a price tag—in fact, different price tags, depending on what alternative course of action is chosen to accomplish the objective. For example, if the objective is to travel from your present location to some place a thousand miles away, there are different ways of accomplishing this. You could go by plane, by bus, by train, or by automobile. Each alternative has advantages and disadvantages associated with it, and each alternative has a different price tag.

The objective that you are supposed to achieve within your organizational budget will come to you in one of two forms:

o You will be allowed freedom to choose the alternative course of action that you wish.
o You will be allowed no freedom of choice in how you achieve the objective.

For example, you may be told to develop Product A. How you develop Product A is left up to you—you can choose from among various alternative courses of action. The figures used in your budget will be from the alternative you have chosen. Or, you may be given a "by name" assignment for one of your subordinates to support someone else's project, as often occurs with a matrix organization. Your support of this objective leaves you no alternative course of action, and your financial budget will reflect this requirement.

If you run an engineering organization, you will typically be given certain objectives and asked to prepare a budget to meet those objectives. If the budget is approved, you will be authorized to expend this fixed amount. You will be able to go over the amounts listed in your budget only when special appropriations are authorized. If you run an organization that has sales, you may be given a more flexible budget. The budget may allow for variations in sales volume by providing for revisions in other variables such as related income, expenses, and cash flows.

If your initial budget is not approved, you may be asked what objectives can be met under a certain fixed amount. It will then be your task to present alternative mixes of objectives that can be accomplished given the budget figure allocated.

Let us look first at a budget for a small research and development organization with no sales for which a fixed budget has been approved.

HOW TO CONSTRUCT A FIXED-APPROPRIATIONS BUDGET

The period for the fixed budget you prepare is typically a year, although it could be for either a shorter or a longer period. The important thing is to make it long enough for effective planning. Since your budget is only one of several or many organizational budgets that must be integrated into a company budget, the period required is usually directed by higher management in the finance department.

The first item with which you will be concerned is indirect salaries of all personnel, including yourself. These are personnel who will not be charging their time to any particular project and who would have to be paid whether or not your organization had any production at all. Note that in Figure 18, the amounts listed for indirect salaries have been increased in the months of May and August. You should attempt to anticipate salary increases and their approximate amounts, although putting them in the budget does not commit either you or the company to giving a raise. The fringe benefits should be figured at a certain percentage of the basic salary. In this example, a 20 percent figure has been used. All figures in the example have been rounded off to the nearest $50. How you round off your figures, or whether you use exact figures, depends on the policies of your company.

Building rent, utilities, insurance, and depreciation are fairly straightforward, since you will know exactly what amounts your organization is being charged. Depending on your organization, utilities may or may not vary with activity level. Be alert to the possibility that these figures are due to rise, in which case you should estimate the increases and make sure adjusted figures based on these estimates go into your budget.

Telephone costs can be a very large expense item. There are two ways of treating this, depending on your circumstances. First, you can look at what your telephone charges have been in the past and multiply these charges by a factor based on the level of activity you anticipate. You must relate level of activity to some known quantity, such as the total number of engineering hours anticipated for project work, the total number of dollars anticipated for project work, or your department's total number of forecast engineering hours. Just be certain to pick a figure that is relevant.

Let's assume that your department's telephone bill for the preceding year looked something like this:

Jan	Feb	Mar	Apr	May	Jun	Jul	Aug	Sep	Oct	Nov	Dec
600	675	610	525	400	410	403	450	550	650	665	500

You've decided to base your budget forecast on forecast engineering hours charged to your projects. The hours forecast to be charged on your planned projects next year are:

FIGURE 18. A budget for a small research and development department.

	JAN.	FEB.	MARCH	APRIL	MAY	JUNE	JULY	AUG.	SEPT.	OCT.	NOV.	DEC.	Total
Salaries (indirect)	$ 5,000	$ 5,000	$ 5,000	$ 5,000	$ 5,200	$ 5,200	$ 5,200	$ 5,500	$ 5,500	$ 5,500	$ 5,500	$ 5,500	
Associated fringe benefits	1,000	1,000	1,000	1,000	1,000	1,000	1,000	1,100	1,100	1,100	1,100	1,100	
Building rent	1,000	1,000	1,000	1,000	1,000	1,000	1,000	1,000	1,000	1,000	1,000	1,000	
Utilities	200	200	200	200	200	200	200	200	200	200	200	200	
Insurance	200	200	200	200	200	200	200	200	200	200	200	200	
Depreciation	100	100	100	100	100	100	100	100	100	100	100	100	
Telephone	800	950	850	700	450	550	500	600	700	850	850	650	
Small tools	300	—	—	—	—	—	—	—	—	—	—	—	
Maintenance	100	100	100	100	100	100	100	100	100	100	100	100	
Office supplies	100	50	50	50	100	100	100	50	100	100	100	100	
Travel	1,000	—	—	—	500	500	—	—	1,000	—	—	—	
Meetings	300	—	—	—	300	—	—	—	300	—	—	100	
Prof. courses	500	500	500	500	—	500	500	500	—	—	—	—	
Project A	2,000	2,000	1,000	3,000	3,800	3,800	2,500	2,500	3,700	1,700	1,900	1,900	
Project B	10,000	5,000	5,000	1,000	1,200	500	500	500	1,000	4,000	6,000	2,000	
Project C	5,000	1,000	1,000	1,000	3,000	2,000	500	500	1,000	500	2,000	3,000	
Project D	3,000	1,000	1,000	2,000	1,000	2,000	2,000	500	2,000	2,000	2,000	5,000	
Project E	2,000	2,000	2,000	2,000	1,000	12,000	13,000	15,000	15,000	11,000	11,000	11,000	
Misc. expense	100	100	50	50	50	50	150	150	200	100	100	100	
Totals	$32,700	$20,200	$19,050	$17,900	$19,200	$29,800	$27,550	$28,500	$33,200	$28,450	$32,150	$32,050	$320,750

CAPITAL EQUIPMENT	JAN.	FEB.	MARCH	APRIL	MAY	JUNE	JULY	AUG.	SEPT.	OCT.	NOV.	DEC.	Total
Precision grinder	25,000												
Impactor						70,000							
Minicomputer											5,000		
Totals	25,000					70,000					5,000		100,000
													$420,750

Jan	Feb	Mar	Apr	May	Jun
1,975	2,300	2,500	2,350	2,100	2,200

						Jul	Aug	Sep	Oct	Nov	Dec
						1,985	2,190	2,090	2,435	2,287	1,800

Last year, the engineering hours actually charged on your organization's projects were as follows:

Jan	Feb	Mar	Apr	May	Jun
1,500	1,700	1,760	1,750	1,800	1,750

						Jul	Aug	Sep	Oct	Nov	Dec
						1,700	1,650	1,654	1,850	1,720	1,400

If we put last year's figures in the numerator and the coming year's forecast in the denominator, we get the following fractions and can reduce them to monthly factors:

Jan	Feb	Mar	Apr	May	June
$\frac{1,975}{1,500}=1.3$	$\frac{2,300}{1,700}=1.4$	$\frac{2,500}{1,760}=1.4$	$\frac{2,350}{1,750}=1.3$	$\frac{2,100}{1,800}=1.1$	$\frac{2,200}{1,750}=1.3$

Jul	Aug	Sep	Oct	Nov	Dec
$\frac{1,985}{1,700}=1.2$	$\frac{2,190}{1,650}=1.3$	$\frac{2,090}{1,654}=1.3$	$\frac{2,435}{1,850}=1.3$	$\frac{2,287}{1,720}=1.3$	$\frac{1,800}{1,400}=1.3$

Last year's telephone bills are now multiplied by the factors we have developed to produce our telephone budget for the coming year:

Jan	Feb	Mar	Apr	May	Jun
600	675	610	525	400	410
×1.3	×1.4	×1.4	×1.3	×1.1	×1.3
$780	$945	$854	$682.50	$440	$533

						Jul	Aug	Sep	Oct	Nov	Dec
						403	450	550	650	665	500
						×1.2	×1.3	×1.3	×1.3	×1.3	×1.3
						$483.60	$585	$715	$845	$864.50	$650

The forecast factors that have been developed can also be used to estimate other costs that will vary with the relevant factor selected (in this case, engineering hours on projects).

There is another way of making telephone forecasts that is useful in cases where a particular project will have a significant amount of telephone calls associated with it. Instead of using a forecast factor, you can charge the calls directly to the project, in which case this cost would appear as part of the project expenses listed rather than as part of the telephone item.

Small tools, or any other item of significant expense, should be identified and listed as an expense for the month in which purchase is anticipated. Expenditures for maintenance and office supplies either can be a standard amount or can be adjusted by your factor if you anticipate that these items will vary significantly with activity level.

Travel can be a very large item, especially in a small department. Therefore, you should list all planned trips that you are reasonably sure of. With a fixed-appropriation-type budget, it is far better to err slightly on the high side than to go back and have to request a special authorization. Again, if a particular project has a significant amount of travel associated with it, those expenses should be listed as a part of that project.

Meetings and courses are important parts of the professional development of your technical organization. Include meetings that are already planned, and also get approval to include special meetings that you may want to send your people to. Remember that most meetings will require an increase in your travel budget as well. With professional courses, you should plan ahead to send your technical personnel on a continuing basis. Even if you haven't identified the courses or the personnel at the time of budget preparation, you should endeavor to get an approved amount set aside for this purpose.

We now come to the projects. Each project should be documented on a product development form, as in Figure 19 for Project A. Note that for each item, the top line represents planned costs and the bottom line represents actual costs.* The estimates for engineering costs are obtained by multiplying hours for any one task by an hourly charge. This charge may be either the actual salary of an identified engineer, adjusted for anticipated raises and fringe benefits, or the average labor rate computed for engineers in your department, adjusted for an anticipated composite raise and fringe benefits.

There are, of course, other ways of budgeting for projects. Some firms take all engineers together and lump them and their compensation under "Indirect salaries" and "Associated fringe benefits." The disadvan-

---

* The product development schedule can be completed solely in dollars or in some combination of dollars and labor hours, depending on its use at the time.

FIGURE 19. Product development schedule, Project A, as of July 31.

TASK AND DEPARTMENT	JAN	FEB	MAR	APR	MAY	JUNE	JULY	AUG	SEPT	OCT	NOV	DEC	JAN	FEB
Design module														
Engineering department	2,000	2,000	1,000	1,000	1,000									
	1,625	1,970	1,100	1,050	950									
Build prototypes														
Engineering department					500	500	500	500	500					
					450	500	400							
Prototype shop						3,000	2,000	2,000	2,000					
						3,200	2,000							
Drafting department					300	300	200							
					350	300								
Material and small parts				2,000	2,000									
				2,000	2,050									

TASK AND DEPARTMENT	JAN	FEB	MAR	APR	MAY	JUNE	JULY	AUG	SEPT	OCT	NOV	DEC	JAN	FEB
Testing of prototypes														
Engineering department									200	200	200	200	200	200
Prototype shop									500	500	200	200	100	
Testing									500	1,000	1,500	1,500	1,000	500
Totals Planned	2,000	2,000	1,000	3,000	3,800	3,800	2,500	2,500	3,700	1,700	1,900	1,900	1,300	700
Actual	1,625	1,970	1,100	3,050	3,800	4,000	2,600							
Cumulative	+375	+405	+305	+255	+255	+55	−45							

tage of this is that the listed cost of each project in the budget is inaccurate, since it includes only the labor rates from departments. Sometimes, when contracted work is being performed for someone outside the company, everyone is considered direct, including you, and may be required to charge directly to the project under contract. The estimated cost of the project is listed under the line item for the month during which the expense is planned.

The final line item in your budget (refer back to Figure 18) is miscellaneous expense. This is not a slush fund for everything and anything, but should be used for small items that by themselves do not amount to much. Examples would be magazine subscriptions or books.

Capital equipment is usually identifed separately. (Ways of making capital budgeting decisions will be discussed later on.) The amount of purchase is anticipated, although the total cost may be paid out over an extended period.

Your first cut at the budget may or may not be approved. It may come back with additional line items that someone thinks you should add, or with items that someone cannot understand the reason for and you will have to defend. It is also possible for your initial budget to be totally rejected, with an annotation from your boss reading something like: "We cannot afford a budget this high for engineering; what can we get for $200,000?" (when your budget estimate was $350,000). Such a reduction means that you must sharpen your pencil considerably and reduce your line items as much as possible while still doing your job and completing the projects for which you are scheduled.

Sometimes the reduction is so large that you can no longer do all the projects planned within the fixed budget given you. You will then need to present various alternatives regarding what projects you realistically can do, as mentioned previously. It is a mistake to agree to work within an impossible budget, because you will be expected to accomplish what you agreed to within the budget allocated. Indeed, higher management plans may depend on your doing so. Therefore, if you have any doubts about what you think your organization can or cannot accomplish, make certain this is clearly understood by your management.

HOW TO MAKE CAPITAL BUDGETING DECISIONS

Capital equipment can be extremely expensive, and alternative proposals for capital expenditures are mutually exclusive—if you adopt one, you cannot carry out the others. Therefore, engineers, economists, and financial experts have together developed techniques that allow you to make a logical selection from among complex capital budgeting alternatives on a financial basis. To do this requires that you know the cost of capital, or rate that must be paid to obtain the most desirable mixture of debt and equity funds for use within the company. You need not have an in-depth knowledge of debt and equity funding; you can get the cost-of-capital figure to use from your finance department.

There are many capital budgeting procedures for evaluating proposals, but only two are theoretically correct. They are known as the present-value and rate-of-return methods (also called the internal-rate-of-return method). With both these methods, the capital expenditure proposals are expressed in the form of cash flows and the cash flows are then evaluated in terms of the time over which they occur.

Both methods require us to set up our cash flows in a similar fashion, so let's look at how this part of the problem is solved first. Every alternative proposal involves two separate cash flows. The first is the outflow required by the investment for the capital equipment. The second is the annual cash inflow, or savings, as a result of the investment.

Let's assume we're considering the purchase of a special computer. There are two different models available from different firms. Model A costs $50,000 and has a life of 10 years. At the end of 10 years, the firm that sold it to us would be willing to buy it back for $5,000. We calculate that with this model we can save $10,000 a year over the next 10 years, in contrast to the bad old way we're doing things now.

Model B is a similar computer offered by another firm. It costs less, only $30,000. But the Model B computer will last only 5 years, and at the end of that time it is worthless for trade-in. At best we can sell it for scrap for $100. However, Model B does have one advantage over Model A: for those 5 years of operation, it will save us $15,000 a year over our present modus operandi. The question is, which model do we put in our budget, Model A or Model B?

The two cash flows can be set up as follows:

	CURRENT METHOD	MODEL A	MODEL B
Initial cost	0	−$50,000	−$30,000
Salvage value	0	+$5,000 after 10 years	+$100 after 5 years
Savings	0	+$10,000/year for 10 years	+15,000/year for 5 years

Clearly it is to our advantage to buy one of the two computers as opposed to continuing without one. Just adding the numbers up seems to tell us to buy Model A. The total benefit with Model A is 10 years × $10,000 = $100,000 plus the $5,000 salvage value. If we subtract the initial investment of $50,000, that leaves us with a net positive benefit of $55,000. For Model B, our net benefit is only 5 years × $15,000 = $75,000 plus the $100 that we can get for the machine for scrap. That's $75,100. Subtracting our investment of $30,000 leaves $45,100, which is less than the net benefit of going with Model A.

But wait now. Isn't it of some value to be getting more money sooner, even if it's only for five years? It clearly is, and that's where the cost of capital and the time value of money come in. Remember, there are alternative things you can do with money. If you choose to receive $10,000 a year from now rather than today, you forgo money you might earn over the course of a year with that $10,000. You might alternatively have put it in the bank to earn interest, invested it in real estate, or bought a certain percentage of an engineer's time to develop a new invention. Therefore, it is clear that in return for agreeing to accept the $10,000 a year from now rather than today, you should get something in return. You will get the $10,000 a year from now plus some payment for its use that is a percentage of the $10,000. The percentage multiplied by the $10,000 is the cost of capital.

There is a complex formula that can be used to tell you how much you should receive a year from now, depending on what percentage of the $10,000 you feel is fair. From this formula, you can construct a table with not just one percentage but a variety of percentages. In that way if you want to charge different percentages depending on financial and economic conditions at the time, you will be able to do so. You can also calculate values for the table for an infinite number of years. Further, you can construct your table either to tell you what the present value of any sum is at some time in the future, or to tell you the present value of a stream of income in which a sum is received every year for a given number of years.

Fortunately, you won't need to do any of these calculations. These figures have already been worked out for you in Tables 1 and 2. Note that these tables require you to enter with a certain number of years (given in the leftmost column) and a percentage. The percentage to be used at any given time is the cost of capital and is supplied by your finance department.

You can make an accurate capital budgeting decision by using either the present-value method or the rate-of-return method. Let's assume that in the computer example we've been given a cost of capital of 10 percent. Consider present value first.

How to Calculate the Present Values of Conflicting Proposals

To calculate the present value of purchasing Model A or B, we would use the same general format that we used in setting up our cash flows. First the initial cost.

	MODEL A	MODEL B
Initial cost	−$50,000.00	−$30,000.00

There aren't any time-value calculations to be made here because both initial investments are in the present time.

Now let's look at the salvage value. The salvage value of Model A after 10 years is $5,000. We turn to Table 1, which shows the present value of $1 received after different numbers of years. For a 10-year period with a 10 percent cost of capital, we extract a multiplier, or discount rate, of 0.3855. We then multiply 0.386 (rounded) by $5,000 to get $1,930. The salvage value of Model B is $100 at the end of 5 years. For a 5-year period and a 10 percent cost of capital, we extract a multiplier of 0.6209. We multiply $100 by 0.621 to get $62.10. Our cash flow table now looks like this:

	MODEL A	MODEL B
Initial cost	−$50,000.00	−$30,000.00
Salvage value	+$ 1,930.00	+$ 62.10

The final step is to look at our savings. For Model A, we save $10,000 a year for 10 years. We now turn to Table 2, which shows the present value of $1 received annually at the end of each year for n years. For a 10-year period and a 10 percent cost of capital, we extract a multiplier of 6.1446. Multiplying 6.145 by $10,000 gives us $61,450. Similarly, a 5-year period and 10 percent cost of capital yield a multiplier of 3.7908. We multiply 3.791 by the $15,000 a year saved with Model B to come up with $56,865. Our cash flow table is now complete:

	MODEL A	MODEL B
Initial cost	−$50,000.00	−$30,000.00
Salvage value	+ 1,930.00	+ 62.10
Savings	+ 61,450.00	+ 56,865.00
	+$13,380.00	+$26,927.10

TABLE 1. Present value of $1 received at end of n number of years.

n/r	1.0%	2.0%	3.0%	4.0%	5.0%	6%	7%	8%	9%	10%	11%	12%	13%	14%	15%
1	.9901	.9804	.9709	.9615	.9524	.9434	.9346	.9259	.9174	.9091	.9009	.8929	.8850	.8772	.8696
2	.9803	.9612	.9426	.9246	.9070	.8900	.8734	.8573	.8417	.8264	.8116	.7972	.7831	.7695	.7561
3	.9706	.9423	.9151	.8890	.8638	.8396	.8163	.7938	.7722	.7513	.7312	.7118	.6931	.6750	.6575
4	.9610	.9238	.8885	.8548	.8227	.7921	.7629	.7350	.7084	.6830	.6587	.6355	.6133	.5921	.5718
5	.9515	.9057	.8626	.8219	.7835	.7473	.7130	.6806	.6499	.6209	.5935	.5674	.5428	.5194	.4972
6	.9420	.8880	.8375	.7903	.7462	.7050	.6663	.6302	.5963	.5645	.5346	.5066	.4803	.4556	.4323
7	.9327	.8706	.8131	.7599	.7107	.6651	.6227	.5835	.5470	.5132	.4817	.4523	.4251	.3996	.3759
8	.9235	.8535	.7894	.7307	.6768	.6274	.5820	.5403	.5019	.4665	.4339	.4039	.3762	.3506	.3269
9	.9143	.8368	.7664	.7026	.6446	.5919	.5439	.5002	.4604	.4241	.3909	.3606	.3329	.3075	.2843
10	.9053	.8203	.7441	.6756	.6139	.5584	.5083	.4632	.4224	.3855	.3522	.3220	.2946	.2697	.2472
11	.8963	.8043	.7224	.6496	.5847	.5268	.4751	.4289	.3875	.3505	.3173	.2875	.2607	.2366	.2149
12	.8874	.7885	.7014	.6246	.5568	.4970	.4440	.3971	.3555	.3186	.2858	.2567	.2307	.2076	.1869
13	.8787	.7730	.6810	.6006	.5303	.4688	.4150	.3677	.3262	.2897	.2575	.2292	.2042	.1821	.1625
14	.8700	.7579	.6611	.5775	.5051	.4423	.3878	.3405	.2992	.2633	.2320	.2046	.1807	.1597	.1413
15	.8613	.7430	.6419	.5553	.4810	.4173	.3624	.3152	.2745	.2394	.2090	.1827	.1599	.1401	.1229
16	.8528	.7284	.6232	.5339	.4581	.3936	.3387	.2919	.2519	.2176	.1883	.1631	.1415	.1229	.1069
17	.8444	.7142	.6050	.5134	.4363	.3714	.3166	.2703	.2311	.1978	.1696	.1456	.1252	.1078	.0929
18	.8360	.7002	.5874	.4936	.4155	.3503	.2959	.2502	.2120	.1799	.1528	.1300	.1108	.0946	.0808
19	.8277	.6864	.5703	.4746	.3957	.3305	.2765	.2317	.1945	.1635	.1377	.1161	.0981	.0829	.0703
20	.8195	.6730	.5537	.4564	.3769	.3118	.2584	.2145	.1784	.1486	.1240	.1037	.0868	.0728	.0611
21	.8114	.6598	.5375	.4388	.3589	.2942	.2415	.1987	.1637	.1351	.1117	.0926	.0768	.0638	.0531
22	.8034	.6468	.5219	.4220	.3418	.2775	.2257	.1839	.1502	.1228	.1007	.0826	.0680	.0560	.0462
23	.7954	.6342	.5067	.4057	.3256	.2618	.2109	.1703	.1378	.1117	.0907	.0738	.0601	.0491	.0402
24	.7876	.6217	.4919	.3901	.3101	.2470	.1971	.1577	.1264	.1015	.0817	.0659	.0532	.0431	.0349
25	.7798	.6095	.4776	.3751	.2953	.2330	.1842	.1460	.1160	.0923	.0736	.0588	.0471	.0378	.0304
26	.7720	.5976	.4637	.3607	.2812	.2198	.1722	.1352	.1064	.0839	.0663	.0525	.0417	.0331	.0264
27	.7644	.5859	.4502	.3468	.2678	.2074	.1609	.1252	.0976	.0763	.0597	.0469	.0369	.0291	.0230
28	.7568	.5744	.4371	.3335	.2551	.1956	.1504	.1159	.0895	.0693	.0538	.0419	.0326	.0255	.0200
29	.7493	.5631	.4243	.3207	.2429	.1846	.1406	.1073	.0822	.0630	.0485	.0374	.0289	.0224	.0174
30	.7419	.5521	.4120	.3083	.2314	.1741	.1314	.0994	.0754	.0573	.0437	.0334	.0256	.0196	.0151
35	.7059	.5000	.3554	.2534	.1813	.1301	.0937	.0676	.0490	.0356	.0259	.0189	.0139	.0102	.0075
40	.6717	.4529	.3066	.2083	.1420	.0972	.0668	.0460	.0318	.0221	.0154	.0107	.0075	.0053	.0037
45	.6391	.410	.2644	.1713	.1112	.0727	.0476	.0313	.0207	.0137	.0091	.0061	.0041	.0027	.0019
50	.6080	.3715	.2281	.1407	.0872	.0543	.0339	.0213	.0134	.0085	.0054	.0035	.0022	.0014	.0009

n/r	16%	18%	20%	22%	24%	26%	28%	30%	32%	34%	36%	38%	40%	45%	50%
1	.8621	.8475	.8333	.8197	.8065	.7937	.7813	.7692	.7576	.7463	.7353	.7246	.7143	.6897	.6667
2	.7432	.7182	.6944	.6719	.6504	.6299	.6104	.5917	.5739	.5569	.5407	.5251	.5102	.4756	.4444
3	.6407	.6086	.5787	.5507	.5245	.4999	.4768	.4552	.4348	.4155	.3975	.3805	.3644	.3280	.2963
4	.5523	.5158	.4823	.4514	.4230	.3968	.3725	.3501	.3294	.3102	.2923	.2757	.2603	.2262	.1975
5	.4761	.4371	.4019	.3700	.3411	.3149	.2910	.2693	.2495	.2315	.2149	.1998	.1859	.1560	.1317
6	.4104	.3704	.3349	.3033	.2751	.2499	.2274	.2072	.1890	.1727	.1580	.1448	.1328	.1076	.0878
7	.3538	.3139	.2791	.2486	.2218	.1983	.1776	.1594	.1432	.1289	.1162	.1049	.0949	.0742	.0585
8	.3050	.2660	.2326	.2038	.1789	.1574	.1388	.1226	.1085	.0962	.0854	.0760	.0678	.0512	.0390
9	.2630	.2255	.1938	.1670	.1443	.1249	.1084	.0943	.0822	.0718	.0628	.0551	.0484	.0353	.0260
10	.2267	.1911	.1615	.1369	.1164	.0992	.0847	.0725	.0623	.0536	.0462	.0399	.0346	.0243	.0173
11	.1954	.1619	.1346	.1122	.0938	.0787	.0662	.0558	.0472	.0400	.0340	.0289	.0247	.0168	.0116
12	.1685	.1372	.1122	.0920	.0757	.0625	.0517	.0429	.0357	.0298	.0250	.0210	.0176	.0116	.0077
13	.1452	.1163	.0935	.0754	.0610	.0496	.0404	.0330	.0271	.0223	.0184	.0152	.0126	.0080	.0051
14	.1252	.0985	.0779	.0618	.0492	.0393	.0316	.0253	.0205	.0166	.0135	.0110	.0090	.0055	.0034
15	.1079	.0835	.0649	.0507	.0397	.0312	.0247	.0195	.0155	.0124	.0099	.0080	.0064	.0038	.0023
16	.0930	.0708	.0541	.0415	.0320	.0248	.0193	.0150	.0118	.0093	.0073	.0058	.0046	.0026	.0015
17	.0802	.0600	.0451	.0340	.0258	.0197	.0150	.0116	.0089	.0069	.0054	.0042	.0033	.0018	.0010
18	.0691	.0508	.0376	.0279	.0208	.0156	.0118	.0089	.0068	.0052	.0039	.0030	.0023	.0012	.0007
19	.0596	.0431	.0313	.0229	.0168	.0124	.0092	.0068	.0051	.0038	.0029	.0022	.0017	.0009	.0005
20	.0514	.0365	.0261	.0187	.0135	.0098	.0072	.0053	.0039	.0029	.0021	.0016	.0012	.0006	.0003
21	.0443	.0309	.0217	.0154	.0109	.0078	.0056	.0040	.0029	.0021	.0016	.0012	.0009	.0004	.0002
22	.0382	.0262	.0181	.0126	.0088	.0062	.0044	.0031	.0022	.0016	.0012	.0008	.0006	.0003	.0001
23	.0329	.0222	.0151	.0103	.0071	.0049	.0034	.0024	.0017	.0012	.0008	.0006	.0004	.0002	.0001
24	.0284	.0188	.0126	.0085	.0057	.0039	.0027	.0018	.0013	.0009	.0006	.0004	.0003	.0001	.0001
25	.0245	.0160	.0105	.0069	.0046	.0031	.0021	.0014	.0010	.0007	.0005	.0003	.0002	.0001	.0000
26	.0211	.0135	.0087	.0057	.0037	.0025	.0016	.0011	.0007	.0005	.0003	.0002	.0002	.0001	
27	.0182	.0115	.0073	.0047	.0030	.0019	.0013	.0008	.0006	.0004	.0002	.0002	.0001	.0000	
28	.0157	.0097	.0061	.0038	.0024	.0015	.0010	.0006	.0004	.0003	.0002	.0001	.0001		
29	.0135	.0082	.0051	.0031	.0020	.0012	.0008	.0005	.0003	.0002	.0001	.0001	.0001		
30	.0116	.0070	.0042	.0026	.0016	.0010	.0006	.0004	.0002	.0002	.0001	.0001	.0000		
35	.0055	.0030	.0017	.0009	.0005	.0003	.0002	.0001	.0001	.0000	.0000	.0000			
40	.0026	.0013	.0007	.0004	.0002	.0001	.0001	.0000	.0000						
45	.0013	.0006	.0003	.0001	.0001	.0000	.0000								
50	.0006	.0003	.0001	.0000	.0000										

TABLE 2. Present value of $1 received annually at end of each year for n years.

n/r	1.0%	2.0%	3.0%	4.0%	5.0%	6%	7%	8%	9%	10%	11%	12%	13%	14%	15%
1	.9901	.9804	.9709	.9615	.9524	.9434	.9346	.9259	.9174	.9091	.9009	.8929	.8850	.8772	.8696
2	1.9704	1.9416	1.9135	1.8861	1.8594	1.8334	1.8080	1.7833	1.7591	1.7355	1.7125	1.6901	1.6681	1.6467	1.6257
3	2.9410	2.8839	2.8286	2.7751	2.7232	2.6730	2.6243	2.5771	2.5313	2.4869	2.4437	2.4018	2.3612	2.3216	2.2832
4	3.9020	3.8077	3.7171	3.6299	3.5459	3.4651	3.3872	3.3121	3.2397	3.1699	3.1024	3.0373	2.9745	2.9137	2.8550
5	4.8534	4.7135	4.5797	4.4518	4.3295	4.2124	4.1002	3.9927	3.8897	3.7908	3.6959	3.6048	3.5172	3.4331	3.3522
6	5.7955	5.6014	5.4172	5.2421	5.0757	4.9173	4.7665	4.6229	4.4859	4.3553	4.2305	4.1114	3.9975	3.8887	3.7845
7	6.7282	6.4720	6.2303	6.0020	5.7864	5.5824	5.3893	5.2064	5.0330	4.8684	4.7122	4.5638	4.4226	4.2883	4.1604
8	7.6517	7.3255	7.0197	6.7327	6.4632	6.2098	5.9713	5.7466	5.5348	5.3349	5.1461	4.9676	4.7988	4.6389	4.4873
9	8.5660	8.1622	7.7861	7.4353	7.1078	6.8017	6.5152	6.2469	5.9952	5.7590	5.5370	5.3282	5.1317	4.9464	4.7716
10	9.4713	8.9826	8.5302	8.1109	7.7217	7.3601	7.0236	6.7101	6.4177	6.1446	5.8892	5.6502	5.4262	5.2161	5.0188
11	10.3676	9.7868	9.2526	8.7605	8.3064	7.8869	7.4987	7.1390	6.8051	6.4951	6.2065	5.9377	5.6869	5.4527	5.2337
12	11.2551	10.5753	9.9540	9.3851	8.8632	8.3838	7.9427	7.5361	7.1607	6.8137	6.4924	6.1944	5.9176	5.6603	5.4206
13	12.1337	11.3484	10.6350	9.9856	9.3936	8.8527	8.3577	7.9038	7.4869	7.1034	6.7499	6.4235	6.1218	5.8424	5.5831
14	13.0037	12.1062	11.2961	10.5631	9.8986	9.2950	8.7455	8.2442	7.7862	7.3667	6.9819	6.6282	6.3025	6.0021	5.7245
15	13.8650	12.8493	11.9379	11.1184	10.3797	9.7122	9.1079	8.5595	8.0607	7.6061	7.1909	6.8109	6.4624	6.1422	5.8474
16	14.7179	13.5777	12.5611	11.6523	10.8378	10.1059	9.4466	8.8514	8.3126	7.8237	7.3792	6.9740	6.6039	6.2651	5.9542
17	15.5622	14.2919	13.1661	12.1657	11.2741	10.4773	9.7632	9.1216	8.5436	8.0216	7.5488	7.1196	6.7291	6.3729	6.0472
18	16.3983	14.9920	13.7535	12.6593	11.6896	10.8276	10.0591	9.3719	8.7556	8.2014	7.7016	7.2497	6.8399	6.4674	6.1280
19	17.2260	15.6785	14.3238	13.1339	12.0853	11.1581	10.3356	9.6036	8.9501	8.3649	7.8393	7.3658	6.9380	6.5504	6.1982
20	18.0455	16.3514	14.8775	13.5903	12.4622	11.4699	10.5940	9.8181	9.1285	8.5136	7.9633	7.4694	7.0248	6.6231	6.2593
21	18.8570	17.0112	15.4150	14.0292	12.8211	11.7641	10.8355	10.0168	9.2922	8.6487	8.0751	7.5620	7.1015	6.6870	6.3125
22	19.6604	17.6580	15.9369	14.4511	13.1630	12.0416	11.0612	10.2007	9.4424	8.7715	8.1757	7.6446	7.1695	6.7429	6.3587
23	20.4558	18.2922	16.4436	14.8568	13.4886	12.3034	11.2722	10.3711	9.5802	8.8832	8.2664	7.7184	7.2297	6.7921	6.3988
24	21.2434	18.9139	16.9355	15.2470	13.7986	12.5504	11.4693	10.5288	9.7066	8.9847	8.3481	7.7843	7.2829	6.8351	6.4338
25	22.0232	19.5235	17.4131	15.6221	14.0939	12.7834	11.6536	10.6748	9.8226	9.0770	8.4217	7.8431	7.3300	6.8729	6.4641
26	22.7952	20.1210	17.8768	15.9828	14.3752	13.0032	11.8258	10.8100	9.9290	9.1609	8.4881	7.8957	7.3717	6.9061	6.4906
27	23.5596	20.7069	18.3270	16.3296	14.6430	13.2105	11.9867	10.9352	10.0266	9.2372	8.5478	7.9426	7.4086	6.9352	6.5135
28	24.3164	21.2813	18.7641	16.6631	14.8981	13.4062	12.1371	11.0511	10.1161	9.3066	8.6016	7.9844	7.4412	6.9607	6.5335
29	25.0658	21.8444	19.1884	16.9837	15.1411	13.5907	12.2777	11.1584	10.1983	9.3696	8.6501	8.0218	7.4701	6.9830	6.5509
30	25.8077	22.3965	19.6004	17.2920	15.3724	13.7648	12.4090	11.2578	10.2737	9.4269	8.6938	8.0552	7.4957	7.0027	6.5660
31	26.5423	22.9377	20.0004	17.5885	15.5928	13.9291	12.5318	11.3498	10.3428	9.4790	8.7331	8.0850	7.5183	7.0199	6.5791
32	27.2696	23.4683	20.3888	17.8735	15.8027	14.0840	12.6466	11.4350	10.4062	9.5264	8.7686	8.1116	7.5383	7.0350	6.5905
33	27.9897	23.9886	20.7658	18.1476	16.0025	14.2302	12.7538	11.5139	10.4644	9.5694	8.8005	8.1354	7.5560	7.0482	6.6005
34	28.7027	24.4986	21.1318	18.4112	16.1929	14.3681	12.8540	11.5869	10.5178	9.6086	8.8293	8.1566	7.5717	7.0599	6.6091
35	29.4086	24.9986	21.4872	18.6646	16.3742	14.4982	12.9477	11.6546	10.5668	9.6442	8.8552	8.1755	7.5856	7.0700	6.6166
40	32.8347	27.3555	23.1148	19.7928	17.1591	15.0463	13.3317	11.9246	10.7574	9.7791	8.9511	8.2438	7.6344	7.1050	6.6418
45	36.0945	29.4902	24.5187	20.7200	17.7741	15.4558	13.6055	12.1084	10.8812	9.8628	9.0079	8.2825	7.6609	7.1232	6.6543
50	39.1961	31.4236	25.7298	21.4822	18.2559	15.7619	13.8007	12.2335	10.9617	9.9148	9.0417	8.3045	7.6752	7.1327	6.6605

n/r	16%	18%	20%	22%	24%	26%	28%	30%	32%	34%	36%	38%	40%	45%	50%
1	.8621	.8475	.8333	.8197	.8065	.7937	.7813	.7692	.7576	.7463	.7353	.7246	.7143	.6897	.6667
2	1.6052	1.5656	1.5278	1.4915	1.4568	1.4235	1.3916	1.3609	1.3315	1.3032	1.2760	1.2497	1.2245	1.1653	1.1111
3	2.2459	2.1743	2.1065	2.0422	1.9813	1.9234	1.8684	1.8161	1.7663	1.7188	1.6735	1.6302	1.5889	1.4933	1.4074
4	2.7982	2.6901	2.5887	2.4936	2.4043	2.3202	2.2410	2.1662	2.0957	2.0290	1.9658	1.9060	1.8492	1.7195	1.6049
5	3.2743	3.1272	2.9906	2.8636	2.7454	2.6351	2.5320	2.4356	2.3452	2.2604	2.1807	2.1058	2.0352	1.8755	1.7366
6	3.6847	3.4976	3.3255	3.1669	3.0205	2.8850	2.7594	2.6427	2.5342	2.4331	2.3388	2.2506	2.1680	1.9831	1.8244
7	4.0386	3.8115	3.6046	3.4155	3.2423	3.0833	2.9370	2.8021	2.6775	2.5620	2.4550	2.3555	2.2628	2.0573	1.8829
8	4.3436	4.0776	3.8372	3.6193	3.4212	3.2407	3.0758	2.9247	2.7860	2.6580	2.5404	2.4315	2.3306	2.1085	1.9220
9	4.6065	4.3030	4.0310	3.7863	3.5655	3.3657	3.1842	3.0190	2.8681	2.7300	2.6033	2.4866	2.3790	2.1438	1.9480
10	4.8332	4.4941	4.1925	3.9232	3.6819	3.4648	3.2689	3.0915	2.9304	2.7836	2.6495	2.5265	2.4136	2.1681	1.9053
11	5.0286	4.6560	4.3271	4.0354	3.7757	3.5435	3.3351	3.1473	2.9776	2.8236	2.6834	2.5555	2.4383	2.1849	1.9769
12	5.1971	4.7932	4.4392	4.1274	3.8514	3.6059	3.3868	3.1903	3.0133	2.8534	2.7084	2.5764	2.4559	2.1965	1.9845
13	5.3423	4.9095	4.5327	4.2028	3.9124	3.6555	3.4272	3.2233	3.0404	2.8757	2.7268	2.5916	2.4685	2.2045	1.9897
14	5.4675	5.0081	4.6106	4.2646	3.9616	3.6949	3.4587	3.2487	3.0609	2.8923	2.7403	2.6026	2.4775	2.2100	1.9931
15	5.5755	5.0916	4.6755	4.3152	4.0013	3.7261	3.4834	3.2682	3.0764	2.9047	2.7502	2.6106	2.4839	2.2138	1.9954
16	5.6685	5.1624	4.7296	4.3567	4.0333	3.7509	3.5026	3.2832	3.0882	2.9140	2.7575	2.6164	2.4885	2.2164	1.9970
17	5.7487	5.2223	4.7746	4.3908	4.0591	3.7705	3.5177	3.2948	3.0971	2.9209	2.7629	2.6206	2.4918	2.2182	1.9980
18	5.8178	5.2732	4.8122	4.4187	4.0799	3.7861	3.5294	3.3037	3.1039	2.9260	2.7668	2.6236	2.4941	2.2195	1.9986
19	5.8775	5.3162	4.8435	4.4415	4.0967	3.7985	3.5386	3.3105	3.1090	2.9299	2.7697	2.6258	2.4958	2.2203	1.9991
20	5.9288	5.3527	4.8696	4.4603	4.1103	3.8083	3.5458	3.3158	3.1129	2.9327	2.7718	2.6274	2.4970	2.2209	1.9994
21	5.9731	5.3837	4.8913	4.4756	4.1212	3.8161	3.5514	3.3198	3.1158	2.9349	2.7734	2.6285	2.4979	2.2213	1.9996
22	6.0113	5.4099	4.9094	4.4882	4.1300	3.8223	3.5558	3.3230	3.1180	2.9365	2.7746	2.6294	2.4985	2.2216	1.9997
23	6.0442	5.4321	4.9245	4.4985	4.1371	3.8273	3.5592	3.3253	3.1197	2.9377	2.7754	2.6300	2.4989	2.2218	1.9998
24	6.0726	5.4509	4.9371	4.5070	4.1428	3.8312	3.5619	3.3272	3.1210	2.9386	2.7760	2.6304	2.4992	2.2219	1.9999
25	6.0971	5.4669	4.9476	4.5139	4.1474	3.8342	3.5640	3.3286	3.1220	2.9392	2.7765	2.6307	2.4994	2.2220	1.9999
26	6.1182	5.4804	4.9563	4.5196	4.1511	3.8367	3.5656	3.3297	3.1227	2.9397	2.7768	2.6310	2.4996	2.2221	1.9999
27	6.1364	5.4919	4.9636	4.5243	4.1542	3.8387	3.5669	3.3305	3.1233	2.9401	2.7771	2.6311	2.4997	2.2221	2.0000
28	6.1520	5.5016	4.9697	4.5281	4.1566	3.8402	3.5679	3.3312	3.1237	2.9404	2.7773	2.6313	2.4998	2.2222	2.0000
29	6.1656	5.5098	4.9747	4.5312	4.1585	3.8414	3.5687	3.3316	3.1240	2.9406	2.7774	2.6313	2.4999	2.2222	2.0000
30	6.1772	5.5168	4.9789	4.5338	4.1601	3.8424	3.5693	3.3321	3.1242	2.9407	2.7775	2.6314	2.4999	2.2222	2.0000
31	6.1872	5.5227	4.9824	4.5359	4.1614	3.8432	3.5697	3.3324	3.1244	2.9408	2.7776	2.6315	2.4999	2.2222	2.0000
32	6.1959	5.5277	4.9854	4.5376	4.1624	3.8438	3.5701	3.3326	3.1246	2.9409	2.7776	2.6315	2.4999	2.2222	2.0000
33	6.2034	5.5320	4.9878	4.5390	4.1632	3.8443	3.5704	3.3328	3.1247	2.9410	2.7777	2.6315	2.5000	2.2222	2.0000
34	6.2098	5.5356	4.9898	4.5402	4.1639	3.8447	3.5706	3.3329	3.1248	2.9410	2.7777	2.6315	2.5000	2.2222	2.0000
35	6.2153	5.5386	4.9915	4.5411	4.1644	3.8450	3.5708	3.3330	3.1248	2.9411	2.7777	2.6215	2.5000	2.2222	2.0000
40	6.2335	5.5482	4.9966	4.5439	4.1659	3.8458	3.5712	3.3332	3.1250	2.9412	2.7778	2.6316	2.5000	2.2222	2.0000
45	6.2421	5.5523	4.9986	4.5449	4.1664	3.8460	3.5712	3.3333	3.1250	2.9412	2.7778	2.6316	2.5000	2.2222	2.0000
50	6.2463	5.5541	4.9995	4.5452	4.1666	3.8461	3.5714	3.3333	3.1250	2.9412	2.7778	2.6316	2.5000	2.2222	2.0000

Totaling the two columns, we see that Model B would be the computer to purchase after all, because the present value of the proposal has a greater positive value than Model A.

Now let's do the same thing using the rate-of-return method.

How to Calculate the Rates of Return of Conflicting Proposals

With the rate-of-return method, we seek to determine the expected annual rate of return to be gained from each conflicting proposal. This rate, which can be viewed as an interest rate, tells us how much income the investment will yield in addition to returning the initial cost or expenditure. We can compare rates of return for different proposals with one another. We can also compare such rates with our cost of capital, since we will certainly look closely at an investment that yields a rate of return lower than the cost of funds.

Finding the rate of return is somewhat different from finding the present value, although the same tables are used. The method involves trial and error. Let us calculate the rate of return for Model A first. We know that our initial investment is $50,000, that our benefits are a saving of $10,000 per year for 10 years, and that the salvage value we will get for turning the computer in after 10 years is $5,000.

Since the $10,000 per year is the largest amount, it will have the greatest impact. Therefore, we will start with Table 2. Reading across the 10-year row, we look for a multiplier that, when multiplied by $10,000, will give us slightly less than $50,000. The reason we are looking for a multiplier that will yield this result is that we must allow some money to be taken care of by the $5,000 to be received at the end of 10 years. Going across the page, we see the multiplier 4.8332 under 16 percent. Under 15 percent is the multiplier 5.0188. Therefore, we realize that for the $10,000 savings alone, these two multipliers rounded off will yield $48,333 and $50,190 respectively. We note these down and turn to Table 1. For 16 percent we see a multiplier of 0.2267. Rounding this off and multiplying it by $5,000 gives us $1,135. For 15 percent, the multiplier is 0.2472. Rounding this off and multiplying it by $5,000 equals $1,235. Therefore, our computations look like this:

MODEL A

16 percent	15 percent
4.833 × $10,000 = $48,333	5.019 × $10,000 = $50,190
0.227 × $ 5,000 = $ 1,135	0.247 × $ 5,000 = $ 1,235
$49,468	$51,425

Since our $50,000 initial cost for Model A lies between these two values, our rate of return for Model A is about 15½ percent.

Now let's look at Model B. Again, the dominant factor is going to be the annual savings, the $15,000 to be received every year for 5 years. So, we again consider Table 2. Moving across the 5-year row, we look for a multiplier that, when multiplied by $15,000, will yield approximately $30,000. Under 40 percent we find the factor 2.0352. When rounded and multiplied by $15,000, this results in $30,525. Normally we would now look at 41 percent, but this figure isn't in the table. Therefore, we must interpolate. The difference between the 40 percent multiplier (2.0352) and the 45 percent multiplier (1.8755) is 0.1597. Dividing 0.1597 by 5 and rounding off the result, we get 0.0319. We can calculate the multipliers for every percentage between 40 and 45 percent as follows:

$$41\% = 2.003$$
$$42\% = 1.971$$
$$43\% = 1.939$$
$$44\% = 1.907$$

From this we can see that the correct multiplier is between 41 and 42 percent. Using these percentages and finding the other multipliers from Table 1 through extrapolation, we come up with the following:

MODEL B

42 percent	41 percent
1.971 × $15,000 = $29,565.00	2.003 × $15,000 = $30,045.00
0.174 × $ 100 = $ 17.40	0.180 × $ 100 = $ 18.00
$29,582.40	$30,063.00

Since our initial cost for Model B lies between these two values, we can estimate the rate of return for Model B to be about 41½ percent.

We now know that the rate or return for Model A is 15½ percent and for Model B is 41½ percent. Both alternatives provide rates of return in excess of the 10 percent cost-of-capital figure provided by the finance department. And Model B provides a rate of return in excess of the rate provided by Model A, which tells us to choose the same alternative that the present-value analysis told us to take, Model B.

Other Considerations in Capital Budgeting Analyses

In actual practice, the procedure is more complicated, since in calculating present value or rate of return, we must also consider maintenance costs, the tax advantages of depreciation, and other factors that affect cash flow for each alternative. Also, if choosing one of the alternatives means doing something with a computer or piece of capital equipment that we are using now, we would have to calculate the present value or rate of return of what we are doing now.

BUDGET PREPARATION FOR AN ORGANIZATION THAT SECONDARILY INVOLVES SALES

If your organization involves sales but sales are not its primary purpose, you will have an additional item in your budget, even if your budget is of the fixed-appropriations type. For example, a research and development organization such as the one for which the budget in Figure 18 was prepared would handle potential research and development sales in the following fashion.

First, there is the cost of sales. For companies selling research and development, this line item might be entitled "New business development" or "Bid and proposal." Regardless of terminology, the item would include all expenditures necessary to win contracts, including visits to potential customers and the cost of preparing bids and proposals. These costs can be significant, so they should be identified clearly under this line item and not buried in other categories. The line item might be developed as per Figure 20. Not that this chart bears a close resemblance to the product development schedule, Figure 19. In fact, the new business development effort should be treated in the same way as a research and development program financially, and plans for winning an externally funded research and development program should be prepared with just as much care as plans for accomplishing it.

Your organization may be involved in R&D work for the government. In this case, your budget would be modified by a sales forecast that reflects the cost of sales as described in Figure 20, plus a potential product development schedule as shown in Figure 19, which includes guesses concerning the magnitude of the contract to be awarded, likely payment points, and their amounts. Obviously there are numerous uncertainties here—the possibility of the program being canceled, of a request for proposal never even being released by the government, and of your losing the bid against significant competition.

All of this puts a considerable strain on your ability to forecast the final outcome accurately. The only thing that can be stated with precision is that everything will not work out exactly as planned. This still

FIGURE 20. Development of the "New business" or "Bid and proposal" budget line item.

	JAN	FEB	MAR	APR	MAY	JUNE	JULY	AUG	SEPT	OCT	NOV	DEC
Development of advanced composite facemask												
Trips to customer	1,000		1,000		500	500	500		500	500		
Internal R&D work on mask	500	500	500	500	500	500	500	500	500			
Preparing bid and proposal									1,000	1,000	20,000*	
Development of solar-powered energy device												
Trips to customer	500		500	500		500						
Testing of our RQ-1 unit		2,000										
Preparing bid and proposal							7,000*					
Totals	2,000	2,500	2,000	1,000	1,000	1,000	8,000	500	2,000	1,500	20,000	41,500

* Expected month of receipt of request for proposal.

should not discourage your best efforts, though. Regardless of which events occur when, make sure you are not caught unprepared because of a lack of prior thinking concerning the budgeting of human or financial resources.

Note that preparation of a budget of this nature requires close coordination between yourself and your company's finance department to alert financial personnel about what you're doing and why. This coordination is especially important in small companies that have potentially very large programs.

BUDGET PREPARATION FOR A TOTALLY SALES-ORIENTED ORGANIZATION OR A PROFIT CENTER

If you yourself are supposed to turn a profit for the company, you have a different problem from the service-type technical organization. Once you have determined the period for which your budget is to be prepared, you will need to make a sales forecast for this period.

There are two ways of arriving at a forecast. One is to sum up the expected sales of each of your salespeople for each month of the period. The other is to look at factors external to the company. For example, if you make a product that goes on new automobiles and can get estimates of how many new automobiles will be sold, you can use historical data (numbers of your product sold per each automobile sold) to come up with expected sales figures for your product for the period. You might use both of these approaches. You will then probably be confronted with the fact that the two forecasts do not agree. In this case, you should develop a forecast based on the relevant data from both projections.

You now have a decision to make about your production. Do you gear up production to meet your sales forecasts, or do you plan for a more or less constant rate? Let's say you've decided to allow for sales forecasts, as illustrated in Figure 21. You would develop an ending inventory for each month by adding production to beginning inventory and subtracting sales. Next, consider required raw materials. The quantities you keep on hand will depend on your production plans and on the safety margin you decide to maintain between raw materials stocked and how much you expect to use. The safety margin decision, in turn, depends on the reliability of your suppliers, the current and expected markets for these raw materials, the costs of storage as a part of inventory, how serious a problem you would have if you ran out of materials, and so forth. In the example given in Figure 21, a decision has been

FIGURE 21. Sales, production, inventory, and purchasing budgets for a sales-oriented technical organization.

UNITS	JAN	FEB	MAR	APR	MAY	JUN
Finished goods						
Beginning inventory	35,000	24,000	18,000	20,000	24,000	18,000
Production	14,000	14,000	20,000	24,000	24,000	24,000
Total	49,000	38,000	38,000	44,000	48,000	42,000
Sales (shipments)	25,000	20,000	18,000	20,000	30,000	30,000
Ending inventory	24,000	18,000	20,000	24,000	18,000	12,000
Raw materials						
Beginning inventory	15,000	15,000	21,000	25,000	25,000	25,000
Purchases	14,000	20,000	24,000	24,000	24,000	19,000
Total	29,000	35,000	45,000	49,000	49,000	44,000
Used in production	14,000	14,000	20,000	24,000	24,000	24,000
Ending inventory	15,000	21,000	25,000	25,000	25,000	20,000
DOLLARS						
Finished goods						
Beginning inventory	$35,000	$24,000	$18,000	$20,000	$24,000	$18,000
Production	14,000	14,000	20,000	24,000	24,000	24,000
Total	49,000	38,000	38,000	44,000	48,000	42,000
Sales (shipments)	25,000	20,000	18,000	20,000	30,000	30,000
Ending inventory	$24,000	$18,000	$20,000	$24,000	$18,000	$12,000
Raw materials						
Beginning inventory	$ 7,500	$ 7,500	$10,500	$12,500	$12,500	$12,500
Purchases	7,000	10,000	12,000	12,000	12,000	9,500
Total	14,500	17,500	22,500	24,500	24,500	22,000
Used in production	7,000	7,000	10,000	12,000	12,000	12,000
Ending inventory	$ 7,500	$10,500	$12,500	$12,500	$12,500	$10,000

Note: Dollar amounts are calculated at $1 per finished goods unit (50¢ for materials, 30¢ for labor, and 20¢ for factory overhead, including depreciation) and 50¢ per raw material unit.

made to maintain a pad of 1,000 units per month. The purchase decisions for raw materials follow automatically from this decision. Since you
plan on using 14,000 units in February, you must have a beginning inventory in February of 15,000 units to maintain your 1,000-unit pad.
This means an ending inventory in January of 15,000 units. If you
produce 14,000 units in January, you must have 29,000 units first in
order to have 15,000 units left over. Since the month of January begins
with an inventory of 15,000 units, you need to purchase 14,000 units in
January. You can compute your other purchases in the same fashion.

You can now proceed to preparation of the cash budget as per Figure 22, the upper portion of which is a worksheet. The sales receipts
come from the sales listed in Figure 21. In Figure 22, these are assumed
to be collected a month later, so that the January sales of $25,000 are
actually collected in February, and so forth. If more accurate information
is available regarding the timing of collections, it is used. Payments are
handled in a similar manner. Wages were calculated by multiplying 30
cents by the number of units produced for that month. Thus in January,
from Figure 21, 14,000 units were produced (14,000 units $\times$ 30¢ =
$4,200).

Now consider the "Direct factory" item. The total overhead for the
six-month period is 20 cents times the 120,000 units produced, or
$24,000. This includes depreciation, which we will assume to be
$4,000. Depreciation should not be included in the type of cash budget
shown in Figure 22. The remaining $20,000 is amortized over the six-
month period. An activity factor can be computed to tie overhead to
production in the same manner as various line items were tied to various
activities in our research and development example earlier. Thus, for
January:

$$\frac{14,000 \text{ units}}{120,000 \text{ units}} \times \$20,000 = \$2,333$$

This becomes the amortized figure (rounded off) for the "Direct factory"
line item for January.

In this example, it has been determined that administrative expenses are unrelated to production. The total figure has been amortized
over the period to yield $500 per month. You could also use actual fig-
ures from a previous period, if it appeared that changes in the figures
were unlikely and if this method had proved reasonably accurate in the
past. Similarly, selling expenses could be related to selling activity (if in
fact a relationship existed); actual figures from a previous period could be
used; or the total figure anticipated could be amortized over the time

FIGURE 22. Cash budget for a sales-oriented technical organization.

	JAN	FEB	MAR	APR	MAY	JUN
RECEIPTS						
Sales	$25,000	$20,000	$18,000	$20,000	$30,000	$30,000
Collections on ac-						
counts receivable	20,000	25,000	20,000	18,000	20,000	30,000
PAYMENTS						
Purchases	7,000	10,000	12,000	12,000	12,000	9,500
Payments on						
accounts payable	6,000	7,000	10,000	12,000	12,000	12,000
Wages	4,200	4,200	6,000	7,200	7,200	7,200
Direct factory	2,350	2,350	3,500	4,000	4,000	4,000
Administrative						
expenses	500	500	500	500	500	500
Selling expenses	1,000	1,000	1,200	1,300	1,300	1,300
Purchase of						
equipment	—	—	1,000	—	—	—
Payment for						
equipment	—	—	—	1,000	—	—

CASH BUDGET

	JAN	FEB	MAR	APR	MAY	JUN
RECEIPTS						
Collections	20,000	25,000	20,000	18,000	20,000	30,000
PAYMENTS						
Accounts payable	6,000	7,000	10,000	12,000	12,000	12,000
Wages	4,200	4,200	6,000	7,200	7,200	7,200
Direct factory	2,350	2,350	3,500	4,000	4,000	4,000
Administrative						
expenses	500	500	500	500	500	500
Selling expenses	1,000	1,000	1,200	1,300	1,300	1,300
Equipment	—	—	—	1,000	—	—
	14,050	15,050	21,200	26,000	25,000	25,000
Net monthly cash						
gain (loss)	5,950	9,950	(1,200)	(8,000)	(5,000)	5,000
Cash balance						
(12/31/xx = 5,000)	10,950	20,900	19,700	11,700	6,700	11,700

period. The purchase of equipment is handled like payables and receivables. If no better information exists, payment is anticipated on the month after purchase. If you have better information regarding terms of payment, use it.

This work-up information is now used to derive the budget, including net monthly gain or loss. Note that you start with a cash balance (or deficit) from the preceding period. In this instance, the cash balance from December 31 was $5,000. Using this information, you can compute the cash balance forecast for each month.

HOW TO COST OUT PROGRAMS AND PREVENT SLIPPAGES AND OVERRUNS

The key to doing accurate costing that will result in technical success without overruns or slippages lies in good technical planning and control. Here's how it's done. Every program anticipated should be formally planned by its anticipated manager. The format used is the product development schedule that was shown in Figure 19. This format forces your project engineer to list every task required, who's going to do it, when it's going to be done, and what it's going to cost. If no one knows when the program will be initiated, or even whether it will be, the names of specific months need not be filled in at the top. Instead, number of months since initiation (1, 2, 3, and so on) would be inserted.

Your project engineer should not fill out this form in a vacuum but should get as accurate estimates as possible from the managers of other organizations in the company that will be accomplishing tasks in the program. This points up another primary advantage of the product development schedule. It not only lets you and the project engineer know what must be accomplished and when, but lets everyone else involved know also. Thus, long before you start a program, everyone involved in it has a pretty good idea of what is expected of them. There is an additional advantage in getting the managers to give you their own documented estimates of how much time and money will be required to accomplish various tasks. This psychologically commits the estimator to accomplishing the work required by your project according to his estimates. The estimator won't always be successful in doing this, but his own estimates can be strong encouragement.

The product development schedule has a wide variety of uses, some of which were discussed earlier. These include:

○ Planning how your organization will be staffed.
○ Planning your budget.
○ Choosing among alternative R&D projects.

○ Costing a program for development.

○ Controlling costs and schedules once you are on contract.

○ Pricing programs to other companies or the government (this is discussed further below).

Once the program has been initiated, accurate charge information must be fed back to the project engineer on a monthly or weekly basis. For large programs this information can be computerized. Actual charges should be written in the product development schedule so that what is happening can be compared with what was planned. If overruns or slippages occur despite the best efforts of participating organizations, the product development schedule should be used as a basis for determining alternative courses of action to bring costs or the schedule under control.

HOW TO USE THE PRODUCT DEVELOPMENT SCHEDULE TO PRICE PROGRAMS

The product development schedule can become the basis for pricing programs accomplished under contract to other companies or the government, since it includes the total labor hours and materials in dollars necessary to do the job. Pricing can be done using the estimation form in Figure 23. The first section provides a place to enter various types of labor hours at the current labor rates in your company. The numbers of hours are taken from the product development schedule (Figure 19). Next, this labor is adjusted for overhead by applying the current overhead rate for your organization. Overhead rate is calculated by dividing actual overhead costs for the year by actual direct labor costs. Thus if overhead costs for the year equaled $1,000,000 and direct labor costs were $1,052,630, the overhead rate would be $1,000,000/1,052,630, or 95 percent.

Beginning with line 7, you should list all outside purchases. These purchases include raw materials, services done outside the company, tooling or equipment necessary to be purchased for the completion of this project, and so on. The resulting subtotal now has a percentage for general and administrative expenses applied to it. General and administrative expenses (or G&A) include such items as executive salaries, office salaries, office supplies, postage, telephone, interest, and repairs and maintenance. The G&A item is calculated in the same fashion as overhead.

FIGURE 23. Estimation form for pricing projects to be done
under contract.

Project Name   Polyethylene Projectile

For   A. M. E., Inc., Pittsburgh

Costing by   A. W. Smith   Date   29 January 1980

1. 1,000 hours engineering   Labor at $14.20/hr. = $14,200

2. 300 hours testing   Labor at $ 9.50/hr. = 2,850

3. 500 hours prototype shop   Labor at $10.10/hr. = 5,050

4. ____ hours _____   Labor at ____/hr. = _____

5. ____ hours _____   Labor at ____/hr. = _____

                           A. Labor subtotal = 22,100

6. (95 % overhead rate + 1.0) × (subtotal #5A)   = 43,095

7. Outside purchase for materials   = 1,200

8. Outside purchase for tooling   = 5,000

9. Outside purchase for consulting   = 2,000

10. Outside purchase for _____   = _____

            A. Overhead and purchases subtotal = 51,295

11. (25 % general and administrative expenses + 1.0)
                              × (subtotal #10A) = 64,118.75
12. (15 % profit + 1.0) × (#11)   = $73,736.56
                                                  Sales price

---

The profit, as a percentage, is figured on the last line. All of the
figures, such as labor rate, overhead, G&A, and profit, can be obtained
from your finance department.

In a large company, you may not be responsible for making these
calculations or coming up with a final sales price. However, as a technical manager, you will frequently be responsible for winning a program
bid in a competitive situation. Unless you understand this process of arriving at a final price, you will have little control over the bid your company offers.

PLANNING—THE KEY TO GOOD BUDGETING AND COST CONTROL

Budgeting and cost control both relate back to planning. The hours you spend planning ahead will return your investment many times over, once you begin putting your plans into operation. To be successful, you must get other organizations involved in the planning, if these organizations will play a part in the program effort. Only in this way will your plans accurately reflect the participation of organizations besides your own. Never accept the excuse from your subordinates or yourself that you haven't the time to do quality planning. In fact, you haven't the time *not* to.

CHAPTER 9

The Secrets of
Winning Any Technical Job

Regardless of your technical specialty, at some point in your career as a technical manager you will be responsible for winning a job with an external organization or will have people reporting to you who must do this. In these instances, you will be judged as a manager solely on your ability to get the contract. It is therefore of no small importance that you understand how to do this before such responsibilities are thrust upon you.

Most guidelines that technical managers are given for winning contractual technical work revolve around the formal written proposal, which tells the prospective customer what you intend to do, how you intend to do it, how long you intend to take, and how much you intend to charge. Some experts call the technical proposal a "sales document" and counsel that it is with this document that you must persuade the reader to buy your service, or whatever it is you are selling. These experts are only partially correct. Research shows that pre-proposal marketing activity—that is, what you do before you prepare a written proposal—has a significant effect on whether you win or lose *aside* from the quality of the proposal you submit or the price you bid. For example, in a study completed by the author of 81 different research and development bids to agencies of the federal government and industrial companies, twice as much pre-proposal marketing activity had occurred for winning proposals as for losing ones. Further, as proposal marketing activity increased, as measured by number of contacts made with the customer, the number of wins increased and the number of losses decreased. The quality of the contacts was also found to have a significant effect on the winning of technical contracts.

THE THEORY BEHIND PRE-PROPOSAL MARKETING

Pre-proposal marketing rests largely on two theories of marketing: consumer acceptance and merchandising. There is an old saying that if you build a better mousetrap, people will beat a path to your door. This is not true today, and very likely it was never true. The Wright Brothers struggled for a considerable period to get their new flying invention accepted, long after they had conquered the technical problems and had actually flown. The automobile was for a long time considered primarily a "rich man's toy." Since it can be assumed that the mere fact of invention will not result in customers, the responsibility for gaining acceptance of the invention by potential buyers is in the hands of the controller of the invention. This theory is known as the theory of consumer acceptance, which goes on to say that there are basically three levels of acceptance for any product:

1. *Acceptance.* The consumer will accept the product as opposed to rejecting it if no other alternatives are offered.

2. *Preference.* The consumer will prefer this product over other alternatives if given a choice.

3. *Demand.* The consumer will accept no substitute. He or she must have this product regardless of alternatives offered.

If a product is to be sold successfully, the consumer must have some degree of favorable interaction with it. Sufficient favorable interaction will achieve the "acceptance" level. Given more favorable experience with the product, the consumer will prefer it over its competition. Still more favorable encounters will finally result in that peak acceptance level where the product is demanded, with no substitute being tolerated. Obviously, in bidding any program, it is to your advantage to achieve the highest level of acceptance that you can. Whatever the technical service you are bidding to provide—be it developing something, building something, testing something, or whatever—you want to stir up a demand for that service.

Merchandising means fitting your product or service to the customer's needs and vice versa. The customer has a certain problem or a certain technical need that he wants fulfilled. We have the product or service that can do this. But, perhaps as it stands right now, our product does not perfectly fill the customer's needs or meet all his requirements.

At the same time, it is possible that the customer does not understand all aspects of his problem. Perhaps he has not defined the problem or his requirements correctly. Potential exists on both sides to make changes that will bring about a better fit between his need and the product or service you are offering.

It should now be clear why you can achieve a far greater win rate by applying the theories of consumer acceptance and merchandising than by merely depending on a formal written proposal to do your selling. The formal written proposal must be injected into an environment in which the sale has already been made. An excellent written proposal should merely document that sale by making explicit the informal and often unspoken agreements that have been reached between customer and contractor.

STEPS IN WINNING—STARTING FROM ZERO

If you had a technical service and wanted to sell this service under contract, starting from point zero you would take the following steps:

1. Identify the potential customer or customers.
2. Develop a marketing plan.
3. Contact the potential customer.
4. Make a presentation to the potential customer.
5. Work on solutions to the potential customer's problem.
6. Present your recommended solution, get feedback, and modify the solution.
7. Submit a bid and proposal for the work.
8. Negotiate the contract.

Identifying the Potential Customer or Customers

There are many ways of identifying potential customers. You can look at a list of potential users of your product or service in a directory such as *Dun and Bradstreet's Million Dollar Directory, The Thomas Register,* or the *World Aviation Directory.* Many industrial or trade association magazines, such as *Plastics, Chief of Police,* and *Aviation Week,* publish an annual issue with a list of the manufacturers, consultants, or operators who serve their industry or profession.

From mailing list brokers, you can get lists of individuals in almost any professional category, such as doctors, steel manufacturers, research and development managers, directors of testing facilities, independent oil drillers, managers in mining companies, glass manufacturing company presidents, uranium prospectors, manufacturers of firearms, and literally thousands of others. Here are a few list brokers taken at random from which catalogs of lists can be obtained:

Project Marketing, Inc.
9000 Sunset Blvd., Suite 710
Los Angeles, Calif. 90069

Ed Burnett Consultants, Inc.
2 Park Avenue
New York, N.Y. 10016

Research Projects Group
Executive Plaza
50 Clenton Street
Hempstead, N.Y. 11550

Network Tests and Data, Inc.
400 Halstead Avenue
P.O. Box 327
Harrison, N.Y. 10528

Dunhill International Test Company
Dunhill Building
444 Park Avenue South
New York, N.Y. 10016

Direct Mail List Rental Service
P.O. Box 12901
Overland Park, Ks. 66212

If you live in a large city, you can find many other brokers under "Mailing lists" in the Yellow Pages of your phone book.

Once you have acquired lists of names, you can mail out brochures describing your product or service and inviting inquiries.

It may also be effective to place display or classified advertising, inviting inquiries, in appropriate magazines dealing with your industry or the type of service or product you are offering. This is usually less productive, however, than a mailing directed at a precise target group of potential customers.

If you are seeking potential customers in the Department of Defense (DOD), you should know about the Technical Industrial Liaison Office (TILO), Navy Research and Development Information Center (NARDIC), and the Air Force Information for Industry Offices. These organizations were put together to help you find individual customers in DOD who might be interested in doing business with you and to acquaint you with research and development work, opportunities, problems, and plans in the army, navy, and air force. For additional information, and a free brochure on their activities, write or contact one of the locations for each of these organizations:

TILO (U.S. Army)

    U.S. Army Aviation Systems Command
    Attn.: DRS AV-EXR
    P.O. Box 209
    St. Louis, Mo. 63166
    Tel.: (314) 268-3821

    U.S. Army Troop Support Command
    Attn.: DRSTS-KT
    St. Louis, Mo. 63120
    Tel.: (314) 263-2346

    U.S Army Tank–Automotive Research and Development Command
    Attn.: DRDTA-REZ
    Warren, Mich. 48090
    Tel.: (313) 573-2372

    DA/DARCOM
    West Coast TILO
    1030 East Green Street
    Pasadena, Calif. 91106
    Tel.: (213) 792-7146

    U.S. Army Armament Research and Development Command
    Attn.: DRDAR-PMP
    Dover, N.J. 07801
    Tel.: (201) 328-3047

    U.S. Army Missile Research and Development Command
    Attn.: DRDMI-IBA
    Redstone Arsenal, Ala. 35809
    Tel.: (205) 876-2598

    U.S. Army Electronics Command
    Attn.: DRSEL-RD-S
    Ft. Monmouth, N.J. 07703
    Tel.: (201) 544-4341

    U.S. Army Training Device Agency
    Attn.: DRCPM-TND-SE
    Orlando, Fla. 32813

NARDIC (U.S. Navy)

    NARDIC/East
    Chief of Naval Material (MAT 03T2)
    Navy Department
    Washington, D.C. 20360
    Tel.: (202) 692-1113

NARDIC/West
Naval Ocean Systems Center
1030 East Green Street
Pasadena, Calif. 91106

Air Force Information for Industry Offices

Air Force Information for Industry Office
AFSC/DLXL
Andrews A.F.B., D.C. 20334
Tel.: (301) 981-2414

Midwest Information for Industry Office
AFAL/TSR
Wright Patterson A.F.B., Ohio 45433
Tel.: (513) 255-6731

Air Force Information for Industry Office
1030 East Green Street
Pasadena, Calif. 91106
Tel.: (213) 643-2280

Incidentally, Pasadena, California, is the only location in the country where the offices of all three services are located in the same building.

Another source of contacts if you anticipate doing business with the government is the *Commerce Business Daily,* or *CBD.* The *CBD* lists opportunities as well as contracts awarded. It offers not only new contacts but important clues as to the types of work different organizations are interested in. The *CBD* can be obtained by writing to the Superintendent of Documents, U.S. Government Printing Office, Washington, D.C. 20402.

Developing a Marketing Plan

A marketing plan must include important information, developed in a logical sequence, that is needed to put the plan into operation. I find this sequence useful:

I. SITUATION ANALYSIS

1. *General situation.* Briefly describe the business opportunity—what it is, why it exists, and what it is expected to lead to.

2. *Demand.* Who is the present customer? Are there any other potential customers? What organizations make up the "customer" and how are they organized to make the R&D acquisition? Who are the key decision-makers in the customer's organization and what are their functions? What is the probable level of funding for this project?

3. *Competition.* What companies are currently competing for this work? What companies have the capability of doing so? What work have they done in the past that might give them an advantage in this area? Do they have any ongoing programs with the customer that would be of competitive advantage to them? How are they doing on these programs? What resources do our competitors have to draw on? What actions are they likely to take in response to our actions?

4. *Environmental factors.* What is happening in the social, economic, political, and technological environments that may affect the demand for this project? Is cancelation or postponement likely? Is funding assured? Does the project have a high priority or a low priority within the customer's organization?

5. *Company resources.* What are our strengths and weaknesses with regard to this project? What financial or other resources can we call on? Have we done work in the past that might give us an advantage? Do we have any ongoing programs with the same customer? Are we doing well with these programs? Do we have the necessary personnel available to do the project?

6. *Legal or policy constraints.* What factors exist that limit our ability to do work on this project? Are there legal factors we must consider? Are security clearances required, and do our people have these clearances? Do we have other contracts whose terms would restrict our doing this work?

II. SUMMARY OF MAJOR PROBLEMS AND OPPORTUNITIES

Summarize the analysis from Section I, emphasizing the main factors, both favorable and unfavorable, that will affect the ability of the company to pursue and win the contract under discussion.

III. MARKETING STRATEGY

1. *Objectives.* State the specific objectives of the marketing plan in terms of the project, the target market, the projected sales value of the contract, and the projected profits on the contract.

2. *Marketing mix.* Define the overall strategy and the program for each element of the marketing mix. Include what is going to be done and why, what each element will cost, and how the program will be evaluated.

3. *Finance.* Document all financial aspects of the program, noting both the acquisition costs and the sales, expenses, and projected profit of the contract itself. If the project is being considered largely because it will result in future profits in production, these projected figures should be documented as well.

IV. TASKS

State specific tasks, action items, and duties for every organization and individual in the company who will participate in acquisition of the contract. This detailed schedule should include everything required in order to accomplish the proposed marketing strategy, including answers to the questions "Who?" "What?" "Where?" "When?" and "How?"

Contacting the Potential Customer

At some point you must initiate contact with the potential customer to exchange information about his problem and your product or service. If you have used a mailing or some kind of advertisement, your potential customer may make the first contact. However, usually the task of first telephone contact must be accomplished by you. During this contact, your objectives are to:

- Understand something of your potential customer's work.
- Determine whether you can help him solve the types of problems he is faced with.
- Set up a firm meeting with him if it appears that you can help him solve his problems.

This first contact is extremely important not only because of any positive or negative first impressions you might make, but also because you need to make an accurate assessment of whether there is a possibility of doing business. Remember that even a single face-to-face meeting will cost money. If this meeting is out of state, a significant amount of resources may be involved: the time you and your technical people will spend, the money for travel, and expenses such as food and lodging. Even if you work for a large firm that can afford to spend significant sums of money exploring possible new business opportunities, there is always some limit on the human resources you can allocate for this purpose.

Explain to your potential customer why you believe it is in your mutual interests to meet. Indicate that you have a presentation you would like to make regarding the type of work you do, and suggest that he invite as many people in his company who might be interested as possible. If he agrees to a larger presentation, either during this call or during later telephone conversations, find out who is going to be at the presentation and what their titles and functions are. (It goes without saying that you should try to understand exactly what your host does and where he fits in.) Suggest that after the presentation you would like to split up into smaller meetings with him, or with other people who are particularly concerned with the potential work, to discuss their problems in detail.

Making Your Presentation to the Potential Customer

Whether or not you have a standard presentation, you should tailor it specifically for this potential customer and the individuals with whom you will be meeting. For example, if you are meeting with technical counterparts, your presentation can be much more technical than if you were meeting with members of management who may have only the vaguest notion of the technical aspects of the work you are doing.

Early in your preparations, you should make some very clear-cut decisions about which members of your organization will go and what their functions will be. Usually it is wise to include the individual who has been your primary contact with the potential customer. This means that if you have been the primary contact, you should go. If you don't intend to go, you should step aside very early on and introduce the primary customer contact by phone to the individual you have selected. When doing this, be sure you don't give the impression that you're stepping out of the picture because the situation or the customer isn't important enough for you. Usually, you will want your primary contact to be the individual who will be in charge of the contract with the potential customer if you get it. Here it will seem natural to get on the phone and say something like: "I want to introduce you to Joe Doakes. Joe is our program manager in charge of this project, and he'll be heading our team that will be giving the presentation."

If the presentation team is to consist of more than one person, you might select other individuals who are likely to be working on the project, good presenters, or simply people who are available at the time. Incidentally, while availability is an important criterion, you should never send people on new business exploration trips who do not interface well with customers. A display of ineptness, or any type of friction or misunderstanding that arises between members of your organization and the customer's organization, can damage your chance of winning the contract.

After a presentation team has been selected (and your "team" might consist of just one person), you should decide exactly what you are going to present and make assignments. Consider whether you're going to use viewgraphs, slides, a movie, or whatever else for this presentation. Before producing these aids, ascertain either that the customer has a device for displaying them or that you'll be able to bring whatever you need with you.

As with every other management activity, you should have a plan for your presentation. Make sure the length is correct for the objective of the presentation and the customer. It's advisable to get some idea from your host of how long the presentation should be, so you can lengthen or shorten your usual program. A typical presentation plan is shown in Figure 24.

After making assignments for the presentation, you should allow sufficient time for each speaker to prepare his presentation, have the presentation reviewed by you, and finally for a number of dry runs to be carried out. These practice sessions are essential for every presentation. If possible, have other members of your department sit in on these sessions and make comments on them. During these practice sessions, you may find that things do not fit together perfectly and must be changed; that some slides, viewgraphs, or other aids are incorrect or do not adequately support the message you are trying to get across; or that some important information has inadvertently been omitted. The dry runs will also allow your speakers to become accustomed to giving their presentations and answering questions regarding them. As a result,

FIGURE 24. Presentation plan.

Basic objective of presentation:
Convince client that we are expert developers of chemical products for use in infant care

SPEAKER	PHASE AND TOPIC	METHOD OF PRESENTATION	TIME
Joe Doakes	Introduction: organization of company, typical successful products developed	Viewgraphs	5 min.
	Film: *The Development of "Infant Clean"*	Movie	20 min.
Janice George	Case histories of three successful programs, including test results and commercial profits realized	Viewgraphs	30 min.
	15-minute break		
William Hill	Demonstration of "Infant Clean," "Diaper Magic," and "Fresh Day"	Live demo	45 min.
Joe Doakes	Summary	Viewgraphs	5 min.

when they give them before your potential customers, they will be better prepared and much more confident.

Always ensure that after the presentation, time has been set aside for you to talk to your potential customers in an informal manner. Only in an informal situation can you get a real feel for what's going on in the customer's organization and what his or her real problems are. During this initial meeting with the potential customer—and, in fact, during all subsequent meetings—you and other members of your team should ask questions and listen very carefully. You will need to find out:

○ How your potential customer is organized.

○ What exact procedures the customer uses in getting a contract or doing business with an organization such as yours.

○ What the real power structure is in the potential customer's organization—especially, which individuals are involved in the decision-making cycle for a new contract and which person gives the final approval.

○ What the potential customer's problems are, and how he thinks he can solve them.

○ Whether the potential customer already has approval for any program he anticipates, or whether approval is forthcoming and when.

○ How much money the potential customer has available to spend or anticipates spending for the work he wants done.

○ Whether there is anyone else in the customer's organization whom your contact feels you should speak with about this work or other potential work.

○ Whether competitors of yours are interested in the same program, or whether you can win this contract through a sole-source bid.

Obviously, there are some questions you can come right out and ask plainly and others you must word carefully and tactfully. For example, unless the contact is an old personal friend, you cannot ask what the real power structure is. What you can do, however, is ask various questions regarding who must approve contracted programs, who will coordinate them, and so on. There are certain other questions you should come right out and ask even if you know that the customer may not answer. For example, there is nothing wrong with bluntly asking how much money the potential customer wants to spend, even if you think he will be prohibited from telling you. Perhaps giving you the information will not be prohibited in this instance, or perhaps he will tell you even if he isn't supposed to. You'll never know unless you ask. If there is any doubt about whether you should ask a question or not, always ask. At worst, the potential customer will tell you that he cannot disclose the information.

If it sounds as if you are supposed to gather as much intelligence as possible at this first meeting, you have read this section correctly. What you find out may greatly affect your future course of action. If the contract turns out to be desirable but highly competitive, your company and organization may need to invest significant resources in order to win it. If the program is actually uncertain because the potential customer may not be able to get funding, or if the program is highly competitive and your competitors are well ahead of you due to previous work, you may want to drop out immediately and not waste your resources. In this case you would do better to allocate your resources toward winning a more likely program. On the other hand, you may detect significant advantages that put you well ahead of any competitors, or you may discover that you are in a sole-source position with no competitors at all. In this case you may immediately want to increase your efforts with this program.

After the first meeting, if you are still interested in the contract you will need to prepare a marketing plan specially targeted for this specific program. You may also want to revise your general marketing plan.

Working Out Solutions to Your Customer's Problem

If you have decided to pursue the contract, you will now work on your potential customer's problem. The magnitude of this effort depends on a number of factors, not the least of which is the magnitude of the anticipated contract. Some smaller programs that will cost your customer under, say, $25,000 can be outlined and potential solutions thought out by one of your engineers in a couple of days. An anticipated multibillion-dollar program, however, may require an investment in the millions of dollars and the best efforts of hundreds of engineers working full time for a year or more, just to come up with a potential solution.

During the period that you are working on the customer's solution, you should not be afraid to discuss your ideas and progress at length over the telephone or to make additional trips in order to do so. Sometimes you will hesitate to discuss information because of its proprietary nature, fearing that a potential customer will use your ideas without your authorization. It is true that this can happen, and you should protect yourself to the maximum extent possible through patenting and statements of disclosure. But, when all is said and done, you must still "sell" your idea to your potential customer, and in order to do this you are going to have to disclose some proprietary information. Your objectives should be to keep your customer informed about what you are doing and to keep yourself informed about how well your solutions are being accepted in his organization, the status of the program, changes, and other pertinent information. Sometimes this close liaison can result in your helping your potential customer to defend his program and get funding approved, or even in your helping him write the statement of work for his planned procurement. You should welcome all such opportunities to provide assistance.

Solutions to the client's problem should be worked out and accepted before you bid the contract. Long before the request for proposal is released by the customer, the following should be established:

- When the potential customer intends to release a request for proposal.
- How much time will be allowed for program completion.
- What the anticipated scope of the effort is.
- How much money the customer plans on spending.
- Confidence that your general approach to the problem is at the very least the approach preferred by the decision-makers in the customer's organization.
- Confidence that the members of your organization who have been assigned to the project are acceptable to the customer.
- Full resolution of any outstanding disagreements between you and the customer.

If you are going to submit an "unsolicited proposal," you should know all of the above, plus be certain that your proposal to do the work is going to be accepted before you submit it.

Submitting Your Bid and Proposal

Through your pre-proposal marketing efforts you have already prepared the environment into which your proposal will be submitted. Still, you must document what you have already sold in order to win.

As with all else, if you want to win, plan ahead. Typically, when you seek to do work for an external organization through competitive bidding, you will have a month or less to respond to a request for proposal. If you allow for delivery time through the mails, production of the proposal, typing, review, and so on, you can see that in reality you have much less time. Therefore, it is important to select and prepare a proposal team before the request for proposal is received. You should designate a proposal manager who is to be responsible for the proposal overall, along with other key members of the proposal team, such as individuals in charge of pricing, production, and so on. Usually the proposal team should be made up of the same individuals who have been the primary contacts with the potential customer and who will accomplish the project if it is done under contract.

Very large companies frequently have proposal departments that do nothing but handle the production of proposals, including artwork, writing, production, reproduction, and other tasks. In a smaller company, this will be in your hands as technical manager. However, even if you have the services of a proposal department, never forget, or let your proposal manager forget, that the ultimate responsibility for winning or losing is still yours and his.

In creating your proposal, you should make maximum use of graphs, charts, and pictures. And while the proposal needn't be extravagant, it should be a quality production.

One good way to organize your proposal is along the following lines:

1. Management proposal: how you will manage the project.
2. Technical proposal: how you will carry out the project technically.
3. Pricing proposal: how much the project will cost.

Each section should have an executive overview that summarizes the contents and the message you are trying to get across in a paragraph or two. These sections are needed because your proposal will frequently be reviewed by managers who are unfamiliar with the technical details or, in some cases, are only conversationally familiar with the objectives of the entire program. Yet their importance in the decision-making process makes it imperative that they understand the basis of what you are trying to do and why.

Brevity is also important. Each paragraph of each section should be included only if it contributes to the message of that section.

The assignment of individuals to write each section should be made prior to receipt of the request for proposal, and finalized when the request for proposal is actually received. The magnitude of some proposals is such that the entire effort can be handled by one person; other proposals will require many more individuals to complete the job. In any event, it is the proposal manager who should organize and orchestrate this effort, and he or she should be given the necessary authority to accomplish this without difficulty.

The proposal should follow the general outline of the request for proposal so that the customer's evaluators can more easily see that all requirements of the request have been met. If all requirements expressed in the request will not be met, you should talk with the potential customer to gain his approval before submitting your proposal. Frequently, however, all contact with technical members of the customer's organization will be prohibited following release of the request for proposal. If you run into a problem, you should attempt to talk with the technical members you have been in contact with before, anyway. The worst thing that can happen is that you will not be given the information. Sometimes you will be referred to the customer's contracting personnel, who will allow you to ask certain questions but not others. If at all possible, you should avoid taking exceptions to a customer's requirement. If you do, you should clearly state the importance of granting this exception and what the impact will be if this exception is not granted.

When you are determined to make major deviations from the requirements of the request for proposal, one way of doing so without risk of losing because of the deviation is to submit an alternative proposal. That is, respond with one proposal that meets all the customer's requirements and an alternative proposal written as you prefer. Price both separately, and explain in a cover sheet that you are offering one proposal that meets all requirements and another that does not but has certain important advantages. Then explain those advantages as you see them.

The reason it is risky to depart from requirements in the request for proposal is that your proposal can be deemed nonresponsive and rejected automatically for what you might consider minor or even ludicrous reasons. I am familiar with a government contractor's proposal that was rejected by a government evaluation team because it proposed to check a new device in 25 different aircraft rather than only 6 aircraft. What the contractor considered to be an enhancement of the requirements of the request for proposal, the government considered to be an increased risk of slippage and overrun and evidence that this bidder didn't fully understand the problem.

Under no circumstances should you introduce new solutions into your proposal that have not previously been "sold" to the customer. Not infrequently, some member of your staff will get a brilliant idea at the last minute, when it is too late to present this to the customer. Resist the temptation to include it in your proposal. Win the contract first. Then if the idea really has merit, you can introduce it after you are on contract and can get the contract changed to permit you to use the idea. If you do introduce it in the proposal, it will be totally new to your potential customer, he will not have sufficient information in your proposal to fully understand it, he will not be able to ask questions, and he probably will not be able to get the opinions of other specialists in his organization or "sell" the solution to his superiors. As a consequence, you risk losing the contract.

Knowing how much money the customer has or anticipates paying, as well as what the likely competition will be, should give you a fair idea of what it takes to win. Having this information, you can scale your effort in order to come up with the "right" price. Every competitive contract should be "scrubbed" to arrive at the lowest price possible within an acceptable range of technical success. As was pointed out earlier, many technical service organizations, such as research and development groups, are not themselves the primary producers of company profits. Rather, they seek to win contracts that will give their companies a competitive advantage in winning more lucrative production contracts. Such organizations can afford to barely break even, or even lose money, on research and development contracts if such business will assist their companies in winning more profitable production contracts, or enable the funded development of proprietary products.

If your organization is seeking engineering contractual work in the hope that your company will later get some profitable production work, you should explore various additional means of lowering the price to your customer. Consider the following techniques.

○ If many engineering drawings are required as a part of the effort, consider offering a free set of drawings coincident with an order for a specified number of developed end items in any one year. For example, if the contract was to develop a new type of spring, and the drawings themselves would add $20,000 to your bid price, you could reduce your bid price by offering the drawings to the customer at no charge coincident with an order for 50,000 springs in one year.

○ Offer to reduce the price by retaining the tooling. On a research and development program, tooling generally becomes the property of the customer, for which he is charged. But if the project is successful, the tooling can frequently be used in production. Offering to retain the tooling serves a dual purpose: it reduces the initial price to the customer and, assuming the project is successful, gives the company that owns it a decided advantage over a company bidding against it that must now develop and build its own tooling.

 o Reduce the price by furnishing a number of engineering hours without charge to the program. This might be done by allocating a certain amount of your department's budgeted indirect hours.

 o Reduce the price by not charging a fee or profit for your work.

Negotiating the Contract

The task of negotiating the contract will rarely be in the hands of the technical manager. However, whoever is negotiating the contract will probably ask you for advice, recommendations, and additional information. In fact, once again you will bear the ultimate responsibility for winning the contract—and for its success or failure once it is won. Therefore, you should insist on being kept informed of any changes in the basic proposal or the price bid.

If you are bidding competitively, very frequently you will be asked for a "best and final." This means that the potential customer is going around one more time to get the best possible price from everyone bidding. The request for a best-and-final offer usually means that you and at least one other bidder have proposals that are acceptable technically and have submitted prices that are within a competitive range, generally plus or minus 10 percent. However, you should not assume this is true. I have seen more than one bidder asked for a best-and-final offer when, in fact, there was no one bidding against him. You may consider this unethical on the part of the potential customer, but it does happen. One manufacturing company in Ohio was asked for a best-and-final offer on its bid of $116,000 for the development of a new detonator cap. The company reduced its offer by 23 percent and won, only to learn several years later that they had been had—there had been no competitor bidding against them.

It should be understood that negotiations are far from a gentleman's game, and are not for the inexperienced or the fainthearted. You can do your job best by seeing that whoever is doing the negotiating has all the information and intelligence you have acquired during your pre-proposal marketing efforts. If it is you who are doing the negotiating, I would recommend the following books to you:

Gerald Nierenberg, *Fundamentals of Negotiating* (New York: Hawthorn Books, 1968).

Chester L. Karrass, *Give and Take* (New York: Thomas Y. Crowell, 1974).

Paul R. McDonald, *Negotiation* (Covina, Calif.: Procurement Associates, 1978).

Chester L. Karrass, *The Negotiating Game* (New York: Thomas Y. Crowell, 1970).

AFTER YOU'RE ON CONTRACT WITH THE CUSTOMER

In addition to doing the best job you possibly can for the customer with whom you have achieved a contract after such a tremendous effort, you should now be thinking about a follow-on contract or additional contracts with the same customer. Once you have won a contract and are doing work for someone, you are now on his team. Information that was once extremely hard to come by will come much more easly. Your understanding of the customer's organization will grow. Relationships will develop between members of your organization and the customer's. You will still have to work and do your pre-proposal marketing homework to win contracts, but this effort will be far easier and can be achieved at much less expense. Therefore, after winning one contract with a customer, do not rest on your laurels but begin work immediately on your next contract with the same outfit.

CHAPTER 10

How to Solve Any Technical Management Problem

The title of this chapter seems to promise that it will contain a unique secret for solving any management problem you might encounter as a technical manager. Unbelievable though it may be, a technique of such power and universality does exist. Did you ever wonder how the management consultant, that mysterious physician of the business world, ever acquired the breadth and depth of knowledge that would enable him to advise any functional manager on any subject and command fees of $50–100 per hour or more while doing so? Yes, the management consultant knows and uses this secret, and in this chapter, you will learn it as well. It will enable you to solve the problems you face with accuracy, precision, and logic. Further, we will apply this technique to a sample case so that you will have no doubt of how to use the technique or what it can do for you.

THE SIX-STEP TECHNIQUE FOR SOLVING ANY PROBLEM

The technique for solving any technical management problem consists of six straightforward steps:

1. Find the central problem in your problem situation.
2. Gather information and write down all factors relevant to the problem.
3. Develop potential alternative solutions and determine the advantages and disadvantages of each solution listed.
4. Weigh the advantages and disadvantages of the alternative solutions against one another.

5. Draw conclusions from your analysis.
6. Identify the actions necessary to implement the solution that you have determined is best.

1. Finding the Central Problem in Your Problem Situation

Finding the central problem you are facing is both the most important and the most difficult part of the whole process. It is the most important because, unless the correct central issue is found, you may improve the general situation as a result of implementing the actions you decide on but will not solve the real problem. It is the most difficult part of the process because the central problem rarely stands out clearly. It is usually surrounded by murkiness resulting from numerous other secondary problems, symptoms, assumptions, long-held beliefs, and so forth. Because of this, you may sometimes get halfway through your analysis and realize that what you've been working on is not the central problem at all. You then have no alternative but to go back to Step 1 and start over. Accordingly, it is worthwhile to spend all the time you can working on Step 1.

Once you have ferreted out the central problem, there are several ways that you can state it for your convenience in proceeding with the analysis:

1. As a fact: The central problem is low pay in engineering, causing excessive turnover.
2. As a question: The central problem is, what should be done about the low pay in engineering that is causing excessive turnover?
3. As an infinitive phrase: The central problem is to find a solution to the low pay in engineering that is causing excessive turnover.
4. As a statement of need: My division needs to find a solution for the low pay in engineering that is causing excessive turnover.

In the above example, you might ask, why isn't excessive turnover the central problem? Excessive turnover is only a symptom—a symptom which, in reasoning the question through, we have decided is caused by low pay in engineering. We can differentiate between a central problem and a symptom by asking ourselves the question "What causes that?" When we no longer have an answer, we have arrived at the central problem. If we cannot answer the question, then answering it becomes our first central problem. For example, if we look first at the question of turnover and cannot say with certainty what is causing this problem, then our first central problem might be "to determine what is causing excessive turnover."

2. Gathering Information and Writing Down All Factors Relevant to the Problem

Your next task is to gather all information that seems pertinent to the central problem and to write down the relevant factors. These can include many different types of information, including facts, criteria, definitions, and, most important, assumptions. You should take note of and write down every significant assumption bearing on the central problem. Omitting a single important assumption can change the nature of your central problem completely, resulting in entirely different conclusions and different actions to be taken to solve the problem.

Keep the word "relevant" in mind in this part of your problem analysis. There will always be many factors in the environment of your problem—so many, in fact, that if you write them all down you can soon get lost in meaningless information. Only write down factors that will affect your thinking and resolution of the central problem.

3. Developing Potential Alternative Solutions and Determining Their Advantages and Disadvantages

As a first cut, write down every possible solution that meets the criteria set forth under relevant factors, no matter how far out the solution appears to be. Next list the advantages and disadvantages of each solution. Do not go into a discussion of each alternative at this point. Your job is merely to think up different possible ways of solving the problem, to write them down, and to list the advantages and the disadvantages of each one.

4. Weighing the Advantages and Disadvantages of the Alternative Solutions Against One Another

In this step, you will compare the advantages and disadvantages of your alternative strategies for solving the central problem. To do this successfully, you should strive for brevity and clarity while maintaining a logical sequence of thought as you reason the problem through. Indicate in writing how you weighed the different advantages and disadvantages against one another, and note which alternative solution you feel is best.

5. Drawing Conclusions from Your Analysis

In this phase of the analytical process, you merely extract conclusions that were obvious, stated, or implied in the preceding phase. Be careful not to introduce new information or discussion. Just summarize your findings and briefly restate what you think is the best possible solution to the problem.

6. Identifying the Actions Necessary to Implement the Solution

This is the final step in the process. You note down those actions that are imperative if you are to implement the solution you have decided on.

HOW TO USE THE MAGIC PROBLEM-SOLVING TECHNIQUE

Some years ago, a young salesman with a technical bent became disgusted with the problems of shaving with his razor. The blade became dull rapidly, it was far from convenient to use, and even if shaving was done with great care, it could produce a painful cut. In a flash, he visualized a new type of razor, one that was constructed in such a fashion that these problems would be overcome. Rushing to a Boston hardware store, he purchased the basic materials and equipment to build a mock-up of the invention he had conceived in his mind. With great care, he constructed a model that was really more than a mock-up: it could actually be used to shave with, so was more a prototype of the new invention.

But the construction of the prototype was the last good fortune this salesman had for many a year. He believed that the blades used in his new razor could be made inexpensively from standard steel ribbon. But for the new razor to perform as conceived required a very unique quality of steel. Over the next six years, the young inventor spent more than $250,000 on his own experiments in an attempt to harden, temper, and sharpen steel to the standard of quality required to make the razor's blades in quantity production. He was unsuccessful. At this point, the inventor was totally frustrated. He knew he was on to something if he could just solve the problem of producing blades for large-quantity production. His razor was clearly superior to existing models. He had solved the major problems associated with the razors currently in use. On the other hand, he had dropped over a quarter of a million dollars trying to solve the singular outstanding technical problem with no success, and he was out of money and ideas.

At this point, let's apply the magic problem-solving technique and see how it works and what it leads us to.

1. The Central Problem with the Razor Situation

Let's look at the problem from the viewpoint of the inventor. We clearly have some big problems here. The technical difficulty with the blades hasn't been solved, and the inventor has run out of both cash and ideas. Looming on the horizon is the fact that even if the technical problems were solved, the new device would still have to be brought to market before it would net a return, either to the inventor or to other investors if they could be found. What is the central problem here?

One might be tempted to say the central problem is the lack of money to continue. But money to the tune of $250,000 has been spent on the project in the past, and still the invention is not in production. Also, if we assume money is the central problem, it fails to meet the criterion set forth earlier: we can still answer the question "What causes that?" The money problem has been caused by "the problem of the blades in production." Why, in turn, does the problem with the blades in production still exist? Because the inventor, despite the expenditure of $250,000 over a six-year period, has been unable to solve the problem on his own. Aha! Now we have it. It remains only to state this problem as clearly, completely, and succinctly as possible. There are many ways of doing this. I have elected the following:

"The central problem is that the inventor has been unable to solve the problem of hardening, tempering, and sharpening the blades for production on his own, despite the expenditure of $250,000 over a six-year period."

2. Relevant Factors

For convenience, we can categorize the relevant factors according to the invention, technical development, the inventor, and assumptions.

The invention
- The product solves some important problems relating to shaving.
- Since most men shave daily, there is a large potential market for the invention.

Technical development
- The problem of hardening, tempering, and sharpening the blades for production has not been solved despite the expenditure of more than $250,000 and six years in time.
- All other technical problems with the new razor have been solved.
- To date, the inventor has worked alone on the development of the invention.

The inventor
- The inventor is clearly innovative, as demonstrated by the razor idea.
- The inventor's technical background or training may not be sufficient to overcome the remaining technical problem.
- The inventor wants to maximize the return on his investment of time and money and to see as many profits as possible from his invention.

Assumptions
- It is assumed that the invention can be successfully marketed once technical development is complete. (Note: with most new products this would *not* be a valid assumption.)
- It is assumed that additional investors can be found if desired.
- It is assumed that solution of the technical problems is currently possible.
- It is assumed that the invention could be sold under terms recouping the inventor's investment if desired.

3. Alternative Solutions to the Problems and Their Pros and Cons

First, let's consider various solutions that are possible. What can the inventor do to solve the central problem?

He might get more money somehow and press on. Other people have done this and been successful. Thomas Edison, for example, tried more than 1,000 different filaments for the electric light bulb before finally getting one to work. Maybe one more day and another $1,000 would do it. Alternatively, our young salesman-inventor could sell out to someone else for a flat sum, a royalty, or some combination thereof. Let someone else solve the problem—selling out may solve it so far as our inventor is concerned, and it's from his viewpoint that we're considering the central problem. Another possibility is for the inventor to find someone better qualified to handle this part of the technical job while still retaining control over the invention. That way he would stand to make more money if the invention was successful. Finally, he could drop the whole thing and continue as a salesman, a field in which he was very successful. Inventors have dropped more money and time on unsuccessful efforts than this inventor had done to date.

Now let's write these potential solutions down with their advantages and disadvantages in a more organized fashion.

Alternative Solution 1: Get more money and continue to work on the technical problem by himself.

Advantages:
- The inventor currently knows more about the technical problems of the blade than anyone else. This may give him an edge in solving the problem at a lower cost in less time.
- If successful, the inventor will obviously save money by doing this development work himself rather than having someone else do it.
- The inventor would retain much of the control over his invention and, if successful, would make more money than if he surrendered control.

Disadvantages:
- The inventor's limited technical background and training may not be sufficient to solve the problem.
- The fact that $250,000 and six years have been spent on the problem without success implies that the inventor, by himself, may not be able to solve the problem.
- Additional investors would have to be found.

Alternative Solution 2: Sell the invention.

Advantages:
- The technical problem of the blades would become someone else's problem.

- The inventor would still be reimbursed for his efforts, and the terms of the sale could be fixed in such a way that if the invention is commercially successful, the inventor would receive additional compensation in the form of royalties.
- The inventor would be free of the problem and additional financial risk and could concentrate on what he apparently does well: selling.

Disadvantages:
- The inventor would lose control over his invention.
- If the invention were successful, the amount of money that he would make through a lump-sum payment and royalties would be far less than if he continued majority control over the invention.
- Buyers for the invention would have to be sought.

Alternative Solution 3: Find someone better qualified to handle the development of the blade and solve the central problem.

Advantages:
- The inventor would retain much of the control over his invention.
- Giving the responsibility of solving the central problem to someone better qualified technically might result in the problem being solved sooner and at less cost to the inventor.
- The inventor's knowledge and experience in attempting to solve the central problem would not be wasted as it probably would in Alternative Solution 2.

Disadvantages:
- The use of an outsider's services would cost an undetermined amount.
- The inventor would have to share the glory of the success of the invention with someone else.
- Additional investors would have to be found.

Alternative Solution 4: Drop the project.

Advantages:
- The inventor would be free to concentrate on other projects or activities.
- The inventor would not need to assume any additional financial risk.

Disadvantages:
- ○ The inventor would lose his investment.
- ○ The invention has a high potential for profit if technical success can be achieved.

4. Weighing the Advantages and Disadvantages

Dropping the project only makes sense if neither additional investors nor buyers for the invention can be found. However, we have assumed that both these actions are possible. Also, there is no possibility of profits with this alternative. Therefore, Alternative 4 can be eliminated.

The inventor wants to maximize the return on his investment of time and money and the long-run profits on his invention. The results would be maximized with either Alternative 1 or Alternative 3. With Alternative 2, his return would be far less. Against this must be weighed the fact that the inventor would have to find additional investors with either Alternative 1 or Alternative 3, and that with Alternative 2 he would have more time to pursue other, potentially profitable interests. We have assumed that investors can be found, and obtaining additional free time is not being regarded as a factor relevant to the central problem. Therefore, the best action in accordance with the relevant factors recorded in this phase is to implement Alternative 1 or Alternative 3.

The major difference between Alternative 1 and Alternative 3 is that with the former, the inventor is going to attempt to solve the problem himself, whereas with the latter, he is going to find someone better qualified to do this. On one side, then, the inventor pays a sum of money to have someone else work at the problem in exchange for probably a better chance at solving it. Why better? The fact that $250,000 has been spent over six years without success, combined with the fact that the inventor's technical background and training may be insufficient, is evidence that someone better qualified technically would be more likely to solve the problem. Adoption of Alternative 3 would sacrifice none of the inventor's knowledge and experience in working at the problem. Because of the large profit potential of the invention, Alternative 3 offers almost as much profit maximization as Alternative 1, even if a small percentage of the business must be given to the technically qualified individual found to do the job. It is even possible that the specially qualified individual could be paid by a salary plus a bonus contingent on success. This would result in no difference in the total rates of return for Alternatives 1 and 3.

5. Conclusions

○ Alternative 4 is eliminated because no profit is possible with this alternative and because either getting additional investment money or selling the invention is possible.
○ Alternative 2, selling the invention, is eliminated because of its low profit potential compared with Alternatives 1 and 3.
○ Alternative 3 is a better solution than Alternative 1 because the chances of success are increased with no appreciable increase in cost to the inventor.

6. Necessary Actions

○ Obtain additional financing through investors to continue the development and marketing of the invention.
○ Obtain a specially qualified individual to solve the problem of hardening, tempering, and sharpening the blades for production.

Was the inventor successful? He succeeded in raising additional funds of nearly $100,000 and engaged William E. Nickerson, a graduate of M.I.T., to continue with the development of the blade. Nickerson solved the technical problem within two years. In 1903, the first year of sales, about 50 razors and a little under 200 blades were sold. Sales jumped to about 100,000 razors and blades the following year, and then to a quarter of a million razors and over a million blades the year after that. Today, annual sales of both razors and blades are in the billions annually.

King C. Gillette became a multimillionaire because he was innovative and he knew the secret technique of problem-solving that would lead to the right solution. Now you know the secret too.

CHAPTER 11

How to Communicate Effectively

The late Chester I. Barnard, AT&T top executive and author of the classic work *The Functions of the Executive,** conceived of communications as the central theme of management and the dominant factor in the structure of complex organizations. Indeed, Barnard saw the manager as no less than a communication center. What is this important executive function of communication?

Communication is the transference of information from one person to another, with a shared understanding of what is meant. Communication is essential to you as a technical manager. With it, you can staff, direct, plan, issue instructions, organize, recruit, train—in fact, carry out all the other functions required of the technical manager. Further, through communication your subordinates can provide feedback, offer advice and assistance, protest, agree, disagree, and carry out your instructions. Management without communication is not possible. It follows that the quality of your communications will directly affect the quality of your management.

UNDERSTANDING AND THE MEANS OF COMMUNICATION USED

Without understanding, communication as we have defined it does not exist. The issuance of unclear instructions results in bad communication, and the issuance of meaningless instructions does not constitute communication at all. Therefore, if we desire to improve the quality of com-

---

*Cambridge, Mass.: Harvard University Press, 1938.

munications, we should focus on the characteristic called "understanding."

Who is primarily responsible for the understanding of communications, the sender or the receiver? In fact, both bear equal responsibility. The sender, no matter how intelligible, will not be understood if the receiver is not prepared to receive the information. Likewise the receiver, no matter how carefully he or she is prepared to receive, will not understand the transmission if the sender garbles it. Under some conditions a sender will not be able to avoid a garbled transmission, and a receiver will not be able to receive the information properly. For example, a speaker lecturing over a public address system that is malfunctioning and distorts speech will probably not be understood very well. A receiver with poor eyesight may not be able to understand information transmitted through writing very well. Aside from such extremes, each individual tends to prefer some types of communication over others, for either psychological or physiological reasons. For example, some managers prefer to receive information from their subordinates orally while others prefer a written report. Both managers can justify their preferences with good logical reasons.

In any case, the means of communication you use can clearly have an impact on the message's effectiveness and how well it is understood. Therefore, consider the particular circumstances when deciding which method of transmission to employ.

THE IMPORTANCE OF TWO-WAY COMMUNICATION

Communications can go two ways: from you, the manager, to your subordinates, and from your subordinates to you. Both directions of communication are required in technical management. It is not sufficient if you merely issue orders that your subordinates carry out. In any management situation, such an approach assumes that your subordinates are merely extensions of yourself and have no individual contributions to make—through their own unique characteristics and capabilities—toward achievement of your organization's objectives. It is a frequently heard myth that armies function in this manner. Supposedly, mindless obedience replaces rational thought. In fact, no army can afford to function this way. It would probably suffer defeat because the mental potentials of the individuals are barely being tapped.

A technical organization should make use of every mind available in order to achieve its objectives. Yet, without good upward communication this is hardly possible. Therefore, pay attention to the communications that come upward to you as well as those you send down to your subordinates.

WHY COMMUNICATIONS GO WRONG

Communications go wrong for a variety of reasons. If you can eliminate certain communication problems from your organization, you will have gone a long way toward providing the clarity of understanding, both upward and downward, that is the crucial heart of any communication system.

Below are some problems that can impede effective communication within your organization and ways in which you can minimize these problems.

Lack of Established Communication Channels

Communication can take place without established channels of communication. The problem is, these communications will not flow in an orderly fashion; not all communications that are initiated will get through; and some transmissions that should get to a specific receiver will never be initiated. Therefore, without established communication channels you won't have an effective or efficient communication system within your organization.

An established communication channel must meet two criteria: it must exist, and the members of your organization must know of its existence. Let's say you open up a new communication channel in which someone on your staff who reports directly to you is willing to hear complaints from any individual in your organization, regardless of the formal chain of command. This channel does not qualify as "established" unless the members of your organization are aware of this individual's existence and function.

When established communication channels are lacking, the problem frequently is not that you oppose such channels but that you don't realize the need for them. For example, let us assume you are the head of a technical organization that is organized along traditional lines of organization theory, with a pyramid of boxes and your position being the top box of the pyramid. How do you communicate with the people at the bottom level of the pyramid?

In theory, communication flows downward from your box to the bottom boxes through successive levels of management. If someone in one of the bottom boxes wants to communicate with you, he takes his problem one level of management up to his or her boss. This person decides whether the problem is sufficiently important to take up to the next box, and so forth, until—if the problem is sufficiently important and cannot be handled by lower-level managers—it arrives on your doorstep.

How well does this work in practice? Usually, not very well. To begin with, there may be some fear about communicating with the top person. That apprehension (which will be discussed more later) may also be shared by other managers several levels up the pyramid. As a result of this fear, many of your subordinate managers will hesitate to "bother" you about particular communications they have received. They may also feel they should have handled the problem themselves rather than passing it up to higher levels. Any manager between you and the originator of the communication can, for this or any number of other reasons, stop the message or delay it, and discourage or even punish the originator. Originators will catch on to this quickly. They know, or intuitively recognize, that if they initiate a message to you of any import at all, it may not arrive, may arrive too late, or may affect them in some negative fashion. For this reason, they might never initiate such messages. In other words, you are lacking an established channel of communication that could be of some importance.

How do you establish a channel of communication that will take care of a problem like this? Well, you could change the structure of your organization to make it flatter, with more people reporting to you. Now the communicator has fewer obstacles to get through. He may even be fortunate enough to report directly to you. Then, all he has to do is communicate.

The problem with this solution is that a flat organizational structure may not be well suited to the work you are doing, the company, your objectives, or other particulars of your situation as noted during our discussion of organization in Chapter 2. If other factors are more relevant to the structure of your organization, a change may create more problems than it solves. Other solutions that might work for you in a situation like this include: establishing a suggestion system, meeting periodically and privately with members of your organization who do not report directly to you, meeting periodically with representative members of your organization outside of the chain of command, and maintaining an "open door" policy so that members of your organization can see you without getting their immediate supervisor's approval. All these solutions have advantages and disadvantages that should be considered in light of your need for established communication channels and your circumstances.

Subordinate Apprehension

Subordinate apprehension can only be overcome through time and trust. In ancient times, the bearer of bad news was often sacrificed as an offering to appease the gods. Your subordinates will not be enthusiastic about being similarly sacrificed. You can't expect them to promptly come to you with problems, failures, or criticisms of your decisions unless they feel certain they will not suffer for their honesty.

You might invite objective opinions as did the research and development manager in Chapter 6, but you probably won't get these immediately. When they do start coming, you'll have to grit your teeth and accept them with much appreciation and very carefully worded remarks. In the beginning, even the slightest tendency to argue your position may be interpreted as meaning that you don't really want the straight facts, you only like to think you're getting them. You needn't agree with every statement made honestly by a subordinate; you must simply be very tactful if you decide to refute it. Eventually, if you make it clear that no punishments will be forthcoming regardless of what your subordinates say, you will get to the point where you can yell and scream if that is your habit, and your subordinates will still stand up to you until you understand their position and are ready to make a decision.

Once you overcome your subordinates' apprehensions, you will have achieved the ideal. Further, because you will be accepting criticism without viewing it as a challenge to your authority or losing control over your subordinates or the situation, your subordinates will be encouraged to do likewise. In fact, you should actively encourage them to try to get their own subordinates to communicate without apprehension.

Faulty Retransmission

Faulty retransmission occurs when either you or your subordinates receive information from above and fail to retransmit it accurately. This failure usually occurs because (1) the retransmitted message has not been reformulated for the intended recipient, or (2) the meaning of the retransmitted message has been changed.

An example of the first failure might be transmission to an engineering group of a message received from top management that contains a page full of statistics, whereas the only statistics of any interest are those pertaining to engineering. As a result, no one in engineering reads any of the data. An example of the second failure would be transmission of a message that originally stated "Future overtime work must be approved at least two days in advance or will not be paid" in the distorted form "Future overtime work will not be paid."

The key to solving this problem is to be certain that both you and your subordinates who retransmit messages fully understand each message and its intent before you attempt to retransmit it. When you do retransmit it, tailor the transmission for those who will receive it but take care that cuts in the message do not affect its meaning.

To ensure that your subordinates are doing this correctly, spot check their written and verbal messages. Bring any faulty retransmissions you discover to their attention immediately.

Unwarranted Assumptions

Considerable research of a phenomenon known as selective inattention shows a receiver's reaction to information he hears will vary greatly according to whether this information is consistent with what he already believes to be true. As a result, it can be extremely difficult to get through to a listener when what you are attempting to communicate contradicts his previous assumptions.

For example, say that for years you never required a copy of a certain technical progress report to be sent to the company contracting officer. You suddenly decide that this is necessary and send out a memo giving a list of company personnel who are to receive the technical progress report from now on, in which you include the contracting officer's name. About half the time, you will find that the contracting officer won't get the report. Why not? Because the inclusion of that person's name is not consistent with the previous assumption that he is to be excluded from receiving the report.

The solution here is that you must stress the change to ensure that you overcome people's previous assumptions. Do this by drawing attention to the fact, either orally or in writing, that "the distribution list has been expanded to include the contracting officer."

Consider another example. You attend the staff meetings of your company financial officer every week, and are routinely on his distribution list for the announcement of these meetings. Than you miss a string of meetings due to more important commitments. Suddenly, you no longer get the announcements of the meetings because it is assumed that you don't wish to attend. Again, stressing each time that you must miss a meeting but intend to come to every meeting you can will solve this kind of problem. When there is a chance that one party may hold an obsolete or unwarranted assumption, always stress the difference.

Inattention

Inattention is very much a two-way problem, affecting both the sender and the receiver. If you attempt to communicate when the receiver is otherwise occupied or distracted, you will not communicate your message accurately. A major aircraft accident once occurred due to the inattention of a message receiver. The copilot's father had recently died, and the copilot was obviously depressed and inattentive to his duties. On takeoff roll, as the aircraft picked up speed prior to leaving the ground, the pilot turned to the copilot and said, "Cheer up." The copilot, only half listening and thinking he had heard the command "Gear up," raised the landing gear and caused the aircraft to crash.

This example points up very clearly the two-way nature of this problem. It is certainly the responsibility of the receiver to be attentive to the message of the sender, but on the other hand, the sender should transmit the message only when he is reasonably sure the message is going to be received properly. Just as the manager in an earlier chapter demanded that his subordinates pound on his desk or grab him by the coat lapels if necessary to ensure that they were getting through, you as the communicator must do whatever is necessary to get the receiver's attention before you attempt to communicate. In some cases it is better to delay the communication until you're sure you'll have the person's full attention.

In summary, you can solve the inattention problem if you note whether people are being attentive to your communications, take whatever action necessary to get attention, or, if full attentiveness seems unlikely, postpone your attempt at communication until a more favorable time.

Disbelief

Disbelief may arise because of a lack of credibility of the organization, company policies, or even the communicator. This distrust may be based on fact or on prejudice. The point is, the communication is not being believed.

Back in 1962, during the Cuban missile crisis, President Kennedy knew from U.S. intelligence sources that there were Russians missiles in Cuba. But Andrei Gromyko, the Soviet foreign minister, told Kennedy that the only assistance being furnished Cuba was for agriculture and land development, plus a small amount of defensive arms. He emphasized that the Soviet Union would not become involved in furnishing Cuba with offensive weapons. After the crisis was over and the missiles withdrawn, a popular cartoon of the time had a relaxed Kennedy talking to an indifferent Gromyko. "Well," said President Kennedy, "I'm glad that's over and I'm sure the foreign minister will never lie to us again. Say, by the way, what's new, Gromyko?" In the cartoon, the Russian foreign minister turns to Kennedy and says, "There are no Russian missiles in Mexico."

There are two counters to a lack of credibility in your communication:

1. Be scrupulously truthful in your statements and dealings.
2. Take actions that confirm your words.

If you are truthful in what you say to people, you will be believed even if certain elements of your company's policies are not trusted by your people. And actions speak much louder than words. Therefore, if you claim to have a promotion system based on promotion by merit, you had jolly well better promote by merit or you are not going to be believed in your other communications.

Information Overload

Information overload occurs when there is so much information furnished to a receiver that he becomes overburdened and shuts down his end of the circuit. He is now receiving *no* information. An example of partial overload, given earlier, was the faulty retransmitted message in the form of irrelevant statistics sent to engineering. Another overload problem is the needless circulation of messages, magazines, or brochures that have nothing to do with the work of your subordinates and that you circulate because you don't have time to read them yourself.

If we agree with Chester Barnard, then you as a communication center can do the most to solve this problem by:

○ Immediately throwing away material that is probably of no use to you or anyone else in your organization.
○ Not circulating irrelevant information to your subordinates.
○ Clearly marking the single sentence, paragraph, or page in a document that you feel your subordinates must read or know about.

Poorly Constructed Messages

When I first became a manager, an older manager spoke to a group of us ambitious young people. "The most important thing for you as new managers," he said, "is that you be able to write and speak effectively. If you can do that, you can write your own ticket."

That statement is as true today as it was twenty years ago when it was first spoken. Poorly constructed messages are sent because the manager does not know how to send, or will not take the time to send, messages that are developed properly. You don't have to be an English major to do this; you don't even need to be a college graduate. The basic idea is to use simple, accurate, and descriptive words and to express yourself in the most simple, direct way you can.

As a manager, you must have proficiency in reading and writing skills that will allow you to construct a clear and understandable message. If you do not, you are headed for very serious problems in your organization.

John F. was a first-line engineering supervisor at a large aerospace company in California just after World War II. Five brand new engineers were turned over to him for mothering on their first day of employment. To each he assigned a certain task and told the new engineer to report back after the job was done. In those days, many aircraft engineering drawings were engraved on metal so that they could take a lot of rough handling on the job. But though handled roughly, these "drawings" were very expensive to make. As a consequence they were well cared for and were kept clean and locked up when not in use. John handed one such plate that was dirty from use to one of the new engineers with the instruction to "get it perfectly clean." An hour later, John was presented with a brightly shining plate with all the engraving buffed off. The engineer had followed his poorly constructed instruction to the letter, costing the company thousands of dollars.

If your problem is that you're in too much of a hurry and have been unwilling to take the time necessary to properly construct written and spoken messages, swear to yourself that as of now, you will take the time. If you really lack these important skills, let me recommend an excellent book to you—*How to Write, Speak, and Think More Effectively,* * by Rudolf Flesch. This book will teach you to do exactly what the title states. It belongs on every technical manager's bookshelf.

---

* New York: Harper & Row, 1960.

Premature Evaluation or Interpretation of the Message

This problem occurs when the receiver makes a mental decision that cuts off the sender's message before it has been completed. As a result, the message may be partially or even totally misunderstood because the last part of the message was not absorbed. You can probably recall times when you, as a receiver, were so certain of what the message sender was going to say next that you interrupted him and told him so, only to learn that you were totally incorrect.

This problem occurs frequently when you are in a hurry, so the first preventive measure is to slow down and hear every speaker out. Concentrate on being a good listener, and don't second-guess the speaker about what he is going to say. If you are the transmitter of the message, watch the receiver's face. Frequently this will provide clues as to whether he's still comprehending what you are saying.

There are two other actions you can take to prevent this problem: (1) repeat the message, or (2) have the receiver repeat the message. It is said that repetition is the basis of learning. It is also the basis of ensuring that a communication you have sent has been received. Repeat the message a second time, or even a third time, in a slightly different way. For example:

o "We'll have the meeting tomorrow afternoon."
o "When we have the meeting tomorrow afternoon . . ."
o "I'll see you tomorrow afternoon at the meeting."

If you have given complicated directions or instructions to a subordinate, tell him that you know the message is pretty complicated and ask him to repeat it back to you. Merely asking whether a subordinate understands the message is never enough. Too many times, the subordinate is in a hurry, he senses your impatience, or he actually thinks he understood the message fully when in fact he did not. Always ask him to repeat the communication.

Failure to Initiate the Transmission

If the message never gets sent, it obviously cannot be understood. Some possible reasons for this barrier to communication are:

o The sender has not gotten around to sending the message.
o The sender feels apprehensive about sending the message.
o The sender has forgotten to send the message.

Certainly we all have priorities, but if a message needs to be sent at all, it should not be delayed unless you can live with any unfavorable consequences that may result from the delay. If something bad may happen soon that is outside your control, and this something affects or is affected by the message, get the message out at once.

Frequently the sender feels apprehensive about a communication he has to send. This again can be traced back to ancient times, when messengers bearing bad news were dealt with harshly, and many managers today still associate the bearer of bad news with the bad news itself. Whatever the reason, here is a case where you must do the harder right rather than the easier wrong, and you must do it without delay.

My own observations have indicated this to be one of the biggest reasons for problems and failures on government contracts. Something goes wrong, and the engineering contractor is so fearful of telling the government program manager the bad news that, by the time he finally does so, there is nothing the program manager can do to alleviate the problem. As a result, this person gets in difficulty with *his* boss, and since "everything flows downhill," the contractor really gets it in the neck, making him even more apprehensive and hesitant to communicate when things go wrong in the future. Regardless of your apprehension or discomfort, something just has to be done in these situations, and you must see that your subordinates take such actions as well.

Forgetting to make the required communication is a serious problem, and it happens every day. There is one good solution that seems to work better than telling your secretary or a subordinate to remind you: carry a pad and pencil wherever you go, and make a note of every message you need to send. Every morning, go over the items written down in your pad and issue every required communication. Your subordinates can use the same technique. In this way, neither you nor your subordinates need ever forget to send a message.

Rumors

Rumors can destroy your organization. They have, in fact, destroyed many organizations in the past. Several years ago during the recession, an engineering organization in a California division of a company went from 20 engineers to just 7 in less than three weeks due to a rumor. What happened was this: A major contract was lost. One engineer overheard the president of the company tell the director of engineering to wind up the in-house work that was being done and he heard the president say, "That's the last time we'll have to bid one like that."

The engineer spread the word that in-house work would cease and that he had heard the president say they were getting out of this area of business. He added that no doubt they would all be laid off. This word got around the engineering group but was not fully believed until a written communication came down ordering all in-house projects to be closed out. That was all that was needed to start a panic and a mass exodus. What the engineers didn't know was that another division in the company, also in California, had taken on a major project that would last for an indefinite period. Even before hearing of the contract loss, top management had been planning to close down the in-house programs and put all 20 engineers on this other project.

The best answers to rumor are open communications with your subordinates and timely truthfulness. By timely truthfulness I mean that you should keep your subordinates informed on a regular basis and be frank and honest when dealing with them. If you keep communication channels with your people open as suggested earlier, a situation like the one described above cannot happen to you. You'll get to the members of your organization first, before rumors can get started. And if a rumor or two does slip by, your people will go where they should for the truth—to you, and you will be trusted and believed.

CHAPTER 12

How to Choose Among Alternatives for New Product Development

One of the most interesting yet frustrating and resource-absorbing tasks that can face you as a technical manager is having to choose among new product development alternatives. One of the main reasons for the frustration is that there are always more new product opportunities than you will have technical or economic resources to pursue. A frequent result is that no sooner do you decide on one portfolio of new product developments, than new opportunities present themselves which seem to offer returns superior to those you envision from your current projects.

METHODS FOR SELECTING AMONG NEW PRODUCTS

Most companies have long since abandoned intuition as the sole means of selecting potential new products. Development costs are too high and lead times too long to proceed in such a fashion. This does not mean you should no longer use your instinctive judgment as a technical manager in deciding which projects to proceed with and which to drop. You must still do this. But your decisions should be based on facts relevant to your situation.

New product selections are made in the following manner:

1. Document the alternative opportunities and attendant facts.
2. Decide which method or methods of analysis are relevant to your situation.

3. Do the analysis.
4. Compare alternative projects, and select the group of projects for development that appear best in light of relevant criteria and available resources.
5. Review your projects periodically.

ANALYTICAL METHODS OF PROJECT COMPARISON

Below are some of the many analytical methods that may be used to compare alternative research and development projects. Some will be relevant to your situation, others will not. Don't waste time with methods or criteria not applicable to you and your organization.

Return on investment (ROI).
Payback.
Time, cost, and sales-volume goals.
Costs and benefits.
Internal rate of return and present value.
Cost prediction formulas.
Economic allocation methods.
Scoring and ranking methods.

Return on Investment (ROI) Analysis

Return on investment (ROI) is a measure of the profitability with which economic resources required for a project are employed. For a new product development analysis carried out by a research and development group, return on investment equals total anticipated profit over the lifetime of the product divided by total anticipated investment. The latter includes development costs, outlays for capital equipment, and any other expenditures needed to achieve this level of profit. Thus, for an R&D project in which total anticipated profit was $1 million and anticipated investment was $5 million, the ROI would be $1 million ÷ $5 million, or 20 percent. If the results are to be more meaningful, both numerator and denominator should be discounted for the time value of money as described in Chapter 8. What you are looking for is the biggest ROI you can get among your alternative projects.

Payback Analysis

The payback, or payback period, is the time required for the earnings to pay back the cost of the investment. It is found by dividing the investment by the gross annual profit expected. Thus, this measure indicates the number of years required for the gross earnings on the project to pay back the original outlay.

For example, say you are considering two projects that have these characteristics:

> Project A   Investment: $5,000
>   Gross annual profit: $1,000 per year
> Project B   Investment: $2,000
>   Gross annual profit: $200 per year
> Project A   Payback period:

$$\frac{\$5,000}{\$1,000 \text{ per year}} = 5 \text{ years}$$

> Project B   Payback period:

$$\frac{\$2,000}{\$200 \text{ per year}} = 10 \text{ years}$$

Unfortunately, the payback figures do not tell you which project, A or B, is more profitable. You know when a project has returned its investment, but you don't know what happens afterward.

Payback is most useful when you want quick, rough estimates to separate easily discernible high-profit projects from projects so poor that it's not worth spending additional time analyzing them. Payback is also a good type of analysis to do when liquidity is a major consideration.

Time, Cost, or Sales-Volume Goal Analysis

Time, cost, and sales-volume goals may be quite arbitrary, but they can be used as screening devices to eliminate projects that would be unacceptable to management and to compare alternatives. For example, as a screening device, you may be told that no future projects will be started that cannot be completed in three years or less. You may be instructed to disregard projects that would cost more than $100,000. Or you may be given a minimum figure for expected sales volume, with instructions to reject any projects that won't eventually generate the decided volume. For comparison of alternative projects, management could give you any of the following acceptability criteria:

"We want projects that will take the least time to complete."

"We want you to pick projects that will require the least investment."

"We want R&D projects that have the potential of generating the largest sales volume."

If time, cost, or sales-volume goals are used in comparing your alternatives, they can be considered only as indicators of effectiveness in achieving your objectives. You will need to use additional analytical methods if you wish to compare the efficiency of various projects.

Cost-Benefit Analysis

A cost-benefit analysis does not have to be quantitative, although you should endeavor to make it so if at all possible. For example, a comparison of two projects might be as follows:

PROJECT C

Cost: $100,000

Benefits	Value of Benefits
1. Will support our work on Project A	$20,000
2. Will make our firm the technological leader	Unknown
3. Will enable us to get a tax reduction of $5,000	$ 5,000

PROJECT D

Cost: $100,000

Benefits	Value of Benefits
1. Tooling can also be used for manufacture of Widget 001	$25,000
2. Will bring our engineering up to date in finite element technology	Unknown

Rate-of-Return or Present-Value Analysis

These techniques were discussed earlier in Chapter 8. Both techniques yield identical results when a single project is being considered and the issue is whether to accept or reject it. This is because the present value of a project is greater than, equal to, or less than zero when the calculated rate of return is greater than, equal to, or less than the cost of capital. However, for selecting among alternative proposals that are mutually exclusive, the results of a rate-of-return analysis may not be equal to those of a present-value analysis due to differing assumptions implicit in each analytical method. In rate of return the assumption is that the appropriate reinvestment rate of return—that is, the rate of interest at which the cash flows would be reinvested—is the same rate as the internal rate of return, whereas the present-value method assumes that the appropriate reinvestment rate is the cost of capital. Therefore, the method that you will use depends on which assumption you feel to be more appropriate. Consult with your financial people on this before proceeding.

Cost Prediction Formula Analysis

Cost prediction formulas predict the investment required to complete individual R&D projects through use of relevant related parameters, such as sales forecasts and historical data. For example, you could derive a cost formula based on the historical ratio of cost to sales for successful projects in your organization as follows:

$$\text{Cost} = \frac{\text{historical cost for successful profits}}{\text{historical sales for successful project}} \times \text{predicted sales}$$

There are two major problems with this approach. One is that it assumes a relationship does exist in your organization between development costs and sales later on, which may not always be true. The other problem is that the successful product being used as a model would have had to complete its full life cycle before sales could be accurately calculated. You may not have any products that have gone through the complete cycle to look at.

Economic Allocation Methods

Economic allocation methods are among the most sophisticated of the different methods for R&D project selection. Basically, such methods address themselves to the question of how much should be spent for each project rather than just the question of which projects should be developed. Below is a highly simplified example of how economic allocation methods might be used to decide on project selection and funding.

Assume that you have two projects, A and B. Project A has a sales potential of $40 million if successful; Project B has a sales potential of $30 million if successful. The probability of success for either project depends on how much you spend for development in accordance with the schedules contained in Figure 25.

Say your budget limitation is $500,000. At best you will enjoy a probability of success of 60 percent for Project A or 78 percent for Project B. In Figure 26, we compute the expected payoff for each cost below

FIGURE 25. Costs of developing Projects A and B versus probabilities of success.

PROJECT A

Cost	$100,000	$200,000	$300,000	$400,000	$500,000	$600,000	$700,000	$800,000	$900,000	$1,000,000
Probability of success	.30	.40	.50	.55	.60	.65	.70	.75	.80	.83

PROJECT B

Cost	$100,000	$200,000	$300,000	$400,000	$500,000	$600,000	$700,000	$800,000	$900,000	$1,000,000
Probability of success	.50	.60	.70	.75	.78	.80	.85	.87	.89	.90

FIGURE 26. Costs and expected payoffs.

PROJECT A

Cost	$100,000	$200,000	$300,000	$400,000	$500,000
Expected payoff	$12 M	$16 M	$20 M	$22 M	$24 M

PROJECT B

Cost	$100,000	$200,000	$300,000	$400,000	$500,000
Expected payoff	$15 M	$18 M	$21 M	$22.5 M	$23.4 M

$500,000 by multiplying the sales potential by the probability of success for that cost.

From Figure 26, it seems clear that if we have $500,000 for our R&D budget, it would be foolish to pick Project A or Project B alone, since we can maximize our expected payoff by allocating funding to some combination of both of these projects. For example, funding Project A at the $300,000 level and Project B at the $200,000 level results in an expected payoff of $20 million plus $18 million, or $38 million. However, if we allocate the entire $500,000 to Project A, our expected payoff is only $24 million, or if to Project B, only $23.4 million.

Obviously, we have done a lot of assuming in this example. Exactly how do you compute all those probabilities of success for each cost anyway? Nevertheless, this method of project selection may well represent the wave of the future. And although the methodology is not currently available to the average technical manager, it is known that models employing this technique are progressing at several companies. One comprehensive treatment that includes the mathematical theory for going on to calculate funding levels for multiple projects is contained in *The Economics of Defense in the Nuclear Age,** by Charles J. Hitch and Roland N. McKean. Other, more recent treatments of this methodology are available, but Hitch and McKean's discussion is one of the originals and perhaps the best.

Scoring and Ranking Methods

Scoring and ranking can be treated as a separate method for selecting projects, although many of the methods discussed previously may include some type of scoring or ranking. With this approach you simply rank the potential projects according to some list of criteria, and then select projects from the top to the bottom of the list until the cutoff point is reached where you run out of budget. There is nothing new in this. However, the scoring criteria used can make the technique a separate methodology per se. Many additional criteria can be considered that were not previously included, such as product life, patentability, strength of competition in the market, the company's financial position, availability of personnel, or whatever else you feel is relevant and important. In this way, all the other factors that were considered under other methods can also be taken into account.

*New York: Atheneum, 1965.

To accomplish this you must first think of all factors that are relevant to your situation. For example, you may consider the following general areas pertinent to your operations: demand, market, product, company, financial considerations, and product development.

Under each general area, list those factors or analyses that you consider relevant. For example, your relevant factors and analyses might be as follows:

Demand
    Strength of demand
    Anticipated period of demand
    Importance of need to be satisfied by product
Market
    Size of market
    Market location
    Competition in market
Product
    Compatibility with current product line
    Special features or performance capabilities
    Price
    Protection
Company
    Engineering advantages
    Production advantages
    Location advantages
    Facility advantages
Financial considerations
    Capital budgeting analysis
    ROI analysis
    Payback analysis
    Life-cycle cash flow
Product development
    Technical risk
    Producibility
    Development scheduling

You would next evaluate the importance of all these factors and analyses and would assign a relative weight, or percentage of importance, to each. The sum of all the relative weights would have to equal 100 percent. In our example, the weightings might be something like those in Table 3.

TABLE 3.

RELEVANT FACTOR	RELATIVE WEIGHT	RELEVANT FACTOR	RELATIVE WEIGHT
Demand		*Company*	
Strength	6%	Engineering	3%
Period	5	Production	7
Need	5	Location	2
Market		Facility	2
Size	3	*Financial considerations*	
Location	3	Capital budgeting	8
Competition	4	ROI	8
Product		Payback	8
Compatibility	7	Life-cycle cash flow	8
Special features/		*Product development*	
performance	3	Technical risk	5
Price	5	Producibility	4
Protection	1	Scheduling	3
		Total	100%

Remember that the relative weights will differ depending on the importance of these factors and analyses to your organization.

The next task is to assign weights for each product being considered. Let's assume we have three potential products, X, Y, and Z. For each factor or analysis, we will assign a value based on a scale of 1 to 10. For the "Demand" area, our factors are "Strength of demand," "Anticipated period of demand," and "Importance of need to be satisfied by the product." These factors have relative weights as follows:

Strength	6%
Period	5
Need	5

Now let's assume that Product X has a very strong demand over a short period and that the need for the product is also strong. On a scale of 10, we might assign this produt 8 points for strength, 3 for period, and 8 for need. Product Y has a medium demand but for a long period. The need for Product Y is also strong. Perhaps we'll assign this product 5 points for strength, 9 points for period, and 8 points for need. Product Z has a very low strength of demand for a long period. The need for this product is medium. The point assignment might be 1, 9, and 5 points, respectively. A recapitulation of these facts would look like this:

DEMAND	RELATIVE WEIGHT	VALUES FOR PRODUCT X	VALUES FOR PRODUCT Y	VALUES FOR PRODUCT Z
Strength	6%	8	5	1
Period	5	3	9	9
Need	5	8	8	5

Now we need to estimate how confident we are about each value estimate. For example, are we 100 percent certain that demand will be strong or only about 50 percent sure? Let's look only at Product X. We'll assume that we're very certain of the need for the product, less certain about the strength of demand, and not very confident at all about our point value for the period of demand. We might therefore assign confidence percentages of 70 percent for strength, 10 percent for period, and 90 percent for need. We then multiply the relative weight percent-

FIGURE 27. New product development selection matrix.

	RELATIVE WEIGHT	POINT VALUE	CONFIDENCE FACTOR	FINAL VALUE
Demand				
Strength	6%	8	70%	.336
Period	5	3	10	.015
Need	5	8	90	.360
Market				
Size	3	10	70	.210
Location	3	7	80	.168
Competition	4	6	50	.120
Product				
Compatibility	7	8	90	.504
Special features/performance	3	5	90	.135
Price	5	3	60	.090
Protection	1	9	90	.081
Company				
Engineering	3	7	80	.168
Production	7	8	80	.448
Location	2	4	90	.072
Facility	2	9	90	.162
Financial considerations				
Capital budgeting	8	7	60	.336
ROI	8	7	70	.392
Payback	8	5	70	.280
Life-cycle cash flow	8	9	60	.432
Product development				
Technical risk	5	8	60	.240
Producibility	4	8	70	.224
Scheduling	3	5	80	.120
	Total 100%			Total value 4.893

ages by the value and confidence percentages to arrive at a final value. For strength of demand for Product X this would be 6 percent times 8 points times 70 percent or 0.336. These values may be calculated on a new product development selection matrix as shown in Figure 27. The final value score resulting from the matrix for each product is then compared to scores for other products in order to arrive at a selection decision.

THE IMPORTANCE OF PERIODIC REVIEW

All ongoing and potential programs should be reviewed on a periodic basis to establish whether older programs should be continued or dropped and determine what new programs, if any, should be started. This review makes it possible to reevaluate older programs with increasingly more accurate data, including changing values of risk, uncertainty, and discount rates.

EPILOGUE

Technical Managers Must Manage

That the management of technical endeavors will become increasingly complex in the future is inevitable. This complexity means that increased numbers of specialists will be needed to manage functions that either did not exist previously (such as data processing) or that were formerly managed directly by the technical manager.

Despite this growing specialization, the technical manager cannot and must not abdicate his or her responsibility for the attainment of organizational objectives. Regardless of the specialists who may assist you, or who even demand control over areas that affect your ability to manage your organization, you as technical manager do not have the luxury of throwing up your hands and admitting failure because the task is the responsibility of a more specialized organization. You personally are responsible for success or failure. You personally are responsible for doing whatever is necessary in order to accomplish the objectives of your technical organization. You must always do whatever it takes to get the job done.

The concept of your function is utterly stark in its simplicity—it is simply to manage. If you follow the techniques and guidelines set forth in the preceeding chapters, you cannot and will not fail in the endeavor.

INDEX

advancement, offer of, by small firms, 51

advertising
identification of customers through, 163
open versus blind, 54
recruiting through, 53

Air Force Information for Industry Offices, 163, 165

ambition, motivation through, 108

American Management Associations, *vii*

application of management concepts, *viii*

appreciation, motivation through, 108

assessment centers, use of, in recruiting process, 63

assumptions, communications problems due to, 193

authority
assigned in company charter, 18
to budget for training, 80
determination of scope of, 7, 8
in human relations organization theory, 25
levels of, 36
of line personnel, 19
of low-level manager, 36
in matrix organizations, 34
of personal staff, 19, 21
of specialized staff, 21
in traditional organization theory, 22, 23, 24

autocratic leader, definition of, 103

Barnard, Chester, 24, 188, 195

behavior
integration of managerial and employee, 24
leadership, 103
rational, 24

behavioral scientists, criticism of traditional organization theory by, 23

bias in performance appraisal, 120

bid, preparation of contract, 172–176

Blake, R. R., 103

Blanchard, Kenneth, 104–105

bonuses as compensation, 84

budget
allowance for training in, 74, 75, 78
construction of fixed-appropriations, 133–140

Burack, Elmer, 100

capital equipment
budget allowance for, 140–141
computation of cost of, 142

Carnegie, Dale, 82

centralization
versus decentralization, 28–30
in functional organization, 30–31

chain of command
handling problems through, 2–3
interference with, 23, 84
line personnel and, 19
recruiting through, 50

charter, written organizational, 18, 19

climate, leadership success and organizational, 103

Commerce Business Daily (CBD), 165

communications
definition, 188